363. 12365

ED LEISURE + CULTURE
Libraries

www.edlc.co.uk

BISHOPBRIGGS	772 4513	LENZIE	776 3021
BROOKWOOD	777 3021	MILNGAVIE	956 2776
CRAIGHEAD	01360 311925	WESTERTON	943 0780
LENNOXTOWN	01360 311436	WILLIAM PATRICK	777 3141

Please return this book on or before the last stamped
It may be renewed if not in demand.

TRAWLER DISASTERS

1946-1975

From Aberdeen, Fleetwood, Hull and Grimsby

JOHN NICKLIN & PATRICIA O'DRISCOLL

AMBERLEY

First published 2010

Amberley Publishing Plc
Cirencester Road, Chalford,
Stroud, Gloucestershire, GL6 8PE

www.amberley-books.com

British Library Cataloguing in Publication Data.
A catalogue record for this book is available from the British
Library.

ISBN 978 1 84868 841 4

Typeset in 10pt on 13pt Sabon.
Typesetting and Origination by Amberley Publishing.
Printed in the UK.

CONTENTS

INTRODUCTION

This book is an attempt to catalogue the enormous losses suffered by the British trawler fleet, both in ships and men. In compiling the list of lost ships, we have concentrated on the larger type of steam and motor trawler, generally vessels of around 200 tons or more. Many smaller boats were lost, and these losses will regrettably continue, and although the grief suffered by the wives and families of the crews of these boats is no less acute, the fleet of large UK fishing vessels has declined to the point where it no longer exists. Very few large UK trawlers and their crews will be lost in future years. Not because the job has become safer, or that the ships are better built, or that the wind blows less strong and storms are fewer. The reason is that very few fishing voyages to the stormy North Atlantic and Arctic Ocean will be made. Distant water fishing, as far as the UK is concerned, is dead, and in writing this account, we hope to preserve the memory of all those brave men who died trawling in distant waters. An occupation where men sailed to the desolate, stormy waters of the Arctic in search of cod and haddock. Where men pitted their wits against nature in some of the most dangerous waters on the planet to reap the harvest of the seas. An industry that was the fourth largest in the country until the international extension of fishing limits brought about its decline almost overnight in the late seventies.

The principal centres of distant water trawling in the United Kingdom were based at Grimsby, Hull, Fleetwood and Aberdeen, and it is on the losses from these ports that we concentrate. In the period from 1946 to 1975, at least 125 ships and over 400 men were lost. The figure for lost men only includes those men who perished with their ship, and if you add those men washed over the side, or killed through accident, the figure would be much greater. The figure for ships lost would also be considerably increased if we included losses from Lowestoft, Swansea, Milford, Granton, Leith and other smaller ports.

On almost every day of the year relatively small ships left port to venture to northern, ice-infested waters, and others docked to land their catch. For every man that crewed the ships, another dozen were employed ashore to keep them running, and to process and distribute the catch they brought home. The fish the trawlers brought home oiled the wheels of the subsidiary industries that were dependent on that fish and was the lifeblood of the communities. Although fishing had been carried out at small ports and havens all round the UK coast for centuries, it was the build-up of the railway system in the mid-1800s that allowed the nationwide distribution of a highly perishable commodity and made possible the heavy concentration of fishing vessels at the ports served by the rail network. This was particularly true of Grimsby, where new docks were built in 1857 to accommodate the rapidly increasing number of fishing vessels using the port, although the same could be said for every large fishing port in the country.

At that time the fishing boats were built of wood and propelled by the wind. For the most part, they caught their fish by hook and line, this method of fishing being less dependent on the wind than trawling. By 1870, over 1,000 of these fishing smacks were landing their catches at Grimsby, and there was a similar expansion of the fishing industry at Hull and Fleetwood. This vast increase in fishing activity soon depleted the fish stock on banks close to home, and boats had to go further and further afield to maintain catches. New fishing grounds were discovered in the northern part of the North Sea, at the Faroe Islands, Iceland, Greenland and the Barents Sea. In 1873, a seed was planted that revolutionised the fish-catching industry. An iron-hulled vessel was built by a Hull shipbuilder, G. Cooper. This ship, the *Tubal Cain*, was delivered to Grimsby in 1874 and registered as GY288 under the ownership of Mr Fred Rushworth. Originally a sailing ship, she was designed for later conversion to steam propulsion and made several profitable voyages to the Faroes under sail. In 1876, she was fitted with a steam engine and propeller, and soon demonstrated that the iron-hulled vessel was better able to cope with the weather, that she could effectively trawl in calms when her sisters under sail were idle, and could considerably cut down the time on voyages to and from the fishing grounds. Landing huge catches from the Faroes, her progress was watched with interest by the owners of the fishing smacks, and before long, more iron-hulled steam vessels began to arrive at the port. The age of the steam trawler had arrived.

The change over from sail to steam was rapid. By 1890, forty-two steam trawlers were working from the port. Two years later, the number was 113, and by the end of the first decade of the twentieth century, the transition from sail to steam was complete. In 1909, there were 680 vessels fishing from Grimsby, and of these, 654 were steam driven. Throughout this period, the fishing industry was expanding in a similar manner at Hull, Fleetwood and Aberdeen.

There were heavy losses, of both ships and men during the era of sail, and after the introduction of iron-hulled steam vessels, although they were bigger, and better able to cope with the storms, the losses continued. As the trawlers ventured further and further into the Arctic, the size of the new vessels coming from the builders' yards increased. At the end of 1883, the Board of Trade introduced examinations for Certificates of Competency for skippers and mates of fishing vessels in an attempt to ensure that they were capable of navigating their ships safely to and from the distant fishing grounds. Initially, only skippers were certificated, but in 1887, mates also had to hold a certificate. Men already doing the job did not have to take the examination and were granted a Certificate of Service if they could prove appropriate service.

After the Second World War, there was a vast improvement in radio-communication equipment aboard the ships. The technical revolution gave them accurate electronic position-fixing systems, and every vessel was fitted with sophisticated radar equipment, but the loss of ships and men continued year after year. This was because the ships were continuously venturing into the unknown, often working in uncharted, or inadequately charted waters, and because owners expected men and ships to be pushed to the limits of endurance, and beyond. And if a skipper was disinclined to display this ruthlessness of purpose, there were plenty of men ashore willing to replace him. When vessels plying a more sedate trade were hove to, or seeking shelter from the weather, the trawlers were running off to shoot their gear. Homeward bound, when a gale was encountered that warranted the ship being eased down in the interests of safety, the telegraph stayed at Full Ahead, and ship and men were gambled against the fury of wind and sea. Catching the market could make a difference of several thousand pounds to the voyage returns – the difference between success and failure.

Losses, both of ships and men, were always heavy. Despite the fact that bigger, more powerful ships were being commissioned, losses continued. This was because they were continuously extending their range of operations. Both men and ships continued to be pushed to their limit, and economic conditions dictate that to build a ship able to withstand extreme climatic conditions that she may encounter maybe once in a lifetime, if ever, would be so expensive as to make it impossible for her to ever show a profit. There is no limit to the power of the sea, and there is no such thing as an unsinkable ship.

This book is about those steam and motor trawlers that were lost between 1946 and 1975. We have chosen this period because, from 1946 onwards, the ships would be built to stringent Lloyd's specifications, would be equipped with the latest electronic navigation aids, would be required by law to be fitted out with the latest life-saving appliances, and their skippers and mates would have met strict examination requirements. We want to highlight two things. Firstly, that the sea is all-powerful and must be treated with respect – a fact that every experienced seaman appreciates, and disregards at his peril. Secondly, the heavy price in lives that was paid for our fish and chips. Many widows in the fishing ports will insist that the price was too high, but coming from fishing stock, had learned to live with it.

After 1970, the number of losses began to decline, and flags in the dock areas flew at half-mast on fewer occasions. The reason for this was that the British distant water fleet of trawlers had been decimated, and fewer trips were made to the Arctic. Trawling in any area is a highly dangerous occupation, and there will still be loss of life on the small home-water boats that currently make up the UK fishing fleet, but these losses will be less in number than in bygone years simply because there are fewer boats fishing, and being smaller, they have smaller crews. The breed that manned the British distant-water trawler is now an endangered species. Nicholas Monsarrat in *The Master Mariner* (Cassell, 1978) quoted Admiral Sir Charles Saunders when in 1774 he told the House of Commons 'Give up the fishery and you lose your breed of seaman', and that is exactly what we have done.

This book is dedicated to all the men that sailed on the trawlers, especially to those who never returned, and to the families who mourned them. The nation owes them a debt, incurred both in peace and war, and we should never forget them.

John Nicklin and Pat O'Driscoll, 1997

NOTE BY PAT O'DRISCOLL

Skipper John Nicklin, with whom I collaborated in this book, died very suddenly in April 1999, so the manuscript has lacked his final touches.

Readers will note the number of occasions in which men have been successfully rescued by the line-throwing apparatus and breeches buoy, yet in a directive issued on 31 March 1988, Britain's chief coastguard ordered that breeches buoys and line-throwing apparatus be handed in for disposal.

Additional information on the loss of the *Gaul* in 1974 may be found in John Nicklin's book *The Loss of the Motor Trawler* Gaul (Hutton Press, 1998). A year later her wreck was located.

1946

Five trawlers and thirteen men were lost during 1946.

Aberdeen	*Star of the East* A434	218 tons	3 March 1946
Grimsby	*Grimsby Town* GY136	422 tons	23 April 1946
	Earl Essex GY48	225 tons	24 April 1946
	Serapion GY1154	195 tons	5 November 1946
	Virginian GY211	211 tons	5 November 1946

Star of the East was a steel, steam side trawler of 218 gross tons, built in 1912 by Hall Russell, Aberdeen, for Walker Steam Trawler Fishing Company, Aberdeen. She was requisitioned by the Admiralty in 1914 and was minesweeping until 1919, when she returned to fishing under the ownership of the Co-operative Fishing Society, Scarborough, and registered as SH321. In 1941, she was bought by her original owners, Walkers, and returned to Aberdeen as A434. On 3 March 1946, she ran aground on Heimaey, one of the Westmann Isles, Iceland. She was a total loss, but fortunately, the Fleetwood trawler *Lois* was close by, and her crew of thirteen were able to launch the lifeboat and row to her. The *Lois* landed the survivors on the Westmann Isles, where they were lodged until an Icelandic fish carrier, the MV *Helgi*, was able to bring them to Fleetwood.

Skipper Charles L. Buchan commanded the *Star of the East* on her last voyage.

Grimsby Town was a single-screw, steel side trawler built in 1934 by Smith's Dock Ltd at Middlesbrough and owned by the Hull Ice Company and managed by Consolidated Fisheries, Grimsby. She was 157 feet long, 26.7 feet wide, and 12.7 feet deep, with a gross tonnage of 422 tons. She was fitted with hand and steam steering gear and propelled by a triple-expansion steam engine. She carried a lifeboat certified for twenty-one persons, and her life-saving appliances met all statutory requirements. When first arriving at Grimsby in 1934, she was registered as GY81. She was taken over by the Admiralty in January 1940, and when she was returned to fishing in January 1946, she registered as GY136.

Grimsby Town sailed from Grimsby bound for the fishing grounds at Iceland on 15 April 1946 under the command of Skipper George Camburn with a crew of twenty hands. On arriving in Icelandic waters, she started fishing on 19 April, but the next day, she put in to Westmanhaven in the Westmann Isles to put the galley boy, H. White, ashore, as he was suffering badly from seasickness. Returning to the fishing grounds, she dropped a marker buoy 4 miles south of Portland Light on 21 April. She fished to the eastward of this buoy, and about 2.30 a.m., on 23 April, she hauled the trawl in a position with the New Light bearing NE by N and estimated by the skipper to be 5 to 7 miles off. A sounding with the Hughes echo-sounder showed 53 fathoms. The

Star of the East. (W. Dodds Collection)

Grimsby Town. (Welholme Gallery)

skipper, intending to return to Portland Light to pick up the marker buoy, rang the engines full speed, and without any reference to the chart, set a course of WNW, with Herbert Walter Winter, a deckhand, as helmsman. The weather was dark and overcast with occasional snow and sleet. While steaming to the westward, the crew were working on the foredeck clearing the fish caught the last haul, and as a consequence, the deck working lights were switched on, which restricted the vision of the men in the wheelhouse. The skipper stayed on the bridge for about half an hour, leaving orders with Winter to call him at 3.45 a.m. or when Portland Light was sighted. The snow and sleet had ceased, but started again almost immediately after the skipper left. Without any sign of danger being seen, the *Grimsby Town* took the ground with considerable force at 3.40 a.m. on 23 April. Immediately, a heavy swell swept across the foredeck, washing four of the men working in the pounds over the starboard side. One of these men was able to regain the ship, but the other three were drowned. The skipper was knocked off his locker by the force of the stranding, and came up to the bridge immediately. The wireless operator was called and distress messages sent out at frequent intervals. A reply was received about three hours after the stranding. A rescue operation was mounted by the Icelanders who had assembled on shore, and the seventeen survivors were taken off by breeches buoy. Intensive efforts were made to refloat the vessel, which lasted until the end of June without success. Skipper Camburn had signed a contract with Oscar Johnson to undertake the salvage of his vessel on a 'No Cure No Pay' basis. The underwriter's surveyor arrived on the scene on 26 April and quickly formed the opinion that the contractor was concentrating on the salvage of the vessel's cargo of fish rather than preparing the vessel for refloating. He considered that Oscar Johnson had neither the trained personnel nor the salvage equipment capable of refloating the *Grimsby Town* and advised the skipper to call in Hamar Salvage Co. to assist the contractor. This was done, but the *Grimsby Town* was finally abandoned as a total loss.

The Court of Inquiry into the stranding found that the loss was caused by the fault or default of Skipper Camburn. His certificate was suspended for eighteen months, and he was ordered to pay £100 towards the cost of the Inquiry.

*E*arl Essex was a typical North Sea single-screw side trawler built by Cook, Welton & Gemmell at Beverley in 1914 for the Earl Steam Fishing Company and registered as GY48. She was 117 feet long, 22 feet wide, and 12.7 feet deep with a gross tonnage of 225 tons. In the period from being built to being lost, she changed ownership three times. In November 1915, she was bought by H. Croft Baker. In January 1923, she was acquired by the Stand Steam Fishing Company, and in February 1939, was bought by Sir Thomas Robinson Ltd. She was requisitioned by the Admiralty in November 1939 and served as a minesweeper throughout the war, flying the pennant FY852 until she was returned to her owners in February 1946.

She sailed from Grimsby on 17 April 1946 under the command of Skipper Albert Treacher, and on 24 April, she was fishing in the North Sea. Just after dinner, she hauled her gear to find a mine sitting on the bracket of the after trawl door. As the door came up to the gallows, the mine exploded, causing severe damage to the stern, and she sank in minutes. There was only one survivor from her crew of eleven. Joe Taylor, a trimmer, only recently demobbed from the RAF, was at the fore end when the explosion occurred, and with the ship almost vertical, with the bows pointing skyward, Joe jumped into the sea. After a vain attempt to save a crew member who was also in the water, he managed to board a raft that had floated clear from the sunken ship.

The Grimsby trawler *Vera Grace*, Skipper W. Calam, was fishing 5 or 6 miles away. The mate, W. A. Wilson, was on watch and happened to be looking towards the *Earl*

Essex and saw the flash and puff of smoke from the explosion. They immediately hauled the gear and arrived at the scene in about 30 minutes. All they found were a few bits of wreckage, and Joe clinging to the raft.

*S*erapion was built by Cook, Welton & Gemmell in 1900 for Standard SF Co., Grimsby, and registered as GY1154. She had several Grimsby owners prior to her loss, the last registered owner being Diamonds SF Company (Taylors). She was a single-screw side trawler of 195 gross tons, 113.6 feet long, 21 feet beam and 11.2 feet deep.

On 5 November 1946, she collided with the Grimsby trawler *Athenian* in dense fog in the Humber Approaches and sank. The *Athenian* was able to pick up all her crew, and fortunately, there were no casualties.

*V*irginian was built in 1906 by Cook, Welton & Gemmell and registered at Grimsby as GY211 and owned by Onward SF Company. She was a single-screw side trawler of 211 gross tons, 115.4 feet long, 21.6 feet beam and 11.5 feet deep.

On 5 November 1946, she collided with the *Empire Napier*, a troopship, in dense fog in the Humber Approaches and sank. *Empire Napier* rescued all the crew, and there were no lives lost.

Virginian. (Fishing Heritage Centre)

1947

Seven ships and seven men lost this year.

Hull			
	Loch Hope H220	274 tons	11 June 1947
	Thomas Altoft H132	290 tons	8 November 1947
	St Amandus H247	443 tons	25 December 1947
Fleetwood	*Lois* FD424	286 tons	5 January 1947
	Benghazi H66	257 tons	23 April 1947
	Dhoon FD348	323 tons	12 December 1947
	Red Gauntlet LO33	410 tons	10 August 1947

St Amandus was built by Smith's Docks, Middlesbrough, in 1934 for Loch Fishing Company and named *Loch Melfort*. She was requisitioned by the Admiralty at the start of the war, and was demobbed in 1945. Acquired by Firth Steam Fishing Company, a subsidiary of Thomas Hamling & Co. Ltd, she was registered at Hull as *St Amandus*, H247. She was a single-screw, coal-burning steam trawler of 442.63 gross tons, 162.1 feet long with a beam of 26.7 feet. She was fitted with two echo-sounders, one made by Hughes, the other by Marconi, and both were overhauled while the ship was in the Humber, but soon after the vessel sailed, the Hughes sounder was found to be inoperative, and three days later, the Marconi sounder packed up as well.

St Amandus sailed from Hull on 19 December 1947 on a fishing voyage to the White Sea fishing grounds with a crew of twenty-four hands all told, under the command of Skipper R. K. Weightman. From the details revealed at the inquiry into her loss, it appears she was navigated in a haphazard manner. A course was set from Spurn Light Vessel to take her to Svino, but when approaching Svino, it was found the vessel had set to the westward of the intended track. Intending to go into Harstad to get the sounders repaired, a course was set from the position off Svino to make for Skomvoer, the southernmost tip of the Lofoten Islands. (The actual distance from Svino to Skomvoer is about 330 miles.) After steaming 360 miles on this course, it was found that the vessel was to the west of the Lofotens, and she steamed back on a south-easterly course for about four hours. Land was sighted, and she rounded Skomvoer and set a course up West Fjord. On passage up West Fjord, the skipper had seen and identified Tennholmen, Maloy Skarholmen and Flatoy Lights, but no effort was made to plot the sightings to fix the ship's position. At about 10.30 p.m. on 24 December, because of greatly reduced visibility owing to snow showers, she dropped anchor in a position estimated by the skipper to be six or seven miles from Flatoy Light, but after the anchor was down, no attempt was made to verify the position by D/F bearings from Skraaven, Rost or Eggeloysa. While the vessel was at anchor, the snow cleared and a two-flash light was observed bearing E by N ½ N, and the skipper assumed that this light was Tranoy Light. The anchor was weighed at about

11.15 p.m., and a course of ENE was set, which was altered a quarter of a point to starboard to pass close to what was thought to be Tranoy. About an hour later, the vessel grounded about a mile west of Skraaven Light. In fact, the light the skipper took for Tranoy must have been Skraaven. Both Skraaven and Tranoy are two-flash lights, but the intervals of flash are 6 and 15 seconds respectively. A glance at the chart, or reference to the *Norway Pilot* or *Admiralty List of Lights*, all of which were on board the vessel, would have identified the light correctly. According to the evidence given at the inquiry into the stranding, none of the witnesses admitted seeing any lights on the port bow, but the lookout did see lights on the port side but did not report them. For a time before the stranding, the skipper, mate and two deckhands had been on the bridge, one deckhand steering, the other on lookout, and the court was of the opinion that the skipper did not receive the assistance he should have done. In the event, the court found that the loss was caused by the fault of the skipper, who 'failed to appreciate the information that was staring him in the face', and he failed to use the navigation aids that were available to him to fix the vessel's position. Fortunately, no lives were lost, but *St Amandus* was a total loss. The court suspended Skipper Weightman's certificate for twelve months from the date of the loss.

Ken Waudby was seventeen years old and a spare hand on *St Amandus* at the time of her loss. He told the author, 'After we struck, a lot of water was gushing into the after fish room, which still contained a good amount of coal. The ship was sinking fast, and due to a starboard list, the only boat we could launch was on the starboard side. It was cold, pitch dark and snowing. After dragging our mattresses up onto the whaleback and setting fire to them, we all boarded the lifeboat. We had been rowing for about thirty minutes when a snibby, which had seen the fire, came out and towed us to Skraaven Lighthouse. I don't know what became of our lifeboat. We spent the night huddled together in the lighthouse, and the next morning, the same snibby put us ashore at Svolvaer. We remained there for about three weeks. For the first week, we stayed at the Seamen's Mission but then some of us were billeted with Norwegian families. They were kindness itself. We were first told by the agent that we would have to wait for homeward-bound trawlers to take us home. We objected strongly to this – we could have been stranded for weeks – but eventually, we were shipped on the mail boat *Kong Hakken* to Bergen, and from there by boat to Newcastle, where we boarded a train to Hull, arriving home mid-January still wearing our sea gear.'

*L*och Hope was a single-screw coal-burning side trawler built in 1915 at Beverley as the *Princess Marie Jose*. In 1934, her name was changed to *Feughside*, and in 1934, she was acquired by the Loch Fishing Company, Hull, when she was registered as H220, and her name changed to *Loch Hope*. She had a gross tonnage of 274 tons, was 133.5 feet in length and 22.7 feet in beam. *Loch Hope* sailed from Hull on 31 May 1947 bound for the Icelandic fishing grounds with a crew of eighteen hands all told under the command of Skipper Archibald Butler. On 11 June 1947, while fishing on the east side of Iceland, she picked up a mine in the trawl, which exploded while the trawl was being hauled. Severe damage resulted, causing her to sink. One man, twenty-three-year-old trimmer Arthur Cattle, was killed by the explosion and eight others were injured. The Fleetwood trawler *Urka* picked up the survivors and landed them at Seydisfjord. Five of the injured men were flown to hospital in Reykjavik, the other three, being too badly injured to move, were detained in hospital at Seydisfjord.

*T*he *Benghazi* was a Strath-class Admiralty single-screw steam trawler built by C. Rennoldson at South Shields as the *John Bullock*. Some time after 1939, she was acquired by the Boston D. S. Fishing Company, and her name was changed to *Flying Admiral*. She worked from Fleetwood under the command of Skipper Bobby Wright.

About 1945, she was bought by Hull Merchants Amalgamated Trawlers Limited and registered as H66 and her name changed to *Benghazi*. After a brief spell working from Hull, she returned to Fleetwood. Of 257 gross tons, she was 125.3 feet long, 23.2 feet in beam, and 12.5 feet in depth. *Benghazi* left Fleetwood early in April 1947 for a fishing trip to Iceland with a crew of seventeen men under the command of Skipper John Anderton. Homeward bound, she called at Oban for bunkers and provisions, and left there just after midnight on 23 April 1947 to proceed to Fleetwood. About an hour out of Oban, in gale-force wind and driving rain, she ran aground on Bogha Nuadh Rock. The vessel heeled so far over that water rushed through the bridge windows. The lifeboat was quickly launched, and Charles Bevin, the second engineer, was the first man into the boat and found that the bung was missing. In an effort to stem the water flooding in, he jammed his hand in the hole. Twelve other crew members joined him in the lifeboat and, having no idea where they were, allowed the boat to drift until they were washed ashore on Luing. Once ashore, they huddled together to keep warm while they waited for daylight, but Charles Bevin died of exposure during the night. By keeping his hand in the plughole while lying in the water at the bottom of the boat, Second Engineer Bevin saved the lives of his shipmates: without his heroic action, the boat would certainly have sunk before reaching land. The skipper, mate, bosun, and a deckhand, Frank Duncan, had remained aboard the ship and were concerned when she floated off the rocks and was carried by the strong tide down the Sound of Luing. The skipper sent out a distress call, which was answered by the Campbeltown and Tobermory lifeboats, but before help could arrive, the *Benghazi* grounded again on Fladda, a small island in the middle of the Sound. At some time during the night, Deckhand Frank Duncan vanished and was never seen again. At daylight, the other three men succeeded in getting ashore and were later rescued by the lifeboat. Initially, it was considered that *Benghazi* could be refloated, and a salvage tug was sent to pull her off the rocks, but before this could be accomplished, on 26 April, she slid off the reef and sank. Although her starboard side was visible above water at low tide, efforts to raise her failed, and she was a total loss.

Author's Note: The above account of the loss has been compiled from contemporary press reports. I have tried, without any success, to find any of the survivors, and to unearth any DTI Inquiry reports into the casualty. The reason is that I am uneasy about the accuracy of the press reports. As an experienced mariner and trawlerman, I think that we don't have all the details and there are questions to ask. *Benghazi* called at Oban in the afternoon and sailed a little after midnight. Having been at sea three weeks, I suggest that the lads would have been thirsty, and it is probable that at least some of them would be the worse for drink when she sailed. The fact that skipper, mate and bosun declined to take to the lifeboat suggests to me that the vessel was not making water. It could be that the skipper never gave the order to launch the lifeboat, and it was launched in panic. Another indication of this is that, according to the press reports I have seen, it was only after the vessel refloated after grounding the first time that the skipper sent out a distress call. It is fair to assume that, had the crew remained on board and steam in the boiler been maintained, once refloated, the vessel could have been saved.

The *Red Gauntlet* was built in 1933 at Beverley and registered as LO33. From 1939 to 1946, she was on Admiralty service as HMT *Ruby*. She was returned to her owners, Iago Steam Fishing Company, in 1946 and was converted to oil at Barrow before she resumed fishing. She was a single-screw steel side trawler of 410 gross tons and was 154.6 feet long. She carried all the appropriate life-saving equipment for a vessel of her class, all in good order and complying with the regulations. She was fitted with wireless telegraphy and radio telephone, a direction finder and two echo-sounders, all in good working order. All the necessary charts for her intended voyage were on board, and when she sailed on her final voyage, she was seaworthy in every respect.

She left Fleetwood on the morning of 26 July 1947 for her last trip fishing under the command of Skipper William Henry 'Dan Leno' Hicks with a crew of twenty men all told, but en route to the fishing grounds, she called at Honningsvaag and signed on two Norwegian fish gutters, so that at the time of the stranding, there were twenty-two men on board. *Red Gauntlet* commenced fishing west of South Cape, Spitzbergen, and had been fishing there for four or five days when, on the morning of 10 August, the skipper decided to change fishing grounds and move to an area between Bear Island and Seahorse (Hope Island on Admiralty charts). At about noon, a course of SE by E ½ E was set to round Sorkapp (South Cape). In setting this course with the intention of passing the cape 10 miles off, it is obvious that Skipper Hicks had miscalculated the departure point. At about 2.30 p.m., a rock was sighted fine on the port bow, and the mate, Mr Dick Wright, called the skipper. No action was taken regarding altering course or speed, and the vessel took the ground at 3.15 p.m. on the southern tip of the reef off Sorkapp. *Red Gauntlet* began to pound, and a distress call was sent on the radio. Then the crew left the vessel in the ship's lifeboat.

Fortunately, the sea was flat and calm at the time. A number of trawlers, including the *Northern Dawn*, were fishing in the vicinity and proceeded to the scene of the wreck, but *Northern Spray*, Skipper Martin Peterson, was bound home and close to the position of *Red Gauntlet*. He stopped the *Spray* as close to the reef as possible, and the men in the lifeboat rowed to him. *Northern Spray* then took the survivors to Harstad, Norway, where they were given a towel, soap, and a toothbrush and paste. They were offered transport back to the UK on the mailboat via Bergen but decided to return to Grimsby on the *Northern Spray*. Arriving at Grimsby on the Sunday, they spent the night at the Fishermen's Mission still wearing their sea gear. The ship was a total loss, but fortunately, there were no lives lost. At the subsequent official inquiry into the casualty, the court found that the loss was caused by the fault or default of both Skipper Hicks and Second Hand R. Wright. Hicks was suspended for six months and ordered to pay £100 towards the cost of the inquiry. Wright was suspended for three months and ordered to pay £25.

Dhoon was built in 1915 by Cochrane's at Selby for the Cargill SF Co. of Hull and first registered as *Armageddon* H319. In 1920, she was bought by Wyre ST Co., Fleetwood, who changed her name to *Dhoon*, and in 1922 re-registered her as FD348. In 1928, she moved back to Hull, re-registering as H396, but in 1930, she was back in Fleetwood under Wyre ownership and registered as FD54. In 1939, she was taken over by the Admiralty for war service and renamed *Dhoon Glen*. She was returned to her owners in November 1945 and registered as *Dhoon* FD54. She was a steel, single-screw, coal-burning side trawler of 323 gross tons, 137 feet long, 23.5 feet beam, and 12.9 feet in depth. *Dhoon* left Fleetwood on 6 December 1947 for a voyage to Iceland with a crew of fifteen men all told under the command of Skipper Fred Kirby. She was wrecked on the west side of Iceland, close to Patriksfjord, at the base of the 500-foot rock of Látrabjarg, with the loss of three of her fifteen-man crew on 12 December 1947. Two British trawlers and an Icelandic coastguard cutter stood by offshore in response to her distress signals, but with a raging blizzard, a strong south-easterly gale and seas as high as the vessel's masts, there was nothing they could do to help. Meantime, a fifteen-man Icelandic rescue party had assembled on the top of the cliff. By the following afternoon, there was a slight moderation in the weather, and the rescue party managed to get a line down to the wreck. A breeches buoy was

Dhoon. (J. Worthington Collection)

rigged, and the attempt to pull the men up the 500-foot cliff face to safety began. Seven of the survivors were hauled to the clifftop before dark when the operation had to be suspended until daylight. They were sheltered in a heated tent and given food and dry clothing. The remaining five fishermen spent the night on a ledge half way up the cliff. A number of the rescuers climbed down to them, exchanged their own dry clothes for the fishermen's wet gear, and formed a ring round them to protect them from the weather. At daylight, they too were pulled up to safety. They were then taken on horseback to a farmhouse. After resting up, they were conveyed to Reykjavik, from where they were flown to the UK. The skipper, Mate Harry Ellison and Deckhand Fred Wolfenden died of exposure. *Dhoon* was a total loss. This same party of coastguards and farmers were called out one year later, when they rescued the crew of the *Sargon*. The scene of the stranding has the reputation of being the worst place around the Icelandic coast. In January 1935, the Grimsby trawler *Jeria* had stranded in the same place with the loss of all hands.

*L*ois was a single-screw steel side trawler of 286 gross tons built in 1917 by Cook, Welton & Gemmell at Beverley as the *Corinthia*. Her dimensions were 39.68 x 7.01 x 3.72 metres. On being launched, she was taken over by the Admiralty and renamed *John Appleby*. In 1923, she returned to fishing when she was bought by Fleetwood SF Company, who renamed her *Lois* and registered her as FD424. After Admiralty service as a minesweeper throughout the war, she returned to Fleetwood in the summer of 1945. She sailed for the fishing grounds west of Iceland on Monday 30 December 1946 with a crew of sixteen men under the command of Skipper George 'Bobbinhead' Smith and had just arrived when, on 5 January 1947, she grounded near Grindavic, Iceland. In response to her distress signals, a rescue party assembled on shore and managed to take the crew off by breeches buoy. The last man to leave the ship was Skipper Smith, but sadly, while being pulled ashore, he fell out of the buoy into the sea and was lost. *Lois* was a total loss.

Thomas Altoft. (J. Campell Collection)

Thomas Altoft was built at Beverley in 1919 and registered as H132. She was 248 gross tons and her registered dimensions were 125.5 x 23.5 x 12.7 feet. From 1939 to 1946, she was on Admiralty service flying the pennant number FY552. In January 1942, she was bought by J. Marr from the Mills Steamship Company, London, while she was still on naval service. Demobilised in 1946, she was delivered to Marr and worked from Fleetwood.

She sailed from Fleetwood with a crew of fifteen men all told under the command of Skipper Charles Walter on 6 November 1947. In the early hours of 8 November 1947, she stranded on rocks off Glas Island, Scalpey, Harris, about 2 miles from Glas Island lighthouse. *Thomas Altoft* had started fishing off Barra Head, but had only had two hauls when, at about 11 a.m. on 8 November, due to a fresh sou'west gale, she stopped fishing. The skipper decided to proceed through the Minch to the fishing grounds north of the Butt of Lewis. Steaming watches were set and the third hand and a deckhand took the watch until 6.30 p.m. At 6.30, two deckhands, Hennessey and Robinson, took over the watch with the skipper on the bridge. Just after 6.30 p.m., before Ushinish came abeam, and with Neist Point in sight, the skipper decided to turn in for a much needed rest. He retired to his cabin at 7 p.m. after instructing Hennessey, who was at the wheel, to pass Neist Point 2 to 3 miles off, to reset the log and steer NE by N, and to call him when approaching Glas Island. At this time, the weather was clear with a light wind. At the inquiry, Robinson gave evidence that, when Glas Island light was sighted, it was on the starboard bow, and he remarked on the fact to Hennessey. Hennessey replied, 'That is alright,' and although he knew the light should be on the other bow, he was content to leave the responsibility of steaming at full speed with the light on the starboard bow to Hennessey. In the event, *Thomas Altoft* took the ground at about 10.20 p.m. After the stranding, radio operator Charles Brown sent out distress messages, which quickly brought the Fleetwood trawler *Flanders* and Stornoway lifeboat to the scene. The vessel quickly filled with water, and her crew were huddled on the fo'c's'le head for five hours before being rescued. By this time, the fo'c's'le was the only part of the ship above water, and with the engine room flooded, the vessel was in complete darkness. Skipper Tom Kirby of *Flanders* manoeuvred his ship with great skill between two dangerous reefs close enough to the wrecked ship to allow the men to jump from one ship to the other. Only two or three of the men could jump before the *Flanders* drove off and the manoeuvre had to be repeated five times before all the men were safely aboard the *Flanders*. Fortunately, there was no loss of life, but *Thomas Altoft* was a total loss.

At the subsequent inquiry into the casualty, the court found the skipper was at fault in leaving the navigation in the hands of uncertificated men while turning in. This, and the ignorance of the deckhands left in charge of the watch, was the cause of the stranding. The court suspended Skipper Walter's certificate for nine months.

1948

During 1948, seven large trawlers and forty-six men were lost.

Aberdeen	Corena A198	352 tons	September 1948
	St Agnes No.1 SN88	205 tons	8 July 1948
Grimsby	Epine GY7	358 tons	13 March 1948
	Mildenhall GY280	434 tons	1 November 1948
	Sargon GY858	297 tons	1 December 1948
Hull	Lord Ross H496	265 tons	1 December 1948
Fleetwood	Goth FD52	394 tons	13 December 1948

Corena was built in 1924 by Cook, Welton & Gemmell at Beverley as the *Andalusite* for Kingston ST Co., Hull, and registered as H90. In 1933, she was bought by J. Marr, Fleetwood for £7,600, registered as FD195, and renamed *Corena*. She was requisitioned by the Admiralty in 1939 and was used for minesweeping throughout the war until being demobbed in 1946. Bought by Joseph Craig, Aberdeen, in 1946, she was registered as A198. She was a single-screw steel side trawler of 352 gross tons, 42.76 metres long, 7.32 metres in beam and 3.93 metres in depth.

In late August 1948, while on a voyage to Greenland with crew of fourteen hands under the command of Skipper C. H. Winter, a native of Grimsby living in Aberdeen, she grounded while navigating through ice on the west coast of Greenland. She was badly holed near the engine room and started to make more water than the pumps could cope with. The crew took to the lifeboat and were adrift for several hours until a party of Greenlanders in a motorboat took them in tow to Frederikshavn. From there a Danish gunboat took them to Feringhavn, where they obtained passage to Torshavn on Faroese fishing vessels. From there, they were able to obtain passage home on other vessels. The first five survivors arrived back in Aberdeen on 17 September 1948 on Faroese fishing vessels. The *Corena* had been fishing for three days when she grounded. Shortly after stranding, she slid off the rocks and sank stern first. She was a total loss. In addition to her skipper, at the time of the stranding, the crew comprised ten Aberdeen men and three from Grimsby. Two lucky men were E. Ross of Aberdeen and J. Richie, second engineer, of Peterhead. They were put ashore at Stornoway when *Corena* was outward bound and replaced by J. Main and A. Bremner, both of Aberdeen.

St Agnes No.1: The evidence given at the Court of Inquiry into the cause of the loss of this vessel is of particular interest in that it throws light on serious disregard of the regulations by the owners and is the only casualty described in this book where the skipper had his Certificate of Competency cancelled.

St Agnes No.1. (W. Dodds Collection)

St Agnes No.1 was built in 1908 by Jos. T. Eltringham & Co. at South Shields, and at the time of her loss was owned by R. Hastie & Sons, registered at North Shields as SN88, and was working out of Aberdeen. She was a single-screw, single-deck side trawler of 205.45 gross tons, 117.2 feet in length, 21.65 feet beam and 12.4 feet in depth. She was equipped with a Marconi echo-sounder, direction finder and a Marconi radio telephone, all of which were serviced on 28 June 1948. The vessel sailed from Aberdeen on her final voyage on 1 July 1948 bound for the Faroe fishing grounds with a crew of eleven hands all told under the command of Skipper John Muir. She proceeded to Fugelfjord for engine repairs and was there from 3 to 5 July. She went from Fugelfjord to Klaksvig where she landed a sick crew member on the 6th. On 7 July, Fireman R. McPherson burned his leg, and the next day, the injury seemed to be turning septic, so the skipper decided to proceed to Soervaag to place him in hospital. At this time, the trawler was about 8 miles SW of Soervaag, and a course was laid for Dragasund. Skipper Muir was unfamiliar with the navigation of Dragasund, but the second fisherman told him he had been through this passage several times. The only chart of this area aboard the ship was a Blue Back No.016 which was only suitable for track and fishing, and totally unsuitable for inshore navigation. The weather was blustery with clear visibility. At 12.35 p.m., the vessel struck a submerged rock at full speed. The engines were put full speed astern, but she remained fast and started to make water. A wireless distress call was sent out, which was answered by the trawler *Jean Stephen*, who anchored about half a mile off the stranded vessel. Faroese fishing boats arrived on the scene, and they carried a warp from the trawler to the *St Agnes*, and unsuccessful attempts were made to float the stranded vessel. Prior to the arrival of *Jean Stephen*, the crew of *St Agnes* tried to launch their boat but found this impossible, because the swivel chock was solidly rusted up, and the mizzen boom was rusted so solidly that it could not be raised. The sheriff of Soervaag arrived aboard shortly after the stranding and, at about 6.30 p.m., advised the skipper to abandon the ship, as the position seemed hopeless. This advice was taken, and the crew were taken ashore by a Faroese boat. At 9 p.m., the skipper, mate and chief engineer returned to the *St Agnes* and found that the engine room was completely flooded and the decks were level with the water. Soon after, the vessel fell over on her port side. She was a total loss.

At the subsequent inquiry, the court heard that the trawler was under the care of Mr Simon, a superintendent engineer, whose duty it was to see that she was kept in a seaworthy condition. He should have been aware that it was impossible to launch the boat and had the faults remedied. However, the skipper must bear some of the blame because he also should have been aware of the faults, having been in command of *St Agnes* since the previous April. There were no binoculars aboard *St Agnes*. These had been ordered by the skipper, but the owners had neglected to supply them. The skipper must also accept blame that insufficient charts were on board. Had he ordered them, the owners would have supplied them.

Evidence was given that at no time since Skipper Muir took command had he held any boat drill. This was a breach of the Life-saving Appliance Rules 1948 and the Muster Rules 1948. Pamphlets were issued by the Ministry of Transport in May 1948, but these were not provided to the vessel. Responsibility for this must lie with the owners. The court found that Skipper Muir navigated his ship in a reckless manner. He attempted to navigate the passage through Storesund with a totally inadequate chart, and but for the arrival of Faroese boats, there could have been loss of life. With only this chart available, a prudent master would not have attempted the passage through Storesund, but would have proceeded via the western side of Gaasholm, which would have added a distance of only 1.5 miles to the passage via Storesund. After careful consideration, the court decided they had no alternative other than to cancel Skipper Muir's certificate.

The *Sargon* sailed from Hull with a crew of seventeen hands under the command of Skipper Alfred Jenner on 24 November 1948 bound for the fishing grounds at Iceland.

She was owned by the Adam Steam Fishing Company Ltd. of Fleetwood, managed by the Saint Andrew Steam Fishing Company, Hull, and built at Beverley by Cook, Welton & Gemmell in 1913. *Sargon* was a steel-hulled, single-screw, one-deck steam trawler of 296.35 gross tons, 120.64 tons net registered tonnage. She was 130.2 feet long, with a beam of 23 feet, and a depth of 12.2 feet. She was propelled by a reciprocating triple expansion steam engine, which drew steam from a single-ended steel cylindrical multitubular boiler fired by coal. Both engine and boiler were made by Amos & Smith of Hull. Her steering gear was of the rod and chain type and operated by hand or by a steam engine from the wheelhouse. She was fitted with a trawler-pattern stockless anchor and 105 fathoms of 1 1/16-inch stud-link cable. *Sargon*'s electronic equipment comprised a Marconi T.727 radio telephone transmitter, T.950 radio telephone receiver, type 552/537A direction finder, and a Marconi type 421A/B S4 TER echo-sounder. All the above equipment was serviced by the maker and found to be in good order on 20 November 1948.

She had three compasses, one in the wheelhouse in the steering position, a pole compass fore side the wheelhouse, and one in the skipper's cabin. They were adjusted in Hull on 24 June 1948.

The *Sargon*'s life-saving appliances comprised one Class 1A wood lifeboat certified to carry seventeen persons and stowed on chocks aft under the mizzen boom, eighteen lifejackets, six lifebuoys, two buoyant apparatus certified to support a total of forty persons, and a line-throwing appliance type H size 3. These life-saving appliances were inspected and found satisfactory by the Minister of Transport Surveyor at Hull on 17 May 1948. She was a good, well-found vessel, seaworthy in every respect when she left Hull on her last voyage.

Sargon. (*Hull Daily Mail*)

Sargon aground. (Source unknown)

As stated earlier, she left Hull on 24 November 1948. On arriving in Icelandic waters, she put into Reykjavik to have her echo-sounder repaired. These repairs were satisfactorily completed, and she sailed for the fishing grounds on 30 November. On 1 December, *Sargon* was fishing off Staalbierg Huk, and shortly after 10 a.m., the weather had deteriorated to the point where Skipper Jenner decided to seek shelter. At 5.30 p.m. that day, she was in the entrance to Patrix Fjord just off Straumness. There was an easterly gale blowing, a rough sea, and normal visibility. *Sargon* entered Patrix Fjord at about 6 p.m., and at this time, the wind was about ENE Force 10 with bad visibility due to snowstorms. At 7 p.m., she dropped anchor in the fjord with 4 ½ shackles of cable out, but the anchor did not hold and had to be hove up. At this time, it was found that the echo-sounder was not working properly, probably due to the weather conditions. After heaving up the anchor, the skipper kept on various courses at slow speed, hoping for the snow to cease, thus restoring visibility. Throughout this period, the mate took soundings with the lead at thirty-minute intervals, getting continuous depths of 37 fathoms until 10 p.m. when the vessel was felt to strike the bottom. Visibility was still nil, and those on board had little idea of where they had stranded. It was later ascertained that she had grounded at Hafnarmuli, on the south side of the fjord about 8 miles from the entrance.

After stranding, several rockets were fired at intervals of about ten minutes, and mattresses were set on fire on the deck. The weather was so bad that this was very difficult, but at least one of the rockets was seen from ashore. Once the Icelanders ashore had been alerted, rescue attempts were started. At about 2 a.m. on 2 December, a rocket line was fired over the ship between the bridge and the foremast. This line was not seen by the crew, some of whom were sheltering forward and some in the wheelhouse, but even if it had been seen, the severity of the weather would have prevented any use being made of it, and after a while, it parted. Further rockets were sent up from the ship, the last about 5 a.m. Between 10 a.m. and 12 noon, the snow had ceased and the weather was a little better, and another rocket line was fired from ashore. This time, the crew got the line, a breeches buoy was rigged, and six of the crew were pulled ashore. Four of these men had been sheltering in the forecastle all night and, at about 5.30 a.m., had been joined by the mate and another man. The conditions on the bridge were appalling. All eleven men there except one were dead from cold and exposure, and the eleventh one was in such bad condition that the mate was unable to detach his hands from the post he was clinging to. This man must have been at the point of death.

The Court of Inquiry into the loss was of the opinion that the skipper could not be blamed for entering the fjord in snow for the shelter the upper part of the fjord would have provided, nor could he be faulted for dodging on various courses after the anchor refused to hold. The court found that the reason for the loss was due to very bad weather conditions with nil visibility, and expressed admiration for the untiring work done by the shore party, who had to come a long way over difficult country at night, in bitter weather, carrying the rescue apparatus.

Tribute was paid by the survivors to the skipper for his attitude and bearing both before and after the stranding, which the court endorsed, and extended to the survivors and those who perished, who it considered had behaved admirably in the terrible stresses to which they were exposed.

The *Goth* was a single-screw steel trawler built in 1925 at Beverley, and owned by the Wyre Steam Trawling Company, Fleetwood. She was 147 feet long between perpendiculars, her moulded breadth 25 feet, moulded depth 14.5 feet, and had a gross tonnage of 394.48. She was first registered at Hull as H211 but probably after completing Admiralty service, she was bought by Wyre Trawlers, Fleetwood, in

Goth. (J. Worthington Collection)

1948 and re-registered as FD52. She was propelled by a reciprocating steam triple-expansion engine of 700 ihp with a coal-fired multitubular boiler with a working pressure of 200 lb per square inch. She was equipped with all the radio equipment and life-saving appliances required by the regulations, all of which was subject to survey just prior to her last voyage, and found to be in order.

Goth was classed +100 A1 at Lloyd's and had met all the survey requirements to keep her class. She had been inclined for stability in June 1945 with satisfactory results, and her stability was adequate for all stages of a normal fishing voyage to Iceland without any provision of ballast. The Court of Inquiry into her loss was unable to come to a definite conclusion, but stated that the probable cause was heavy weather, but other causes could not be excluded. All we can do is state the details of her last voyage as known and draw our own conclusions.

The *Goth* sailed from Fleetwood on 4 December 1948 for a voyage to the Icelandic fishing grounds with a crew of twenty-one men under command of Skipper Wilfred Elliot. It was Skipper Elliot's first trip in command. She made good time on her outward passage, taking about four and a half days to reach the fishing grounds. On the afternoon of 10 December, she was fishing with the Grimsby trawler *St Melante* about six or seven miles NW of Straumnaes. That afternoon, there was a strong NW wind, a rough sea, and intermittent snow squalls. By 11 a.m. the next day, 11 December, the wind had freshened to gale force from the NE, causing *St Melante* to pull the gear aboard and head for shelter in Red Sand Bay, to the east of Staalbierg Huk. While steaming south for shelter, she observed *Goth* steaming in towards Adalvik, with land in sight. So far as is known, that is the last time the *Goth* was ever seen. The *St Melante* continued to shelter under the land in Red Sand Bay until 8 a.m. on 13 December, during which time she experienced hurricane-force winds and had difficulty using her anchor. The weather began to improve at 8 a.m. and she left Red Sand Bay and sailed for Grimsby. Throughout 14 and 15 December, the weather continued to moderate a little, but on the 16th, the wind again reached Force 9 or

10. So much for the weather during the period the *Goth* disappeared. The wireless operator on *Goth* was making his first trip in that capacity, and in the first part of the voyage was having trouble with his radio telephone apparatus, but after receiving advice from radio officers on other trawlers, these problems seemed to be resolved. The last known official communication with *Goth* was when she acknowledged receipt of a wireless telegraph message sent at 2300 hours on 10 December, but after that her skipper and wireless operator were in contact with other trawlers in the area, and there is reliable evidence that *Goth* was still communicating with other trawlers on the radio telephone until the night of 13 December. It cannot be assumed that *Goth* was lost on the night of 13/14 December because it is remotely possible that weather conditions had brought the wireless aerial down, or salt water may have reached her batteries. There is no conclusive evidence as to when or how *Goth* was lost. The only certainty is that whatever happened to her occurred after late evening of 13 December. The most likely cause seems to be that *Goth* was overwhelmed by the heavy weather, and in the area she was last seen, there are several tide races that are extremely dangerous to ships in bad weather. But there are other remote possibilities. Along the coast from Staalbjerg to Adalvik, there are numerous places a ship could ground and then slip back into deep water leaving no trace. Five or six miles north of Adalvik there was a mine field, which at the time of the loss, had not been declared free of mines, so the possibility that *Goth* had struck a mine exists. There is a slight chance that her boiler could have exploded and an even smaller chance that there could have been an explosion of gas in her bunkers caused by a naked light. The area was systematically searched by sea and air, and no trace of wreckage was ever found, which seems to discredit the loss being due to an explosion. That brings us back to the weather and/or a rocky coast.

Author's Note: In the summer of 1997 the Icelandic trawler *Helga* was fishing on the North Cape ground when she came fast on a wreck. The gear was cleared, and when it was heaved to the surface, a funnel was found in the net. On being brought aboard, the number painted on it showed that it came from *Goth*. The *Helga* landed the funnel at Reykjavik from where it was shipped to Fleetwood via Immingham, where it is proposed to preserve it in memory of the twenty-one men lost in that storm fifty years ago.

The *Epine* was built by Cook, Welton & Gemmell in 1929 for Hull owners and named *Solway Firth*. She came to Grimsby in January 1939 and was registered in that port as GY7, and her name changed to *Epine* in February that same year. Throughout the Second World War, *Epine* was engaged in minesweeping for the Admiralty, returning to Grimsby in 1946. She was a steel, single-deck, single-screw steam trawler, and at the time of her loss was owned by the Premier Steam Fishing Company. Her gross tonnage was 357.55 tons, and her registered dimensions were 140.3 feet x 24 feet x 13.2 feet. She carried all the life-saving equipment, including a lifeboat, required for a vessel of her class, and it was all in good order and complied with the regulations. She was equipped with wireless telegraphy and telephony, a direction finder and an echo-sounder.

Epine sailed from Grimsby on 1 March 1948 for a fishing trip to Icelandic waters with a crew of nineteen hands all told under the command of Skipper Alfred Loftis. She had on board all the necessary charts and sailing directions for the proposed voyage and was well found and seaworthy in every respect. During the early part of the trip, fishing was plagued with bad weather, but on 13 March, she was fishing about 40 miles west of Hvalsnes on the west side of Iceland in about ninety fathoms. Fishing was bad and the weather was deteriorating, so the skipper decided to put

Epine on naval duty. (W. Dodds Collection)

into Keflavik Bay for shelter, and at 5.30 p.m., a course of ESE was set, and the vessel proceeded towards the land at a speed of 9 knots. At about 6.50 p.m., the skipper spoke to the skipper of the trawler *Hargood* who was fishing at Adalvik, who told him the weather at Adalvik was good and so was the fishing. He therefore decided to proceed to Adalvik, and at about 7.25 p.m., the course was altered to N by E ½ E and the log was set. The mate was on watch with one deckhand. At about 7.30 p.m., the skipper told the mate he was going to turn in and gave him orders that he was to be called if the weather deteriorated, if there were any snowstorms, if any ships or lights were sighted, or when the log read 40. The mate reminded the skipper that he was due to go off watch at 8.30 p.m. and was told to inform him (the skipper) when the watch was changed. The watch was changed at 8.30, the new watch consisting of two deckhands, Yates and Maul. The instructions regarding calling the skipper were passed on to Yates, except that he was told to call the skipper when the log read 39, not 40, and that he would get this log reading about 11.30 p.m. The mate then took soundings and found a depth of just over 70 fathoms, and informed the skipper that he was going off watch. The skipper told him to go below and that he would be coming up to the bridge in a few minutes. The mate turned in at 9.10 p.m., but the skipper did not come up to the bridge, and the two deckhands were left in charge of the ship. Shortly after 9.30 p.m., the skipper called up to the bridge and asked what the weather was like, and was told it was clear. About 10.45, the two deckhands saw a light about 2 ½ points on the starboard bow, but they did not report it, as they were unable to ascertain whether it was a ship, a buoy or a shore light. Visibility was patchy with periodic snow showers. At 11.35 p.m., the log reading was 39, and this was reported to the skipper, who came up to the bridge very shortly afterwards. When the skipper arrived on the bridge, he was told about the light on the starboard bow, but was unable to locate it with the glasses. At 11.50 p.m., the *Epine* hit the rocks just to the west of Malariff Light without anyone on board realising she was dangerously close to the land. The wind was a moderate gale with a rough sea, and the vessel pounded heavily and took a big list to starboard. Water entered the vessel in large quantities, and in less than ten minutes, the engine room was flooded and the lights were extinguished. The crew came out on deck wearing lifejackets with the exception of one man, and the skipper gave this man his own lifejacket. Seas were sweeping the deck, and the lifeboat was found to be stoved in. Six distress rockets were fired, and fires were lit on top of the wheelhouse and on the whaleback. Some of the crew were washed overboard, but others managed to climb up the rigging. The wireless operator stuck to his post and sent out a distress call, and made contact with the trawler *Spurs*. Shortly after the vessel struck, Malariff Light was seen at times on the starboard beam. The place the vessel stranded was rocky with high cliffs, but with a small beach at the foot of the cliffs. After some time, a light was seen ashore, first on top of the cliffs and later on the beach. Soon after daylight, the Icelandic rescue party managed to get a rocket line to the ship, and a breeches buoy was rigged. Four members of the crew were pulled ashore with the buoy, and one man jumped overboard and swam, or was washed, ashore. The other fourteen hands had already perished, either from drowning or exposure. The skipper was one of the casualties. This was another stranding where heroic service was rendered by an Icelandic rescue party.

At the subsequent inquiry into the loss, the court found that the stranding was due to the fault or default of Skipper Loftis. He had probably made an error in fixing his point of departure, and he should never have allowed the ship to be in the charge of two uncertificated deckhands, especially in an area where it is well known that compasses are affected by magnetic disturbance.

The *Mildenhall* was built in 1934 by Cochrane's at Selby for the Rinovia Steam Fishing Company. She was registered at Grimsby in January 1935 as the *Dragney* with the port number GY126. In January 1940, she was taken over by the Admiralty for minesweeping and escort duties, being returned for fishing in 1946 and registered

Mildenhall as *Dragney*. (J. Worthington Collection)

as GY280. In March 1947, under the ownership of H. Croft Baker, her name was changed to *Mildenhall*.

Mildenhall was a single-screw coal-fired steam side trawler of 434 gross tons, 156 feet long, 25.9 feet beam, and 14.1 deep. She was fitted with modern radio and echo-sounding devices, regulation life-saving appliances, and magnetic compasses. The ship and her equipment were in good condition and compasses were adjusted before she sailed on her final voyage.

She sailed from Grimsby, bound for Bear Island, on 18 October 1948 with a crew of twenty-one hands all told under the command of Skipper Harold Edward Brennan. When about 300 miles out from Grimsby, Skipper Brennan received information concerning the fishing from the owner's office which decided him to proceed to the White Sea fishing grounds, rather than to Bear Island. At 1100 hours on 1 November, he dropped a buoy with Cape Nyemetski bearing SE ½ S at an estimated distance of 3.75 miles in 52 fathoms of water. The vessel commenced fishing, towing in a south-westerly and north-easterly direction, hauling the trawl at the completion of each run at the north-eastern end of the tow. Darkness fell at 1300 hours, and no definite observation or recognition of any part of the land was made after the buoy was dropped. At about 2118 hours, breakers were sighted bearing about NE on the starboard bow, and although the engines were stopped, the vessel stranded on Laassat Reef. Attempts were made to refloat the trawler, but her hull was so badly damaged by contact with the rocks that she was a total loss. An SOS was sent out and answered by HMS *Romula*, who arrived on the scene at about 1300 hours on the morning of the 2nd. *Romula* launched a motorboat and succeeded in rescuing all the crew, most of them being taken aboard the motorboat, the others in *Mildenhall*'s starboard lifeboat, the port boat having been smashed by the sea.

The verdict of the Court of Inquiry into the stranding was that the loss was caused by the failure of Skipper Brennan to check his position from the time of dropping the buoy until the time of the stranding, and they suspended his certificate for six months.

*L*ord *Ross* was built in Germany by Deutsche Schiffs und Maschinenbau, AG Seebeck, Wesermünde, in 1935. One of the 'Northern Boat Pups', she was 127.6 feet long, 24.1 feet in beam, and 12.9 feet in depth, with a gross tonnage of 266 tons. She was first registered in Aberdeen as the *Neil Mackay* A316. She moved to Hull in late 1946 or early 1947 under the ownership of the Lord Line and was renamed *Lord Ross* H496.

Lord Ross had left Hull with a crew of seventeen hands under the command of Skipper Ellis White. She sank in Faxe Bay, off Alftanes, South West Iceland, after striking a submerged rock in a snowstorm on 2 April 1948. After the stranding, the crew launched and boarded the lifeboat. The bosun kept the boat's head to wind while the other occupants bailed out with milk cans and sou'westers. The survivors were in the lifeboat for 1½ hours until the Icelandic trawler *Juni* arrived on the scene and picked them up. There was no loss of life, but *Lord Ross* was a total loss.

1949

Four ships lost this year.

Grimsby	*St Clair* GY387	255 tons	23 August 1949
Hull	*Spaniard* H366	542 tons	22 March 1949
Fleetwood	*William Mannell* LO370	276 tons	22 February 1949
	Pintail H982	198 tons	2 April 1949

The *Pintail* was built at Goole in 1908, and her engine was supplied and installed by Earle's Shipbuilding & Engineering Company Ltd, Hull. At the time of her loss, she was owned by Brixham Trawlers Ltd., Fleetwood. She was a steel, single-screw, single-deck steam trawler of 198 gross tons, 110 feet in length, 21.6 feet beam, and 11.67 feet deep. She was steered by hand-operated steering gear and had two compasses, an overhead compass in the wheelhouse, and a hanging compass in the skipper's berth. These were last adjusted in Fleetwood on 15 October 1948, and were practically without deviation.

The vessel was fitted with a Marconi echometer, Type 424, which had been serviced on 12 January 1949, but which went out of order a few days before the stranding. She had leads and lines on board, and her life-saving appliances complied with mandatory requirements. When she left Fleetwood on her last voyage, she was seaworthy, and had adequate charts on board for her proposed voyage.

The *Pintail* left Fleetwood on 15 February 1949 for a fishing trip in Donegal Bay with a crew of twelve hands all told, under the command of Skipper Robert Staffard. On 25 February at about 1.30 p.m., she left the fishing grounds and set course for home. Between 8 and 9 p.m., she passed Tory Island Light at an estimated distance of 5 miles off, and steered east, passing Garvan Islands at an estimated distance of between one and two miles. When about two miles WSW of Inistrahull Light at 1.10 a.m. on the 26th, the course was altered to ESE, the log was set, and the skipper marked the position on the chart. At this time, there was a WSW gale and heavy sea, with periodic rain and hail squalls reducing visibility. At about 1.45 a.m., the skipper went below leaving orders he was to be called at 4.30 a.m. The bosun, who was on watch, called the skipper at 4.30 a.m. as ordered, informing him that he had sighted Bull Point Light about a point and a half on the starboard bow. The skipper came immediately to the bridge, saw the light, and estimated its distance to be about seven miles. At about five o'clock, a squall obscured the light and it was not seen again. Navigating purely by guesswork or 'estimate based on experience', the skipper set a course of SE ½ S in order to pass through the middle of Rathlin Sound. From then on, nothing was seen or heard until the ship ran aground about 300 yards southward of Bull Point Light at 5.30 a.m. On stranding, the engines were run full speed astern without result, and as the engine room was rapidly filling with water, the engineers

Pintail. (J. Worthington Collection)

were ordered on deck. Rockets were fired, and the whistle sounded as long as there was steam. At dawn, two men from the lighthouse were seen on shore and a line was passed to them by rocket pistol. They hauled the end of a 3-inch line ashore, which they secured to a rock, and one of the trawler crew reached the shore along this line. Portrush lifeboat arrived on the scene but could do nothing, and at about 10.30 a.m., the remaining eleven members of the crew were safely landed by the Rathlin Island Life-Saving Company.

The Court of Inquiry expressed the view that the skipper was lacking in proper care in failing to take better measures to ascertain the ship's position by laying off bearings on the chart, and by not hauling his ship further away from the danger which he last sighted only half an hour before stranding. The court suspended the skipper's certificate for a period of six months, and ordered him to pay £100 towards the cost of the inquiry. Today, the *Pintail*'s boiler and part of her bow can still be seen at low water.

*S*paniard H366 was built at Beverley in 1942 for the Admiralty as the *Dunkery*, an RN Hills-class ship. Her name was changed to *Spaniard* in 1946 when she was registered under the ownership of Northern Fishing Company, a subsidiary of Hellyer Bros. She was a single-screw oil-burning side trawler of 542 gross tons, 167.7 feet long and 28.1 feet in beam.

She sailed from Hull on 7 March under the command of Skipper Ben Ashcroft for a voyage to the Barents Sea grounds and, on the night of 22 March 1949, ran aground close to Sletnes Lighthouse just west of the entrance to Tanafjord, Finmark, Norway. Responding to her distress call, the Grimsby trawler *Indian Star*, owned by Northern Trawlers, Grimsby, succeeded in taking all her crew off. There were no casualties. At first, it was thought she could be salvaged, but over the next few days, she was pounded by heavy seas in fierce westerly gales, and was eventually abandoned as a total loss.

Spaniard. (P. Whiting Collection)

St Clair. (Fishing Heritage Centre)

St Clair was built for Fleetwood owners in 1904 by Cook, Welton & Gemmell at Beverley. She was a single-screw steel steam trawler of 255 gross tons, 128.3 feet long, 22.2 feet in beam, and 12 feet deep, and registered as FD15. She was taken over by the Admiralty in June 1940, and after being fitted out for minesweeping, was renamed HMT *Sunspot*. Demobbed at the end of the war, she returned to Fleetwood under the ownership of Dinas Steam Trawling Company, but in November 1946, she was acquired by Northern Trawlers, Grimsby, and registered as GY387. In May 1948, she was bought by Yarmouth owners, and on 23 August 1949, she stranded on Swona, Pentland Firth, in thick fog and was a total loss.

She had left Yarmouth on 11 August with a crew of Lowestoft and Yarmouth men under the command of Skipper Frederick Thomsett on a voyage to the westerly grounds and was homeward bound with a good catch of 6,000 stone of white fish when the mishap occurred. In fact, she took the bottom twice. First, she grounded on the Isle of Stroma in the Pentland Firth and fired distress rockets and sent out a distress call on the radio. A short time later, she refloated and the tide carried her across the Firth. With a damaged rudder probably making it impossible to steer her, she again grounded. In response to the distress call, the Longhope lifeboat put to sea and found *St Clair* aground on the rocks off Swona, 5 miles north of her first mishap. She was heeled at a 45-degree angle and was in a very exposed position about eighty yards offshore. The lifeboat managed to take off all the crew and there was no loss of life, but *St Clair* was a total loss.

William Mannell was built by Smith's Dock at Middlesbrough in 1917 for the Admiralty. She was a single-screw steel side trawler of 276 gross tons, 125.5 feet long, 23.4 feet in beam, and 12.8 feet deep. She was registered at London as LO370. After the Second World War, she worked from Milford Haven for a while under the ownership of Yolland Bros, but in 1948, she was sold to J. Marr and moved to Fleetwood.

She sailed from Fleetwood on a fishing voyage on 9 February 1949 under the command of Skipper Reuben John Melhuish with a crew of thirteen men all told and was seaworthy in every respect.

On 21 February, while fishing on the Dubh Artach fishing ground, a gale warning was received. As a consequence, the gear was pulled aboard and she proceeded to Culdaff Bay for shelter and anchored at 2.30 p.m. in the bay just south of Glengad Head in 7 fathoms about 200 yards offshore. At about 4 a.m. on 22 February, the weather showed signs of improving and Skipper Melhuish decided to weigh anchor and resume fishing. He was alone on the bridge, and the mate and two deckhands were on the fo'c's'le head weighing the anchor. When the mate signalled that the anchor was aweigh, the skipper increased speed from 'Slow' to 'Half Ahead' and put the wheel to what he thought was hard-aport and secured it with a becket. At this time, a heavy squall had reduced visibility to nil. After securing the wheel, the skipper looked out ahead and on returning looked at the compass and found that the ship had only turned about three points, much less than she should have done with the helm hard over. As he was about to ring the engine to 'Stop', the vessel took the ground and took a list to port. The engine was put 'Full Astern' for a few minutes with no result, and then the ship's boat was put in the water. The port list made this difficult. The trawler *Gava* was anchored nearby and, hearing the *William Mannell*'s SOS on her whistle, launched her boat, which proceeded to her. The skipper and crew of the stranded vessel proceeded to *Gava* in these two boats. No attempt was made to assess possible damage or to start the pumps. About two hours later, the skipper and chief engineer returned to the wreck in a small boat that had arrived from ashore. It was found that the engine room, bunkers, and forepeak were dry, but the fish hold had water to sea level. At about 12.15 p.m., the *William Mannell* refloated on the rising tide. She retained the port list and continued to fill with water. The *Gava* moved alongside her, and a tow was rigged. The attempt was then made to tow the sinking ship to the nearest beach in Culdaff Bay. One tow rope parted and was replaced, but progress was slow, and at about 2.30 p.m., those men on *William Mannell* returned to *Gava*. Towage continued until about 3 p.m., when *William Mannell* heeled to port and sank by the head about 2 ½ miles east of Dunmore Head in 14 fathoms of water.

Evidence given at the inquiry revealed that there had been previous trouble with the steering gear earlier that trip. Skipper Melhuish was criticised for having no lookout on the bridge with him. The court was of the opinion that he should have waited for better visibility before weighing the anchor, and after the stranding steps should have been taken to keep steam and operate the pumps. The court was satisfied that, even if these measures had been taken, the vessel would still have sunk within three or four hours of refloating. No fault could be found with the efforts of *Gava* to beach her. Skipper Melhuish's certificate was suspended for six months.

1950

Four ships and one man were lost this year.

Aberdeen	Kuvera A384		202 tons	26 January 1950
Grimsby	Ogano GY69		265 tons	24 April 1950
	Preston North End GY82		419 tons	14 April 1950
	Pollard GY244		350 tons	17 February 1950

*K*uvera was a Strath-class trawler built by Ouse Shipbuilding Co., Goole, in 1919 as the *John Heath* for the Admiralty. Completed too late for war service, she was sold to F. Pearce, Grimsby, who registered her as GY381 and renamed her *Kuvera*. In October 1922, she was bought by Consolidated Fisheries, Grimsby. In 1936, she was sold to R. Baxter, Aberdeen, and registered as A384. Taken over by the Admiralty in 1940, she served as an armed patrol vessel until September 1945, when she returned to fishing under the ownership of a Granton company. She was 202 gross tons, 115.4 feet long, 22.1 feet beam, and 12.1 feet deep.

On 26 January 1950, *Kuvera* was fishing 110 miles north-east of Buchan Ness when she sprang a leak and foundered. Her thirteen-man crew were rescued by Skipper John Paterson on the Granton trawler *Chiltern* and landed at Granton.

*O*gano was a non-standard Castle-class Admiralty trawler built by Cook, Welton & Gemmell in 1917 as the *Hugh Black*. On being released from naval service, she went to Hull, where her name was changed to *Macbeth*. In 1929, she was bought by Taylors, Grimsby, (Diamond SF Co.) and registered as *Ogano* GY69. In June 1939, her registered owners were St Andrews SF Co., Hull, but by February 1945, she was back in Grimsby with Taylors (Ogano SF Co.), who were the registered owners at the time of her loss. She was a single-screw side trawler of 265 gross tons, 125.5 feet long, 22 feet beam, and 12.8 feet in depth.

She sailed from Grimsby bound for the fishing grounds at Iceland with a crew of fifteen hands under the command of Skipper Len Green. On 24 April 1950, she ceased fishing to proceed to Sydisfjord to land a decky with a broken leg, when she grounded on Brokur Rock off East Horn, and was badly holed. After fifteen minutes, Skipper Green was able to refloat her, and with her pumps going and the crew baling her out with buckets, she limped into Stoedvarfjord, where she was beached. Here, she was abandoned and was a total loss. Throughout, the trawler *Lombard* had stood by her and took the survivors to Seydisfjord. There was no loss of life.

*P*ollard was built by Cochrane's at Selby as the *Consbro* in 1930 for Crampin SF Company, Grimsby. She was on naval service throughout the war, after which, she returned to Grimsby. She was registered as GY244 and, in June 1947, was renamed

Ogano. (Welholme Gallery)

Pollard. (Welholme Gallery)

Pollard. She was a single-screw steel side trawler of 350 gross tons, 145.5 feet long, 24.1 feet in beam and 13.2 feet deep.

She sailed from Grimsby on 13 February 1950 bound for the White Sea fishing grounds with a crew of twenty-two hands all told under the command of Skipper George Peacock. At about 8 p.m. on the evening of 17 February, she ran aground on Trannoy in Westfjord. She was badly holed and making water in the engine room. The Norwegian vessel *Ornes* answered her distress call and succeeded in taking off all her crew, but *Pollard* was a total loss.

*P*reston North End was built in 1934 by Smith's Dock, Middlesbrough, for Consolidated Fisheries, Grimsby, and registered as GY82. She was a single-screw steel side trawler of 419 gross tons, 157 feet long, 26.7 feet beam, and 12.7 feet deep.

She sailed from Grimsby for the Icelandic fishing grounds on 1 April 1950 with a crew of twenty-one hands under the command of Skipper Jack East. On 14 April 1950, she ran aground on a submerged reef on the west side of Iceland, about 35 miles west of Reykjanes. An attempt was made to abandon ship, and a lifeboat was launched. Ten men had boarded the boat when the painter parted and the boat drifted away. The boat was leaking badly, and the men in it bailed out all night until they were picked up by a Hull trawler, the *Bizerta*, Skipper F. Rasmussen. The remaining eleven crew members got off her at daylight. Twenty crew members survived, one deckhand died of exposure, but *Preston North End* was a total loss.

1951

Two ships lost this year.

Hull	*St Leander* H19	658 tons	9 January 1951
Grimsby	*Aucuba* GY117	211 tons	5 September 1951

The *Aucuba* was built in 1906 by Cook, Welton & Gemmell for W. Grant, Grimsby, and registered in March 1906 as GY117. She was a steel, single-screw side trawler of 211 gross tons. She was 115.4 feet long, 21.6 feet in beam, and 11.5 feet in depth. During her life, she had several owners and, at the time of her loss, was owned by Derwent Trawlers, Grimsby.

She sailed from Grimsby on 3 September 1951 with a crew of ten men all told under the command of Skipper Thomas Darwood for a fishing trip in the North Sea. She was trawling 11 miles south of South Cheek, Robin Hood's Bay, at 9 p.m. on 5 September 1951 in conditions of poor visibility. The 4,400-ton Italian cargo vessel *Maria Bibolini*, outward bound from Middlesbrough to Rotterdam, collided with her. Aboard the badly damaged *Aucuba*, attempts to launch the lifeboat failed when the topping lift parted. Six members of the crew jumped into the sea and were picked up by the *Bibolini*'s boat, which also rescued the four men remaining on board the *Aucuba*. In response to a radio message from *Bibolini*, salvage tugs were dispatched from the Tees, but after searching in thick mist for several hours, they found no trace of the *Aucuba*. The *Bibolini* proceeded to Rotterdam, where the survivors were landed. The British Consul fitted the men out with new clothes and arranged passage for them on the SS *Bury*, which sailed for Hull the following day. A short trip on the Humber ferry and they arrived back in Grimsby. There were no casualties, but the *Aucuba* was a total loss.

The *St Leander* H19 was built at Beverley by Cook, Welton & Gemmell in 1949 for Thomas Hamling & Company, Hull. She was an oil-fired single-screw steel side trawler of 658 gross tons, was 181.0 feet long and 30.6 feet in beam.

On the night of 9 January 1951, just before high water, a number of homeward-bound trawlers were manoeuvring in the Humber just off the entrance to St Andrews Dock waiting to enter. Among these ships were the *St Leander* with about 1,400 kits of fish on board from the Norway Coast grounds, and the *Davy*, who was at anchor, with about 1,200 kits. In pitch darkness, and with a strong flood-tide, the *St Leander* collided with the *Davy*. The *Davy* suffered extensive damage to her bows but was able to edge alongside the West Pier. The *St Leander* was badly holed below the waterline and immediately started to flood with water. At the time, the dock harbour master was on the end of the lock pits. Hearing the crash, and the subsequent SOS sounded on the *St Leander*'s whistle, he realised the seriousness of the situation and immediately

Aucuba. (Fishing Heritage Centre)

St Leander. (W. Dodds Collection)

ordered oil barges moored in the locks and harbour tugs to proceed to the stricken vessel. The first rescuer on the scene was the oil barge *Gainsborough*, who took off seventeen members of the crew including her skipper, M. Shaughnessy. Three crew members had jumped into the river and were picked up by the oil barges *Martindale* and *Orthdale*. The *St Leander*, listing heavily, drifted away into the darkness followed by a pack of tugs. Eventually, they managed to take her in tow off Barton Ness, but while towing her back to Hull, she grounded on Hessle Flats, about a mile offshore. By the morning of 11 January, the *St Leander* was completely submerged, and she was a total loss. There were no casualties, but the three men who had jumped into the water were taken to the hospital suffering from shock and immersion.

1952

Eight ships and twenty-three men were lost this year.

Aberdeen	*Loch Lomond* A299	310 tons	23 October 1952
	Strathelliot A46	211 tons	23 October 1952
	Braconlea A227	200 tons	5 October 1952
Grimsby	*Trojan* GY848	141 tons	17 May 1952
	Magnolia GY482	260 tons	20 August 1952
Hull	*Norman* H289	628 tons	4 October 1952
	St Ronan H86	568 tons	12 October 1952
Fleetwood	*Wyre Law* FD48	313 tons	23 October 1952

The *St Ronan* was built at Beverley in 1948 as the *Princess Elizabeth* for Boston DSF Company and was registered in Grimsby as GY590. In 1949, she was sold to Firth Steam Trawling Company, a subsidiary of Thomas Hamling Ltd, re-registered as H86, and renamed *St Ronan*. Her gross tonnage was 567.88 tons and her registered dimensions were 170.25 feet x 29.2 feet x 14.45 feet. She was fitted with a triple-expansion reciprocating engine, which drew steam from an oil-fired boiler giving her a speed of 12 knots.

She was equipped with wireless telegraphy, radio telephone, a direction finder and radar. She had an echo-sounder and three compasses. The compasses had been adjusted on 15 September 1952, and radio gear, sounder and radar had been inspected on 8 October 1952 and found to be in good working order. She carried adequate life-saving appliances, which were in good condition.

The *St Ronan* sailed from Hull on the early afternoon of 11 October 1952, bound for the Greenland fishing grounds. She was under the command of Skipper John C. Gibson and had a crew of twenty hands all told. Her mate, Jens K. Nielsen, also held a Skipper's Certificate. The voyage proceeded without incident until the afternoon of 12 October, when the vessel was approaching Duncansby Head. At about 1800 hours, she rounded Duncansby Head, and thereafter the mate took charge of the navigation. He decided to pass through the Inner Sound between the island of Stroma and the mainland. This channel is unlit, and at about 1840 hours, the *St Ronan* stranded on the outermost rock of the Men of Mey, off St John's Point on the mainland.

At the Court of Inquiry, it was revealed that the mate had been drinking with the skipper that afternoon before coming to the bridge. The skipper was asleep, and the amount of alcohol the mate had drunk had probably affected his judgement on attempting to navigate the inner channel in the dark and also his decision on when to alter course at the western end of the channel in order to clear the Men of Mey. The *St Ronan* was a total loss, but fortunately, all her crew were taken safely off by a Stroma motorboat and landed at the harbour of Mey. The court found that the stranding was

St Ronan. (P. Whiting Collection)

Norman. (P. Whiting Collection)

due to fault or default of the skipper and the mate. The skipper was suspended for fifteen months and the mate for twelve months.

The *Norman* was built at Beverley by Cook, Welton & Gemmell in 1943 for the Admiralty. One of the Military class, she was named *Bombardier* and was on convoy escort duties until the end of the war. She was bought by Hellyer Brothers Ltd, Hull, in 1946 and registered at Hull as H289, and her name changed to *Norman*. She was a single-screw, steel, oil-fired steam trawler of 629 tons gross, 178.5 feet long, 30 feet in beam and 15.2 feet deep. Her life-saving appliances complied with the regulations, she was equipped with radio telegraphy and telephony, echo-sounders and radar, and when she left port on her last voyage, she was well found and seaworthy in every respect.

The *Norman* sailed from St Andrew's Dock, Hull, on 17 September 1952, bound for the Greenland fishing grounds with a crew of twenty-one hands all told, under the command of Skipper Jack Dukes. At about 7.30 on the morning of 4 October, she grounded in thick fog on the rocks close in to Cape Farewell. She sent out a distress call and attempted to launch the lifeboats. The port boat was smashed by the sea as it was being launched and the starboard boat overturned. Then the vessel took a list and started to slide, and the crew, thinking that she was about to slip off the reef into deep water, jumped overboard and tried to reach the temporary safety of the rocks. In the turbulence and very strong tide, they had little chance. Only one man, Norman Spencer, the young decky learner managed to climb on to the rocks. A number of trawlers in the area, which included *Northern Isles* (Skipper Tommy Booth), *Northern Princess* (Skipper Jimmy Nunn), *Thornella* (Skipper Charlie O'Neill) and the Norwegian salvage vessel *Skull*, approached the scene of the wreck, but the dense fog, according to Charlie O'Neill, reduced visibility to less than a cable and prevented them from getting close enough to help. In the event, Spencer was on the rock for about seven hours before the Norwegian vessel *Poseidon* – Skipper Ole Vindenes – was able to rescue him. Skipper O'Neill recovered eight bodies from the sea, including that of Skipper Dukes, and brought them back to the UK. The *Poseidon* landed the only survivor at Bergen, Norway. The rock that the *Norman* stranded on is now known to fishermen as Norman Rock, whether in honour of the survivor or the ship, I don't know. The vessel remained stuck on the reef for two days after the stranding before she slid off and sank. According to skippers in the vicinity, had the men remained on board the vessel, they would probably have been rescued.

The *Braconlea* was built at Aberdeen by Alexander Hall & Sons as the *Donum Maris* for Great Yarmouth owners in 1920 and first registered as YH227. Soon after launching she was bought by the Don Fishing Company, Aberdeen and re-registered as A227, and in 1921, her name was changed to *Braconlea*. She was a single-screw steel side trawler of 200 gross tons.

In 1941, she was bought by the Boston company and transferred to Fleetwood, but in 1946, she returned to Aberdeen under the ownership of J. W. Johnston, who was the registered owner at the time of her loss. On 5 October 1952, while under the command of Skipper William Summers, she was running for shelter from gale-force winds when she struck submerged rocks at the Baas of Hascosay in the entrance to Mid Yell Sound. Water began to flood the vessel from her damaged bottom, and a distress call was immediately broadcast on the radio. The North Shields registered trawler *George H. Hastie* NS274 was sheltering in Mid Yell Voe and was quickly on the scene. Local motorboats from the village of Mid Yell were able to get alongside the *Braconlea*, and they took the crew off and ferried them to the *George H. Hastie*. They were landed at Mid Yell and taken home to Aberdeen the following day by the trawler *Strathleven* A47.

There were no casualties, but the *Braconlea* was a total loss.

Loch Lomond. (Aberdeen Library)

The *Loch Lomond* was one of two sisters, the *Lune* and *Fane*, built at Smith's Dock, Middlesbrough, in 1930 for Wards Fishing Company, Fleetwood, which had the distinction of being the first cruiser stern trawlers to sail from that port. In September 1938, both ships were bought by Earl Steam Fishing Company, Grimsby, the *Lune* being registered as GY538. On Admiralty service from 1939 till 1946, she returned to Grimsby, but was moved to Aberdeen in April 1947. In March 1948, she was registered as A299, and her name was changed to *Loch Lomond*. At the time of her loss, she was owned by Malcolm Smith Ltd. She was a single-screw steel side trawler, 310 gross tons, 131 feet long, 24.5 feet in beam and 13.4 feet deep.

The *Loch Lomond* sailed from Aberdeen on 23 October 1952 for a trip to the Faroe fishing grounds. She didn't get far. There was a heavy sea running in the harbour entrance channel, and she seemed to hit her rudder on the bottom halfway along the channel. The damage sustained prevented her from being steered, and she was swept on to the concrete ledge that runs along the foot of North Pier, where she remained fast. The duty watch in the Roundhouse had seen her predicament and alerted the rescue services. All thirteen crew members were got ashore safely though some suffered slight injuries. However, the *Loch Lomond*, battered by heavy seas, was too badly damaged to be refloated and was broken up were she lay.

The *Strathelliot* was built by Hall Russell at Aberdeen for the Aberdeen Steam Trawling Company in 1915 and registered as A46. She was a single-screw steel coal-burning side trawler of 211 gross tons. She saw naval service in both world wars and returned to Aberdeen in 1946. At the time of her loss, she was owned by Clova Fishing Company Ltd, Aberdeen. She sailed from Aberdeen under the command of Skipper George Simpson and a crew of twelve hands all told. On 23 October 1952, she was running for shelter in a severe gale when she grounded on the Taing of Selwick at the western entrance to Scapa Flow. The Stromness Lifeboat answered her distress call but was unable to get alongside the wreck. However, the Hoy Life-saving

Strathelliot. (W. Dodds Collection)

Strathelliot aground. (W. Dodds Collection)

Magnolia. (Welholme Gallery)

Company succeeded in taking all the crew off by breeches buoy. The *Strathelliot* was a total loss.

The *Magnolia* was built by Cook, Welton & Gemmell in 1909 for Danish owners and named *Kong Frederick III*. She was first registered in Grimsby in April 1915 as GY482, and in 1919, presumably after completing naval service, was renamed *King Frederick III*. She had several Grimsby owners and was renamed *Magnolia* in March 1928. After service with the Admiralty in the Second World War, when she was called *Glacier*, she returned to Grimsby again called *Magnolia*. She was 260 gross tons, 125.3 feet long, 22.1 feet beam and 12 feet deep.

On 19 August 1952, while fishing in the North Sea under the command of Skipper Arthur Stanley Wing, she sprang a leak. Another Grimsby trawler, the *Rose of England*, Skipper Alf Walker, had completed landing her catch that morning and was sent out to assist her. By the time he arrived, the fires on *Magnolia* were out, and at 4 p.m., a tow was rigged and the tow towards Grimsby started. Despite continuous pumping, the water was gaining, and at 7.15 p.m. on 20 August, a nineteen-hour struggle to save the ship ended when *Magnolia* sank stern first. The crew jumped into the sea and were hanging on to rafts and other wreckage. The *Rose of England* picked up the survivors, but unfortunately, three men, her Skipper, the Chief Engineer Albert Forster, and deckhand Roland Willis, were lost.

Later, the widows of Skipper Wing and deckhand Willis sued the owners, claiming that the loss of their men was due to the owners' negligence. After a lapse of three years, an Admiralty court found in their favour, awarding them undisclosed damages and costs. Mr Justice Willmer found that the *Magnolia* had put to sea in an unseaworthy condition, which made her unfit for the ordinary perils of a voyage.

The *Trojan* was built in 1898 by Cook, Welton & Gemmell at Hull for T. Robinson, Grimsby, and registered as GY848. She fished from Grimsby for several owners until 1932, when, in July of that year, she was sold to Plymouth owners. At the time of her loss, she was owned by Mr Percy Turner and was one of only three trawlers working from Plymouth. She was a single-screw side trawler of 140 gross tons, 93.2 feet long, 20.6 feet beam and 10.7 feet deep.

She sailed from Plymouth on a fishing trip with a crew of ten men under the command of Skipper Dan Taylor and, on 17 May 1952, was in collision with the Liberian tanker *Kiki Naess* in the English Channel. The *Trojan* sank almost immediately, but all her ten-man crew were saved.

The *Wyre Law* was registered at Fleetwood as FD48. She was a steel side steam trawler of 313 gross tons and built by Livingston & Cooper at Hesle in 1915 as the *Miletus*. After war service, she was renamed *Lowther* and worked from Fleetwood until 1940 when she was again taken over by the Admiralty. On returning to fishing after the Second World War, she was acquired by Wyre Trawlers and renamed *Wyre Law*. She was 135.3 feet long, had a beam of 26.6 feet and was 12.5 feet in depth.

On the evening of Wednesday 22 October 1952, she was fishing off the coast of Lewis when a severe SE gale sprang up. She had left Fleetwood the previous week with a crew of thirteen men under the command of Skipper George Wood and was expected home that weekend. Pulling the gear aboard, the *Wyre Law* headed for the sheltered anchorage in Broad Bay on the east side of Lewis. At 0300 hours, on the morning of 23 October, she ran aground in the bay in pitch darkness, and immediately water began to flood the stokehold. Skipper Wood ordered the mate, Wally Mitchinson to launch the lifeboat. The Fleetwood trawler *Charles Doran*, Skipper Charlie Robinson, was anchored only 200 yards from where the *Wyre Law* grounded and, hearing

Wyre Law. (J. Campell Collection)

her distress signal on the whistle, immediately weighed anchor and moved in closer. The *Wyre Law*'s boat made two trips ferrying all her crew to the *Charles Doran*. There were no casualties. The survivors were landed at Stornoway, where the British Sailors Society arranged food, accommodation and travel to Fleetwood for them. The Shipwrecked Mariners Aid Society provided them with clothing to replace the oddments they were wearing at the time of the stranding. Skipper Woods and Chief Engineer L. J. Snape remained in Stornoway to assist in salvage attempts. The trawler *Wyre Corsair* brought up pumps from Fleetwood and a salvage tug joined them, but bad weather delayed the salvage for over a week. The *Wyre Law* was finally abandoned and the seas broke her up where she grounded.

1953

1953 was a bad year. Ten trawlers and fifty-four men were lost during the year.

Aberdeen	*Sunlight* A221	203 tons	15 January 1953
	River Lossie A332	201 tons	27 March 1953
Grimsby	*Sheldon* GY696	278 tons	31.1.53
	Leicester City GY106	411 tons	22 March 1953
	Riviere GY14	226 tons	10 June 1953
	Hassett GY499	349 tons	18 September 1953
	Belldock GY367	236 tons	16 November 1953
	River Leven GY293	202 tons	13 December 1953
Fleetwood	*Michael Griffith* FD249	282 tons	31 January 1953
	Hildina H222	324 tons	1 December 1953

The *Sunlight* was an Admiralty Strath-class trawler built in 1918 and named *Thomas Graham*. Released from Admiralty service in 1921, she was sold to Grimsby owners, Bunch Steam Fishing Company, and registered as GY1320. In 1927, she was sold to North Shields owners, and her name was changed to Tynemouth Abbey. She was moved to Aberdeen in 1932 and was renamed *Sunlight* – A221 – and continued to fish from that port until she was again taken over by the navy in July 1940. She was demobbed in 1944 and returned to Aberdeen. At the time of her loss, she was owned by the Harrow Baxter Steam Fishing Company, Aberdeen. She was a single-screw steel side trawler of 202.81 gross tons and was 115.5 feet long, 22.2 feet broad and 12.25 feet deep.

The *Sunlight* sailed from Aberdeen for the fishing grounds at 3 p.m. on 13 January 1953 with a crew of thirteen hands all told under the command of Skipper Alexander Souter. Although Skipper Souter had held a skipper's certificate since 1928, the *Sunlight* was his first command, and he had been in charge of her for about two years. When the vessel left Aberdeen, she was well found in every respect. Initially, the *Sunlight* fished east of the Pentland Skerries, but on 14 January, she sailed west through the Pentland Firth and shot the gear off Dunnet Head and fished there until midnight. The weather was then deteriorating, so the skipper decided to proceed for shelter under the lee of Holburn Head, the most northerly and westerly point of Thurso Bay. He arrived there at about 2 a.m. on the 15th and stopped her with Little Head Light bearing SW by W about half a mile off. This brought her just inside Holburn Head, further north. When running in, he was accompanied in the wheelhouse by the second fisherman, Mr J. Sutherland, and when stopped, he ordered Sutherland to call out the crew and clear the fish off the deck. The skipper had had no rest for twenty-two hours, so then went to his cabin, lay down on his bed, and fell asleep. He had not anchored the vessel, nor had he given anyone instructions to keep watch on the bridge. With the prevailing

Sunlight. (W. Dodds Collection)

westerly wind, the *Sunlight* drifted across Thurso Bay in an easterly direction, falling slightly towards the shore on the south side.

The skipper awoke at 4 a.m. and proceeded to the bridge. The only thing he could then see in the darkness were lights to the WNW about 2 miles away, which he took to be the lights of other trawlers. He put the engines slow ahead and proceeded in a WNW direction towards the lights at a speed of about 4 knots. Fifteen minutes later, she struck the ground. In fact, the vessel had drifted to the eastward of Murkle Point on the south side of the bay and grounded on the east side of the Point. The skipper had seen the lights over the land. She made water very quickly and sent out a distress call and fired flares. The Grimsby trawler *Loch Park* came to her aid but was unable to get close to the wreck. Thurso Lifeboat was launched and managed to get alongside the stranded vessel and took off all her crew.

The *Sunlight* was a total loss. At the Court of Inquiry into the casualty, it was found that the loss was caused by default of the skipper. Firstly, when he decided not to anchor, he should have ensured that there was a watch on the bridge. Later, when he came to the bridge at about 4 a.m., he had no idea of the ship's position and should have dropped the anchor and waited for daylight before attempting to move the vessel. The court suspended Skipper Souter's certificate for two years.

*R*iver Lossie was an Admiralty Strath-class trawler built by Fleming & Ferguson, Paisley, as *Arthur Herwin* in 1920 – too late for war service. She was bought by Montrose Fishing Company and registered as *River Lossie* ME121. In May 1923, she was bought by Consolidated Fisheries, Grimsby , and registered as GY279. She moved to Aberdeen in 1935 and was registered as A332 under the ownership of Skipper J. K. Robertson. She was requisitioned by the Admiralty in 1940 and used as an armed patrol vessel until February 1945, when she was demobbed and returned to Aberdeen. *River Lossie* was a steel, single-screw side trawler of 202 tons gross, was 115.5 feet in length, 22.1 feet in beam and 12.1 feet in depth.

She sailed from Aberdeen in late March 1953 for a fishing voyage to the Shetland grounds with a crew of eleven men under the command of Buckie Skipper Alexander

River Lossie. (W. Dodds Collection)

Clark. On 27 March 1953, she was running for shelter and attempting to enter Lerwick Harbour through the tricky north entrance when she ran on to Robbie Ramsay's Baa. Although Lerwick lifeboat was standing by her within an hour of her stranding, the crew decided to remain on board, hoping to refloat her. However, by the next day, she was half full of water, and was abandoned, becoming a total loss. There were no casualties.

The *Sheldon* was a steel, single-screw trawler of 278 gross tons, was 130.1 feet long, 22.2 feet in beam and 12.2 feet deep. She was built by Cook, Welton & Gemmell at Beverley for Standard Steam Fishing Company, Grimsby, in 1912, and registered as GY696. In January 1940, she was bought by Sir Thomas Robinson & Son Ltd, Grimsby, who owned her up to the time of her loss. She was equipped with a Marconi Seagull radio telephone and an Invicta broadcast receiver, which had a range of about 1,250 miles. Her navigational aids comprised a Type 195B Decca Radar, Type MS/24 Kelvin-Hughes Echo-Sounder, Fischlupe Sounding Device, Marconi Type 977/552 Direction Indicator, Pelorus Position Finder and two aneroid barometers. Her life-saving appliances met all current regulations, and she was supplied with all the necessary charts for the proposed fishing voyage. When she left port for her final voyage, she was well found and seaworthy in every respect.

The *Sheldon* sailed from Grimsby, bound for the Faroe fishing grounds, on 26 January 1953. She had a crew of fourteen hands all told and was under the command of Skipper T. R. Beesley. On her way northward, she encountered bad weather and sought shelter in Lambs Bay, Shetland, where she anchored. Skipper Frank Goddard on the trawler *Burfell* also entered Lambs Bay seeking shelter at about 11.30 a.m. on Wednesday 28 January and saw the *Sheldon* at anchor. In a radio conversation at about 12.30, Skipper Beesly told Skipper Goddard he was proceeding to Kirkwall to land two sick seamen, and it was arranged that they would communicate at ten o'clock mornings and evenings. At 1300 hours, *Sheldon* picked up her anchor to proceed to Kirkwall, and that was the last time she was seen by the *Burfell*. *Sheldon* put into Kirkwall late on Wednesday 28 January where two crew members, A. Algar and K. Hotson, were put ashore sick. Two substitutes were sent to Kirkwall from Grimsby, and the *Sheldon* left Kirkwall just after noon on 30 January to resume her passage to the Faroes.

At 2100 hours on 28 January, the *Burfell* left Lambs Bay and proceeded to the Faroes, where she commenced fishing at 2100 hours on the 29th. The weather was fine with no wind, but by 1945 hours on 30 January, the wind had increased to gale force, and she was forced to seek shelter at Klaaksvig in Straight Fjord. At 2200 hours on 30 January, the skipper of the *Burfell* spoke on the radio to the skipper of the *Sheldon*. During the conversation, Skipper Beesly reported that he was steaming full speed, that the wind was light from the SSW, and that he gathered from the reports of other skippers on the Faroe grounds that the weather there was NNE gale about Force 10, thick snow and visibility nil. So far as is known, that was the last time the *Sheldon* was heard on the radio. The *Burfell* called her on a number of occasions at the agreed times but received no answer.

On the night of 30/31 January and the morning of the 31st, the wind veered from SW to NNE and increased to storm Force 10 with very heavy snow reducing visibility to nil. Skipper Jack Shepherd, skipper of the *Cunningham*, was off Dennis Head and estimated that the *Sheldon* was about three hours ahead of him in a position about 70 miles NW by N of Dennis Head. He came head to wind and dodged out the storm, which continued to get worse until about noon on the 31st, when the wind backed to NW and moderated.

On 23 February, a lifebuoy marked 'SHELDON GRIMSBY' was found off the west coast of Shetland, and on 12 March, part of the bow of a lifeboat marked GY696 was found on the Norwegian coast between Kraakeness and Statt. No other trace of the *Sheldon* and her crew was ever found.

The exact cause of the loss remains unknown, but it is probable that she was overwhelmed by wind and sea of exceptional force during the night of 30/31 January 1953. Wind force in the locality was the greatest recorded in the previous seventy years, and at least eight other small ships, including the Fleetwood trawler *Michael Griffith*, were lost that night around the British coast.

The *Leicester City* was built in 1934 by Smith's Docks Ltd, Middlesbrough, and was owned by Consolidated Fisheries, Grimsby. She was a single-screw steam trawler of 422 gross tons. Her registered dimensions were length 157 feet, beam 26.7 feet, depth 12.2 feet. She was classed at Lloyd's and insured with Grimsby Trawlers Mutual Insurance Company and had been subjected to regular surveys. When she left port on her final voyage, she was equipped with all the life-saving equipment required by the regulations, and she was well found and seaworthy in every respect.

Leicester City sailed from Grimsby for a fishing voyage to Icelandic waters on the morning of 3 March 1953 under the command of Skipper G. Johanason, with a crew of twenty men all told. On 22 March, homeward bound, she ran on the rocks off Breibuster Head in dense fog, just after midnight. Immediately after stranding, the vessel took a 45-degree list, and after firing distress flares, the skipper gave the order to abandon ship. This proved to be an error because later the ship righted herself, and had the men remained on board, they could have been taken off by lifeboat when the fog lifted later that morning. The skipper later explained that, at the time, with the vessel so heavily listed, and having no idea how far from land they were, 'Abandon ship' seemed the only sensible course of action to take. The skipper and nine of the crew boarded the lifeboat, but it overturned and one man was washed away. The

Leicester City. (Bill Taylor)

Leicester City. (Bill Taylor)

Leicester City. (Bill Taylor)

River Leven. (Fishing Heritage Centre)

rest of the crew tried to board the rafts but were swept from them by the seas. The upturned lifeboat drifted ashore with the men clinging to it. The mate, Edward Young, was a strong swimmer and attempted to swim ashore to get help. He actually reached land, but was later found on the shore dead from exposure and exhaustion. Ashore, crofters had seen the distress flares and alerted the coastguard. Stromness Lifeboat was quickly on the scene and picked up four men clinging to a raft, but one of these men died on the way into Stromness. An air search continued all day by RAF Hastings, and the last man, the wireless operator, was picked up dead by Thurso Lifeboat. In all, seven men were lost.

The *River Leven* was an Admiralty Strath-class trawler built as the *John Edsworth* in 1918 by J. Fullerton at Paisley. In May 1923, she was bought by Consolidated Fisheries, Grimsby, and registered as *River Leven* GY293 and worked from Grimsby, but in March 1943, she was sold to a North Shields owner. She had a gross tonnage of 202 tons and was 115.4 feet long, 22.1 feet in beam and 12.1 feet deep.

She was working from Hartlepool, fishing in the North Sea, when, on 13 December 1953, she sprang a leak. The Hartlepool trawler *Friarage* came to her assistance and attempted to tow her into harbour. However, she foundered about 33 miles NE by E ½ E of the Tyne. The *Friarage* took off all her crew and landed them at North Shields.

The *Riviere* was built by Cook, Welton & Gemmell in April 1916 for Sir Alec Black and registered at Grimsby as GY893. She moved to Hull in March 1918, returning to Grimsby in February 1919 when she registered as GY14. Between then and her loss in 1953, she had no less than seven different owners. At the time of her loss, her registered owner was Parkholme Trawlers, a subsidiary of Derwent Trawlers (Grimsby)Ltd. She was a single-screw steel steam trawler of 226 gross tons, 117 feet long, 22 feet wide and 12.7 feet deep.

Riviere sailed from Grimsby on 30 May 1953 bound for the fishing grounds at the Faroes with a crew of thirteen men all told, under the command of Skipper J. B. Dunham. On the morning of 10 June, at 0520, she was bound home, and steaming in thick fog when she collided with the 2,841-ton collier *Firelight*, a vessel that supplied coal to the Thames riverside power stations. The *Firelight*'s bows struck the *Riviere* amidships on the port side with considerable force, making a large gash. As the sea flooded into the stricken trawler, *Riviere* sank in about four minutes. Her crew had no time to launch the lifeboat and jumped into the sea. The *Firelight* launched her boat and managed to pick up three survivors, the other ten, including the skipper, were lost. In response to a radio message from the *Firelight*, Flamborough Lifeboat, the collier *Suntrap*, and pleasure steamers from Bridlington were quickly on the scene, and after a fruitless search for bodies, the lifeboat took the three survivors off the *Firelight*. She then proceeded to Flamborough and, on the way in, recovered the body of the third hand, William Duncan, from the sea. Another body was sighted in the water, but it sank before it could be recovered. An RAF Lincoln aircraft from Manby also took part in the search but had to abandon the operation because dense fog over the area made searching impossible. After being landed, the survivors were taken to the North Star Private Hotel. Here they were fed, had a bath and then retired to bed for a sleep before being returned to Grimsby. *Riviere* sank 5 miles off Flamborough Head, less than forty miles from home.

The *Hassett* was built in 1929 by Cook, Welton & Gemmell for Grant and Baker Steam Fishing Company, Grimsby, and named *Gambri*. In 1934, she was sold to Hull owners and her name was changed to *Runswick Bay*. After service with the Admiralty throughout the war, she returned to Grimsby and was registered as GY489

Hassett. (Bill Taylor)

Hassett. (Fishing Heritage Centre)

and renamed *Hassett*. Her owners were Perihelion Steam Fishing Company, a Crampin subsidiary. She was 349 gross tons, and 140.2 feet long, 24.6 feet wide and 13.2 feet deep. She was classed +100 A1 at Lloyd's, and fitted and equipped to the same high standard as the other Crampin's 'Cricketers'. Her life-saving appliances comprised one lifeboat for twenty-one persons, two buoyant apparatus to hold a total of twenty-four persons, four lifebuoys, twenty-three lifejackets, six distress rockets and sticks, two parachute distress flares and a line-throwing apparatus. This equipment was inspected by the Grimsby Fishing Vessels Mutual Insurance's surveyor on 18 December and found to be in good condition. However, it did not comply with the regulations because of failure by the owners to meet requirements of new regulations that came into force on 19 November 1952. Under these regulations, she should have carried twelve new-type parachute rockets in a watertight container. The vessel was equipped with a radio transmitter and two receivers, direction finder, and echo-sounder. She also had a Decca Marine Radar Type 159, which was operative when the vessel sailed but was found to be faulty soon after sailing.

   Hassett sailed from Grimsby, bound for Iceland, at noon on 16 September 1953 under the command of Skipper Arthur Almond, with a crew of twenty hands all told. Shortly after midnight on 18 September, she ran ashore in heavy weather at Auckengill, 10 miles north of Wick. Shortly afterwards, Wick Radio picked up the following distress message from *Hassett*: 'I am ashore north of Noss Head and need immediate assistance. We have Noss Head Lighthouse bearing south-west.' They alerted the rescue services. Wick Lifeboat was launched and found the *Hassett* after a four-hour search. Unable to approach the vessel on account of the rough sea and shoal water, the lifeboat contacted the coastguard and a rescue party assembled ashore on the cliffs. The destroyer HMS *Scorpion* arrived on the scene and floodlit the wreck with her searchlights to assist the rescuers. Aboard the *Hassett*, immediately after the stranding, fifteen men got to the bridge, the other five crew members being swept away by the seas breaking over her. At 5 a.m., two lines were fired across the vessel from the cliff top, but the crew were unable to reach them on account of the heavy water washing across the decks. Commander Gilbert and Coastguard George Hepple then climbed down to the rocks and fired three lines with a pistol. One of these lines passed over the wheelhouse and hung on the wireless aerial. The mate, Malcolm Smith, showing exceptional courage in taking the risk of being washed away, climbed onto the top of the wheelhouse and managed to secure this line. This line was passed down to the men in the wheelhouse at 6.10 a.m. and a breeches buoy was quickly rigged. The first man was pulled ashore at 6.30 and the last at 7.15. In all, fifteen men were saved by breeches buoy; there were two dead and three missing, presumed drowned.

   The official inquiry into the stranding was held in Grimsby on 15-16 June 1954 and found that the cause of the stranding was negligent navigation by her skipper, Arthur Gabriel Almond, and suspended his certificate for a period of twelve months from that date.

The *Belldock* was built in 1917 by Smith's Dock Company on the Tees for Fleetwood owners and named *Leam*. She left Fleetwood, and after a spell working from North Shields, when her name was changed to *Belldock*, she was bought by Crampin Steam Fishing Company, Grimsby, in 1941 and registered as GY367. She was a coal-fired, steel, single-screw side steam trawler, 235 tons gross, 117 feet long, 23 feet in beam and 13.1 feet in depth. Her triple-expansion engine gave her a maximum speed of about 10 knots. She was a well-found seaworthy vessel, and fitted with wireless, echometer and Decca Navigator. Her compasses were adjusted in August 1953.

   The *Belldock* sailed from Grimsby on 12 November 1953 for a fishing voyage to the Shetland Isles with a crew of thirteen hands all told under the command of Skipper

John Robert Dobson. She began fishing on 14 November about 5 miles east of Lamba Ness and continued trawling until 1330 hours on the 16th when a SSW gale caused the gear to be pulled aboard. The vessel then made for shelter in Harolds Wick Bay, but conditions there were not to the skipper's liking, and he proceeded further to the southward and entered Balta Sound by the south entrance. Dusk was just falling and the flood-tide was setting to the southward at about half a knot. The skipper, the mate, a deckhand called Sherriff, and the third-hand, Brown, were on the bridge, the latter steering the vessel.

Brown told the Court of Inquiry that, when approaching Swarta Skerry, the Skipper took the wheel from him and put it hard aport, despite Brown protesting that he would go ashore, and shortly afterwards, the *Belldock* grounded in the vicinity of Swarta Skerry. At this time, Sherriff had left the bridge to call the hands to prepare for anchoring and the mate had also left the bridge. The mate, who was the skipper's brother, quickly returned to the bridge, used bad and uncomplimentary language to the skipper, and worked the engines ahead and astern. The *Belldock* quickly refloated, and while the two brothers were still arguing, with the engines still going ahead, and with no one at the wheel, she ran ashore on the other side of the channel. Efforts to refloat her were unsuccessful, and a Mayday call was sent out and distress rockets were fired. The ship's lifeboat was launched but was found to be making a lot of water. Two men from the *Belldock* climbed down into the boat and began to bail it out with tin cans, but the boat's painter parted and the boat drifted away with the two men in it. These two men eventually reached the shore. A fishing boat, the *Village Maid*, was tied up to the quay in Balta Harbour and was contacted by radio. She searched for the two men in the boat, and later took the crew off the *Belldock*. The following day, the 17th, with the assistance of the *Village Maid*, the *Belldock* was kedged off the ground and towed into Balta Harbour. Subsequently, she was towed to Aberdeen, where an examination showed that damage to her hull was so extensive that she was considered a constructive total loss.

At the formal Court of Inquiry held at Grimsby on 11 and 12 March 1954, testimony was given that a considerable amount of intoxicating liquor was consumed on the bridge of the *Belldock* on the afternoon of the stranding, and this was found to be a contributory cause of the casualty. Skipper Dobson's certificate was suspended for two years, and the mate, Arthur Leonard Dobson, was suspended for six months and ordered to pay £50 towards the cost of the inquiry.

The *Michael Griffith* was a steel steam trawler built by Cook, Welton & Gemmell at Beverley in 1919 and was one of the 'Castle' type. After being released from Admiralty service, she was substantially reconditioned in 1947. She was owned by Clifton Steam Trawlers Ltd of Fleetwood and registered as FD249. Her gross tonnage was 282 tons, and she was 125.5 feet long, 23.5 feet wide and 12.7 feet deep. She was classed +100 A1 at Lloyd's and had passed her last special survey in June 1951. Like all the Castle-type ships, she had three watertight bulkheads – a collision bulkhead abaft the fore peak, one between the fish hold and the bunkers, and the third fore side the after peak. She had a raised fo'c's'le, her bridge was about amidships, and her engine and boiler rooms were abaft the bridge. The fo'c's'le was 21 feet long, and she had steel bulwarks all round the ship abaft the fo'c's'le. Running aft from the after end of the bridge was a 4-foot-high steel engine casing, which terminated in a deck-house, which contained the galley, and she had a bar keel. She was fitted with a triple-expansion engine drawing steam from one single-ended cylindrical boiler with three furnaces, which were built by Amos & Smith Ltd of Hull. She was steered by hand gear. Pumping equipment consisted of two ram bilge pumps driven off the main engine, a bilge injection on the main circulating pump, one steam ejector, one general-service donkey pump, and one donkey pump for boiler feed. Also, she had four hand pumps on deck. Electronic equipment consisted of a radio telephone transmitter and receiver, a direction finder and an echo-sounder. Her lifeboat and life-saving appliances were adequate and in good condition. She carried no wireless operator, but the skipper was competent to operate the equipment.

The *Michael Griffith* sailed from Fleetwood on 29 January 1953 for a fishing trip off the west coast of Scotland, under the command of Skipper Charlie Singleton and with a crew of thirteen hands all told. Shortly after sailing, she had trouble in the after-feed pump delivery valve chest. She returned to Fleetwood, where repairs were satisfactorily and efficiently carried out. She set sail and resumed her voyage at 12.30 a.m. on 30 January. The Court of Inquiry into her loss was satisfied that at this time she was fit in every way for the intended voyage. At 8 p.m. on 30 January, the *Michael Griffith* was seen by the crew of the trawler *Aigret*, which was then 20 miles W ½ S of Dubh Artach Light. At that time, *Aigret* had the fishing gear aboard due to the weather and was remaining on the ground in the hope that the weather would moderate sufficiently to allow her to resume fishing. A little later, she received an adverse weather forecast, and the skipper decided to seek shelter and set a course to the East of Skerryvore. The *Michael Griffith* passed close to her, steaming in a northerly direction, and her stern light was visible to the men on the *Aigret*'s bridge until about 11.10 p.m., at which time, she must have been a few miles south and west of Skerryvore. That is the last time the *Michael Griffith* was seen.

On the evening of 30 January, the south-west wind started to veer and freshen, and by 11 p.m., there was a NW gale of about Force 9 blowing. The wind continued to veer, and by midnight was between NNW and north, and had increased to Force 10. There were heavy snow squalls and a very rough sea. In the area in which the *Michael Griffith* was in the early hours of 31 January, the height of the waves was at least 30 feet, with a very confused sea. At 9.23 a.m. on 31 January, the trawlers *Velia* and *Wyre General* picked up a distress message sent out by the *Michael Griffith*: 'All ships – *Michael Griffith*, 7 to 8 miles south of Barra Head – full of water – no steam – am helpless – will some ship please come and help us.' Both trawlers were a considerable distance from the position given in the distress message, so they relayed the call to coast radio stations. The trawlers *Wardour*, *Braconbank* and at least one other trawler, being much nearer than *Velia* and *Wyre General*, who were at least 85 miles away, proceeded in horrendous weather conditions to the position given in the SOS call to search for the stricken ship. Barra Lifeboat was launched and proceeded to the area, and later, the Islay lifeboat, which was at sea answering another distress call, joined the search. Two crew members of the Islay Lifeboat were overcome by fumes and lost their lives during the search. The destroyer HMS *Tenacious* was ordered to leave port in Northern Ireland to search the area, and two RAF aeroplanes conducted an air search. An observer on the *Tenacious* reported wind gusting over 100 mph, 50 feet waves and blinding snowstorms.

All that was ever found of the *Michael Griffith* was a lifebuoy washed ashore in Loch Foyle, Ireland, a week later. The Court of Inquiry into the loss was unable to come to a firm conclusion as to the cause but decided that the most probable cause was exceptionally heavy weather. In the area that the *Michael Griffith* was on the morning of 31 January, there was a north-easterly gale of Force 10 with squalls of hurricane force, and very high, confused seas. From the distress message, it seems certain that the ship was without power and had a lot of water in her. Although it is a guess, it seems probable that she was struck by a very heavy sea, and the ingress of a large quantity of water put the fires out, causing the loss of steam. Without power, she would be laid broadside to the weather, and with her stability already reduced by the free surface effect of the sea water on board, she would be unable to cope with the water; she must have shipped while laid.

Hildina. (J. Worthington Collection)

The *Hildina* was a steel, single-screw motor trawler built by Cook, Welton & Gemmell at Beverley in 1952. Although working out of Fleetwood at the time of her loss, she was registered as H222. She was owned by the City Steam Fishing Company Ltd of Hull and was one of Marr's 'banana' boats. She was classed with Lloyd's and insured with Hull Steam Trawler Mutual Insurance, and both Classification Society and the Insurance Company carried out regular surveys of hull and machinery.

The vessel was 296.06 gross tons, and her registered dimensions were length 128.25 feet, breadth 26.6 feet, depth 12.2 feet. She was powered by a five-cylinder internal combustion diesel engine of 700 bhp, giving her a speed of 11 knots. She was equipped with the most modern navigation aids and radio communication apparatus. She had one 18-foot lifeboat for nineteen persons, one Nott type P.T. buoyant apparatus for twenty persons, four lifebuoys, and enough lifejackets for every person on board. She was a fine, well-found modern trawler, well equipped and well manned in every respect when she left Fleetwood on her last voyage.

As you will see later, the piece of equipment most involved in her loss was her trawl winch, so I will describe this winch in some detail. This winch was built by James Robertson & Sons, Fleetwood, and had two barrels, each capable of holding 1,200 fathoms of 2 7/8-inch circumference steel warp. It was driven by a 126-bhp electric motor made by Laurence, Scott & Electro Motors Ltd, and operated through a worm reduction gear. The power for the electric motor was supplied from a JAS five-cylinder diesel generator situated in the fore part of the engine room on the starboard side, made by Mirrlees, Bickerton & Day Ltd, Stockport. It was fitted with a cut-out device designed to operate when lubricating oil pressure fell below 10/12 lb per square inch. This 'cut-out' is a safety device to prevent the diesel engine overheating in the event of shortage of lubricating oil.

The *Hildina* sailed from Fleetwood in the early morning of 25 November 1953 bound for the fishing grounds off the north-west of Scotland under the command of Skipper George Goodwin Clarkson, with a crew of fifteen men all told. It was her first trip out of Fleetwood, having previously worked from Hull. On the late evening of 26 November, *Hildina* commenced fishing in position 55 degrees 57 minutes north, 9 degrees 10 minutes west. She continued fishing until 30 November, when a westerly wind freshened to gale force, causing her to pull the gear aboard, and lay and dodge. By 1 a.m on 1 December, the weather had moderated and fishing was resumed. At about 6.45 a.m., the trawl on the starboard side was shot away on the 100-fathom line with Sule Skerry bearing SE by S ¾ S, 350 fathoms of warp being payed away. The vessel proceeded to tow downwind before a W by S breeze of about Force 4, with a moderate sea and heavy swell. The skipper was on the bridge at about 7.55 a.m. when the trawl came fast. He rang the telegraph to 'Stop engines', and the bosun immediately proceeded to the winch and shipped the fore clutch. As soon as the skipper gave the order, the deckhand aft knocked out, and the bosun hove in three or four turns on the fore warp. Hearing the skipper call out 'Don't heave too much for'ard, she has pulled the after warp out,' the bosun stopped heaving on the fore warp, shipped the after clutch, and commenced heaving on both warps. When about twenty-five fathoms had been hove in a very heavy sea struck the starboard, and weather, side of the vessel, filling the deck and causing the vessel to take a 40-degree list, and putting her rail under water. She never recovered from this position. From that moment, the seas piled aboard and found their way into the accommodation through an open storm door on the starboard side of the main deck-house. As soon as the skipper realised that the rail was under water and the vessel was not returning upright, he ordered the bosun to reverse the winch. The bosun, who had been joined by the mate, reported to the bridge saying, 'It won't work.' The skipper then shouted, 'Unship the clutches.' The mate and bosun struggled hard to carry out the order but found it impossible either to reverse the winch or to unship the clutches. Once the vessel had sufficient list to submerge the rail, she was virtually gone. She continued to heel over until she eventually capsized. With the skipper giving no orders, and with the mate and bosun at the winch until a late moment, the other members of the crew were left to make their own decisions about leaving the ship. Some of them went to the lifeboat, which was stowed on the poop under the mizzen boom, and cut the gripes, allowing it to slide into the sea. In the process, it was damaged and floated bottom up. The other crew members went to the bridge top where the Nott buoyant apparatus was stowed and were joined by the mate and bosun. They managed to launch the Nott, and eleven men managed to board it, but a big sea overturned it. Two of the men lost their hold and were carried away by the sea. The trawler *Velia* was fishing close by, and at 8.12 a.m., her wireless operator picked up part of *Hildina*'s call sign, followed by 'SOS' sent once and 'Turning over. We fast'. The Skipper of *Velia*, Charlie Pennington, immediately hauled and proceeded to the position in which he knew *Hildina* to be, arriving about 9 a.m. They found the buoyant apparatus and the upturned lifeboat and picked up ten men. After ensuring that two other trawlers, *Monimia* and *Margaret Wicks* would search the area, *Velia* then proceeded to Stornoway to land the survivors, making advance arrangements with the hospital over the radio. Unfortunately, one of the survivors died on the way in.

Author's Note: With considerable hindsight, this tragedy needn't have happened. It was caused by two avoidable occurrences. 1. The vessel was allowed to come broadside to the weather with her gear fast, and 2. the storm door into the after accommodation was probably secured in the open position. Had the bosun been ordered to heave on the fore warp and slack the after warp until the weight came on the fore warp, the vessel would have swung head to wind and sea, and the sea which caused the initial list would probably never have come aboard. I say this with hindsight because weather conditions at the time hardly warranted this precaution, and by the time the vessel listed, it was too late to do anything. In the case of the open door, with the gear being hauled, a procession of men would be coming out on deck, and it was natural to bolt the door back. It takes a list of over forty degrees to allow ingress of water through this opening, and in the prevailing weather conditions, such a list could hardly be anticipated.

The reason it was impossible to reverse the winch and/or unship the clutches was probably due to the lub oil swilling to one side of the tank when the ship took the list, creating the impression that there was an oil shortage, and causing the power 'cut-out' to operate.

1954

Four ships and thirty-two men were lost during the year.

Aberdeen	*Koorah* A18	227 tons	11 February 1954
Grimsby	*Laforay* GY85	609 tons	8 February 1954
Fleetwood	*Evelyn Rose* GY9	327 tons	31 December 1954
Hull	*Kingston Aquamarine* H520	613 tons	11 January 1954

The *Koorah* was a nomad. In addition to serving on Admiralty service as a mineweeper throughout the First World War, she fished from five different ports for various owners and never had a name change. The *Koorah* was built in 1912 by Hall Russell at Aberdeen for Milford owners and was first registered as M120. She was 227 tons gross, 117.4 feet long, 22.6 feet in beam and 12.2 feet deep. She fished from Milford Haven until August 1914, when she was taken over by the Admiralty and converted for minesweeping. Demobbed in 1919, she was bought by T. Robinson, Grimsby, and registered as GY122. She fished from Grimsby until 1934, and in that period, she had two other owners – E. Cox and the Earl Steam Fishing Company. In January 1935, she was bought by Granton owners and registered as GN14. She was bought by Regent Fishing Company in 1941 and moved to Aberdeen, registering as A249. In 1944, she was bought by A. & M. Smith Ltd and moved to Hull, registering as H77. The year 1946 found her back in Aberdeen, owned by Brebner Fishing Company Ltd and registered as A18.

She sailed from Aberdeen on her final trip in February 1954, with a crew of twelve men all told, under the command of Skipper James Findlay. She was fishing off Strathy Point when the wind freshened to gale force, and she ceased fishing and ran for shelter under the lee of Dunnet Head. In the early hours of 11 February, she ran ashore on rocks 5 cables west of Dunnet Head. A distress message was sent on the radio and distress rockets fired. The crew launched the lifeboat and left the stranded vessel and were picked up by the Thurso seine-netter *Our Lassie*, who landed them at Scrabster. Later in the day, Skipper Findlay and his crew returned to the *Koorah* to prepare for a salvage attempt with the assistance of a salvage tug, but it was found impossible to drag her off the rocks, and she was a total loss.

The *Laforay* was built in 1949 for Trawlers (Grimsby) Ltd by J. Lewis at Aberdeen and registered as GY85. At the time of her loss, her registered owners were Derwent Trawlers Ltd, Grimsby. She was a single-screw steel trawler of 609 gross tons. Her registered dimensions were length 170.4 feet, breadth 29.2 feet, depth 14.3 feet.

She sailed from Grimsby on 18 January, bound for the Norway Coast fishing grounds, under the command of Skipper Billy Mogg, with a crew of twenty men all

Koorah. (W. Dodds Collection)

Laforay. (Welholme Gallery)

Laforay. (*Grimsby Evening Telegraph*)

told. She arrived at the Andanes ground on 22 January and continued fishing until the afternoon of 5 February, when she pulled the gear aboard and set course for home with a catch of 1,500 kits of cod on board. From 6 to 8 February, the weather along the Norwegian coast was very bad – SW gale Force 9 gusting up to Force 10 or 11. Shortly after midnight on 8 February, a Norwegian coast station, Floroe Radio, picked up an SOS message from the *Laforay*: 'Ashore at Yttero. Immediate assistance required.' And a few minutes later, 'Listing heavily and capsizing.' Norwegian coastal rescue services were alerted, and several trawlers from Grimsby, Hull and Fleetwood who were in the vicinity joined in the search, but nothing was found. On Monday morning, 9 February, a Norwegian search party found the *Laforay* upside down on the rocks at Sendingane. There were no survivors.

The *Kingston Aquamarine* was built in 1948 by Alexander Hall & Company at Aberdeen for the Boston Deep Sea Fishing Company, Hull, and was called *St Mark*. In 1952, she was bought by Kingston Steam Trawling Company, Hull, and renamed *Kingston Aquamarine*. Her gross tonnage was 612.75 and her registered dimensions were 180.1 feet x 30.2 feet x 15.15 feet. She was a steel, single-screw steam trawler propelled by a triple- expansion reciprocating engine that drew steam from a cylindrical, multitubular oil-fired boiler, which gave her an operational speed of about twelve knots. She was fitted with steam-hydraulic steering gear, with alternative rod-and-chain-type hand steering gear. Her life-saving appliances comprised two lifeboats, four lifebuoys, thirty lifejackets, twelve parachute distress flares, and a Schermuly line-throwing apparatus. This equipment was inspected by a Ministry of Transport Surveyor at Hull on 13 August 1953 and found to be satisfactory. The vessel was equipped with a Redifon marine deep sea trawler radio installation type M.I. 2030 comprising

Kingston Aquamarine. (P. Whiting Collection)

Transmitter: Type G. 80 100 watts.
Main Receiver: Type R. 50
Emergency Receiver: Type R. 55
Control Unit: Type RC. 12/A 137
Direction Indicator: Redifon KD.I with R.18A receiver and modified DFL 4A rotating
loop.

All the above were tested by the makers in Hull and found to be in good working order
on 20 December 1953. Navigation equipment comprised a Marconi Radiolocator IV
marine radar. This was tested by the makers at Hull on 21 December 1953 and found
to be satisfactory, but was believed to be inoperative at the time of the stranding. She
had a Loran receiver type AN/APN.4 and two echo-sounders – one type MS 21 E
with a maximum range of 2,250 fathoms and one type MS 24J/CTR with a range of
240 fathoms. Both sounders were serviced in December 1953 and were in good order.
She was classed +100 A1 Steam Trawler at Lloyd's, and the last classification survey
was carried out during October 1952. When she sailed on her last voyage, she was
seaworthy in every respect.

   The *Kingston Aquamarine* sailed from Hull, bound for the White Sea fishing grounds
on 22 December 1953 with a crew of twenty hands all told under the command of
Skipper Dennis Albert Cornish. On 10 January 1954, she was fishing in the vicinity of
Malansgrunden Bank off the north-west coast of Norway. At 2230 hours that night,
the skipper decided to change ground and steam to Svensgrunden, a bank he calculated
was 30 miles to the southward of his then position. Accordingly, he set a course south
magnetic. The mate, Mr John Stanley Parkinson, came up to the bridge at midnight to
take over the watch, when the vessel was steering south. Before leaving the bridge, the
skipper told the mate he wanted calling when they got to the 100-fathom line, or in
three hours, whichever came first. Admiralty chart No. 2313 of the area was laid out
on the chartroom table, but there was no discussion between the skipper and mate as
to the ship's position, and the mate made no attempt to ascertain the ship's position.
At about 0015 hours on 11 January, a few minutes after the skipper left the bridge,
the mate read a depth of 140 fathoms on the echo-sounder, and realising that the ship
was very close to the 100-fathom line, he called the hands to get the gear ready for
shooting. A little later, when the sounder showed 100 fathoms, he rang the engine-
room telegraph to stop engines. The ringing of the telegraph was heard by the skipper
in his cabin who called, 'That is not the 100 fathom I want. I want the next one.' The
mate then rung the ship on full speed and continued on the same course. Throughout,
visibility was generally poor – a dark night with frequent snow squalls. At about 0200
hours, Mr Stephenson, a spare hand who was on watch, drew the mate's attention to
a white light on the port beam. On seeing the light, the mate ordered the helmsman
to go hard-a-starboard and bring the ship's head to south-west. He then went to
the skipper's cabin and reported seeing the light, and told the skipper he thought
something was wrong. The skipper followed the mate to the bridge and saw two lights
on the port beam – one white and one red. He looked at the sounder and saw that
it had been shoaling rapidly and was now showing zero. He immediately rang 'Stop
Engines' and ordered the helmsman 'hard-a-starboard', but before the order could be
carried out, the vessel grounded. A few minutes after stranding, the engines were put
full speed astern and ran for 45 minutes in an attempt to refloat. Shortly afterwards, a
wireless message was sent out asking for assistance. Within an hour of the stranding,
the mate and chief engineer had made an inspection for damage, and water was found
to be entering the after end of the fish room and the after end of the engine room.
The bilge ejector was started but could not cope with the ingress of water. At 0530
hours, the entire crew left the vessel in the two ship's boats, which had already been

lowered. The *Kingston Aquamarine* had grounded at Strandby on the west side of Steinfjord. The Court of Inquiry into the casualty found that the loss was due to the fault or default of both her skipper and mate. With regards to the skipper, he failed to indicate to the mate the estimated position when handing over the watch, and when, at 0015 hours, he was informed that the 100-fathom line had been reached, his omission to go to the bridge and satisfy himself of the vessel's position each amounted to a default or wrongful act, which in a large measure caused the loss of the vessel. In the case of the mate, he was guilty of three wrongful acts or omissions. He should have informed himself of the approximate position of the vessel when he first took over the watch; he failed to verify the ship's position at 0015 hours when he crossed the 100-fathom line and was instructed to proceed to the next 100-fathom line; and his use of the echo-sounders in the last hour before the stranding in poor visibility was inadequate and inept, when, by paying attention to them, it would have been obvious from the shoaling that the ship was standing into danger. He entirely failed to appreciate his responsibility for the safety of the vessel. Both skipper and mate had their certificates suspended for twelve months. The *Kingston Aquamarine* was a total loss.

The *Evelyn Rose*, though registered in Grimsby as GY9, worked from Fleetwood and was owned by the Cevic Steam Fishing Company Ltd, Fleetwood. She was a single-screw steam side trawler built in 1918 by Cochrane & Sons Ltd at Selby for the Admiralty as the *William Jackson* and was a Mersey-type ship. Sold to Hull owners (Lord Line), she was renamed *Lord Byng* and worked from Hull until January 1929, when she was bought by Bunch SF Co., Grimsby, and re-registered as GY9. In 1936, she was acquired by Boston DSF Co. and her name was changed to *Evelyn Rose*. After being on Admiralty service throughout the war, she was bought by Cevic Fishing Company, Fleetwood, in August 1945 and worked from Fleetwood initially under the command of Skipper Jim Pegler. She was classed * 100 A1 Steam Trawler at Lloyd's. Her registered dimensions were length 138.5 feet, breadth 23.75 feet, depth 12.8 feet, with a gross tonnage of 326.52. Her hull was divided into compartments by four watertight bulkheads as follows: a collision bulkhead sited abaft the forepeak, one abaft the for'ard crew space, one abaft the fish room, and one abaft the engine room. She had a triple-expansion engine, which gave her a speed of 10 knots. She was fitted with three power-driven pumps and four hand pumps. Her steam steering gear was of rod and chain type, and she had emergency steering gear fitted. Her life-saving appliances comprised one wooden lifeboat for nineteen people stowed under the mizzen boom, two buoyant apparatus each for fourteen persons, four lifebuoys, twenty lifejackets, distress rockets and a line-throwing apparatus. These appliances had been inspected in December 1953 and were then found to be in good order. Communication and navigation equipment comprised a radio telephone, a Decca Marine Radar No. 159B, echo-sounders, Walker's logs, and three magnetic compasses.

The *Evelyn Rose* sailed from Fleetwood for the Faroe fishing grounds on 30 December 1954 under the command of Skipper William (Jerry) Dawson, with a crew of fourteen men all told. By 10.30 p.m. on 30 December, the ship was in a position 10 miles NE of Rudha Mhail on the northern tip of the Isle of Islay. It was at this position that the mate, Mr W. R. Crowford, handed over the watch to the bosun. At that time, the skipper was on the bridge. There was a fresh southerly breeze; it was a dark, clear night, and there was a choppy sea. So far as is known, these weather conditions persisted all night. The events between the changing of the watch and the stranding are a matter of inference, because the only two survivors, the mate and a deckhand, were below from shortly after 10.30 p.m. until the vessel grounded. At some time after 12.30 a.m. on 31 December, the two survivors were awakened by the vessel

Evelyn Rose. (Welholme Gallery)

Evelyn Rose aground in 1949 on a previous occasion to her loss. (P. Whiting Collection)

running on the rocks at Ardtornish Point in the Sound of Mull, about fifteen yards from the light. The light was functioning normally at the time, and it seems probable that the *Evelyn Rose* was proceeding on a north-westerly course towards Ardtornish Light in the white sector and that the skipper intended to alter course to port to pass between Eileanan Glasa and Fiunary rocks when close in to the light. This is perfectly safe and proper providing the alteration of course to port is made at a safe distance from Ardtornish Light. How the ship was allowed to get so close in on a clear night is again a matter of inference, but it seems probable that the skipper was using the radar to ascertain his distance off, and the radar was picking up the high ground further inshore, the controls being set in a manner that the low shore line was not being picked up. This would lead him to believe he was farther off than he actually was. On being awakened by the crash of the vessel grounding, the mate went to the bridge, where he saw the skipper, bosun and deckhand on watch. He said to the skipper, 'What's up?' to which the Skipper replied, 'We're ashore in the sound. The radar is bonked.' The radar had been working normally at 10.30 p.m. when the mate had gone off watch, and the Court of Inquiry expressed the opinion that the casualty was due to a misinterpretation of the radar image rather than a defect in the equipment. The mate was then ordered to go and try to ascertain the extent of any damage. On going up on the fo'c's'le head, accompanied by the bosun and the deckhand on watch, by looking over the rail, he saw that the fore end of the ship was clear of the water. After reporting to the skipper, the mate suggested launching the lifeboat, and was told to carry on. The mate then went aft, and with two other men, began to try to launch the boat. Before the boat could be launched, the vessel slid off the rocks and sank stern first. When the vessel ran ashore, she rode up for'ard, which would lower the stern. The engine space quickly filled with water, either from a breached hull, or from the deck, and the weight of this water aft caused the vessel to slide stern first off the rocks. The mate was carried under with the ship, but came to the surface and was able to swim ashore, picking up a lifebuoy on the way. He got ashore and scrambled up to the foot of the light. A deckhand who had been helping to launch the boat also managed to get ashore at the same place, and shortly afterwards, one of the firemen was seen to get ashore. The mate and the deckhand proceeded to go to find assistance, but had to go some distance to get help. Mr Henry, the factor of Ardtornish Estates, telephoned the police and organised a search party to go to Ardtornish Point. A search in the darkness using torches found no trace of the *Evelyn Rose* or any survivors, but a lifebuoy from the vessel was found. Later, a search party at daylight found the body of the fireman, who had apparently died of exposure. It is a matter for considerable thought to understand why, with about half the length of the ship high and dry, so close to the shore, and in fine weather, twelve men from a crew of fourteen perished. It is clear that the men on the *Evelyn Rose* could not have anticipated the vessel sliding off the rocks so quickly after stranding, but many more would probably have been saved had the buoyant apparatus been thrown overboard, or if the men had climbed down a rope over the stem. The skipper was last seen in the wireless room trying to call Oban Radio and was probably trapped when the ship sank. Not expecting the vessel to slide off so quickly, some of the other men may have gone below to get lifejackets or retrieve personal effects and went down with the ship.

The final stranding was not the first time the *Evelyn Rose* had been ashore. On the night of 22 November 1949, when bound home from Iceland with a crew of twenty-one men under the command of Skipper Jim Pegler and 1,000 kits of fish on board, she ran aground on the Jura side of the Sound of Islay in rough seas, pitch dark and heavy rain (see photo). A schoolboy, Charles Darroch, saw her distress flares and ran through the rain to Port Askaig Lifeboat Station to raise the alarm. Only 3 miles away, the lifeboat was quickly on the scene and took off twelve of her crew, the other nine deciding to remain on board. After landing the survivors at Port Askaig, the lifeboat returned and stood by the wreck all night. The *Evelyn Rose* had sustained a 20-foot gash in her bows, and at daylight, 2 tons of cement was poured into the hull to try to seal the hole. She remained aground for ten days while emergency repairs were carried out and a salvage vessel was able to refloat her and tow her to the pier at Port Askaig. Half of her 1,000-kit catch was offloaded into the trawler *Cevic* and brought to Fleetwood. The remainder was dumped into the sea. After repairs were completed, Skipper Pegler brought her safely back to Fleetwood, where, after slipping, she continued fishing.

1955

Eleven ships and fifty-three men were lost during the year.

Aberdeen	*Doonie Braes* A881	213 tons	20 April 1955
	Sturdee A219	202 tons	19 October 1955
Grimsby	*Daniel Quare* GY279	440 tons	9 September 1955
	Remindo GY1089	358 tons	28 April 1955
	Barry Castle SA33	380 tons	1 November 1955
	Reggio GY368	285 tons	6 November 1955
Hull	*Lorella* H445	559 tons	26 January 1955
	Roderigo H135	810 tons	26 January 1955
	Stella Orion H379	575 tons	7 November 1955
	Prince Charles H249	514 tons	23 December 1955
Granton	*Euclase* GN51	295 tons	22 September 1955

The *Doonie Braes* was a Strath-class, steel, single-screw side trawler built for the Admiralty in 1918 by Alexander Hall & Company at Aberdeen as the *George Coulston*. Released from naval service in 1922, she worked for a short time from Glasgow, being registered as GW38. In July 1922, she was registered in Aberdeen under the ownership of Miss H. W. Lewis and took the number A881 when her name was changed to *Doonie Braes*. From 1940 until 1945, she was again on naval service as a minesweeper, after which she returned to Aberdeen. Although originally designed for conversion to trawling, in fact, she was employed as a long line fishing boat.

On 20 April 1955, when bound home with a good catch of line-caught halibut, she ran aground on the west coast of the Orkneys 120 yards north of the Old Man Of Hoy in poor visibility. It would seem that her skipper, Robert Bruce, was doubtful of her position because in the distress call he sent out, he gave his position as on the North Shoal, which is about 10 miles north of where she actually stranded. Stromness lifeboat was launched as a result of the distress call and proceeded to North Shoal, and by the time she located the wreck, the crew had already been picked up by a naval MFV and taken to Lyness. Later that day, Skipper Bruce returned to the wreck with the lifeboat and the steamer *Orcadia* to attempt to pull her off but found her full of water and impossible to salvage. She was then abandoned and was a total loss.

The *Sturdee* was an Admiralty-built Strath-class trawler built by Hall, Russell & Company at Aberdeen in 1919 as the *Michael Brian* and completed too late for naval service. She was a steel, single-screw side trawler of 202 tons gross, 115 feet in length and 22 feet beam. In 1919, she was sold to Hull owners when her name was changed. After a brief spell working from Hull, she moved to Lowestoft, where she was registered as LT988. In 1932, she was bought by Gore & Spence, Aberdeen, and

Doonie Braes. (Fishing News)

registered as A219. In 1937, she was acquired by A. Davidson, Aberdeen, with whom she remained, apart from a short period of naval service between November 1939 and January 1940, until 1946, when she was sold to Looker Fishing Company, Aberdeen, who were the registered owners at the time of her loss.

The *Sturdee* sailed from Aberdeen on 11 October 1955, for a fishing trip to the North Sea fishing grounds, with a crew of eleven hands all told, under the command of Skipper William Wilson. She was equipped with an echo-sounder, direction finder, Decca Navigator, radio transmitter and receiver and radar. All of these aids to navigation were in efficient working order at the time of her stranding. She was supplied with adequate, well-maintained life-saving appliances, and when she left Aberdeen, she was seaworthy in every respect bar one. I make this point because the mate, Reuben Rae, did not hold a Certificate of Competency as required by the regulations, and it is probable that the insurance company would consider this a breach of warranty, expressed or implied, of the condition that the vessel would be properly manned. He had done three voyages on the *Sturdee* as Second Hand, and had told the Ship's Husband he had the appropriate certificate, and when he signed on at the Marine Office he gave a fictitious certificate number and was not asked to produce the certificate. In this respect, the company was also at fault, because there is a mandatory obligation to see a man's certificate before signing him on. The Court of Inquiry into the casualty were satisfied that the owners and the skipper believed he held such a certificate. Having completed her fishing, the *Sturdee* arrived off Aberdeen at 1730 hours on 19 October. She could have docked on arrival but did not do so. Instead, her skipper decided to remain offshore until after midnight. The reason for this was probably to qualify for an extra day's subsidy. The Skipper stopped the vessel half a mile east of Girdleness just south and east of the harbour entrance and, having stopped, left her in charge of Charles Trowbridge, the Second Fisherman. At 1830 hours, Trowbridge was relieved by the mate, Reuben Rae. The skipper left the wheelhouse at 1900 hours and was playing cards in the cabin up until the time of the stranding. The weather was a west to south-west moderate wind, heavy ground swell, and occasional rain showers with moderate to poor visibility. No attempt was made to check the vessel's position during the evening, and she took the ground at about 2130 hours on Aberdeen beach just north of the Beach Ballroom and half a mile from the North Breakwater. The skipper came immediately to the bridge and worked the engines astern but was unable to free the vessel, so a distress call was made on the radio. The Aberdeen lifeboat, *Hilton Briggs*, Coxswain George Flett, was soon on the scene and succeeded in taking off the crew. The next day, the vessel's catch was unloaded, but the *Sturdee* was a total loss.

The findings of the Court of Inquiry were that the loss was due to the fault of Skipper Wilson and Mate Rae. In the case of the Skipper: 1. He failed to take her in to port on arrival when the port was ready to receive him, and after deciding not to do so, he failed to anchor her. 2. He failed to see she had sufficient offing, and when she was inside half a mile from land he failed to check her position from time to time.

Rae's contribution to the loss was that he failed to keep a proper, or any, lookout. Had he done so, he must have seen the vessel was driving ashore. The court suspended Skipper Wilson for one year and censured Rae and ordered him to pay £15 towards the cost of the inquiry.

The *Reggio* was built as the *Lord Knollys* in 1911 by Cochrane's at Selby. First working from Hull, and later Fleetwood, she moved to Grimsby in 1941 and registered as GY368 under the ownership of Sir Alec Black. Being owned in turn by J. Harrison (February 1943), J. Ross (May 1943) and Grimsby Merchants Amalgamated Trawlers (July 1946), she was bought by G. F. Sleight in August 1953, who renamed her *Reggio* in January 1954. She was a steel, single-screw steam side trawler of 285 tons gross, 133.5 feet long, 23 feet in beam and 12 feet deep. She was fully equipped with navigational aids, which included a radio transmitter and receiver, direction finder, Decca radar, Decca Navigator and a Marconi Echo-sounder. Her life-saving appliances were adequate and well maintained, and she was supplied with all the appropriate charts and nautical publications for the intended voyage.

The *Reggio* sailed from Grimsby, bound for the Westerly fishing grounds, on 24 October 1955, under the command of Skipper George Fredrick White with a crew of fourteen hands all told. She completed fishing on the ground west of Nun Bank, north of Cape Wrath at about 1500 hours on Sunday 6 November 1955. At 1730 hours, Sule Skerry was abeam, distant 2 miles by radar, and the skipper set a course of SE by E nothing southerly. This course was steered until the vessel stranded. It is a course that leads directly to the southern end of Hoy Island and is a dangerous course to steer unless the position is carefully checked during the last hour of the vessel's approach to land. At 1830 hours, the mate, James Barnett Butters, took charge of the bridge watch, and before turning in, the skipper gave him orders to start the echo-sounder and use the radar from 2000 hours. The weather was fine and clear, with little or no wind, and Hoy, on account of it being mainly very high land, is an excellent radar target. On the bridge with the mate was one hand at the wheel and another looking out. No land was seen either visually or on the radar until the vessel grounded at full speed, about 10 knots, probably in Rack Wick. In this respect, the vessel was fortunate. The shore of Rack Wick consists of a sandy beach and is one of the very few places on Hoy where a ship can ground without sustaining extensive bottom damage. That no land was seen on the radar was probably due to the fact that the mate had no training in the use of the equipment and was unable to set it up and tune it in correctly. Despite this, he knew from previous experience in these waters, the distance between Sule and Hoy, and the reduction of soundings should have warned him of the approach to land. In the circumstances, he should have realised something was wrong and called the skipper. However, he took no action at all. At the time of the stranding, the skipper was asleep in his berth but came up to the bridge immediately. It was low water at the time, and soon after, the vessel refloated. A course of north-west was set until clear of the land and then the vessel proceeded to Scrabster. Her bottom was examined by a diver and a Certificate of Seaworthiness obtained, after which she proceeded to Grimsby, arriving there on 11 November 1955. That was presumably the end of her fishing career. In January 1956, she left Grimsby for Belgium to be scrapped.

At the subsequent Court of Inquiry, held in Grimsby on 10-11 April 1956, it was found that the stranding was due to her improper navigation by both the skipper and the mate. The skipper was suspended for eighteen months and the mate for twelve months.

The *Remindo* was built in 1926 by Cook, Welton & Gemmell for Hull owners and was renamed a number of times. She started life as *Lady Beryl*, and in turn became *Ocean Duke*, *Stella Rigel*, *Alamein*, and *Lady Olwen*. For a short time after the Second World War, she worked from Milford Haven and was transferred to Grimsby owners, G. F. Sleight Ltd, registered as GY252 and had her final name change – *Remindo* – in 1952. She was a single-screw, steel, coal-burning steam trawler. Her registered tonnage was 358 tons gross, and she was 140.4 feet long, 24 feet beam, and 13.2 feet deep.

Remindo left Grimsby on the morning of 21 April 1955 bound for the Faroe fishing grounds under the command of Skipper W. Bridges with a crew of fifteen men all told. On 28 April, she was at anchor sheltering from a storm at Nypubakka, Faroe Islands, when she parted her anchor cable and drove ashore. Almost immediately, she began to fill with water and slid off the rocks and sank in deep water. There was no time to launch the lifeboat. The Aberdeen trawler *Ben Meidie* was at anchor nearby,

Remindo. (Fishing Heritage Centre)

Daniel Quare. (Fishing Heritage Centre)

Daniel Quare aground. (W. Taylor)

saw the *Remindo*'s distress flare and immediately weighed anchor, quickly arriving on the scene. On approaching, she put her lifeboat in the water manned by the mate and four seamen. The lifeboat picked up three men from the sea, one man being lost in the darkness. The *Ben Meidie* recovered eleven men clinging to a small raft. She then proceeded to Thorshaven to land the survivors, but unfortunately, three of the men died on the way in. On arrival at Thorshaven, the eleven survivors were taken to hospital to recover from their ordeal before being transported back to Grimsby. The rescue was accomplished in a south-east gale with heavy rain, and it is fortunate that the *Ben Meidie* was in the vicinity, otherwise there would have been no survivors.

*D*aniel Quare was a single-screw steel side trawler built by Cochrane at Selby in 1936 as the *Ocean Monarch* for Hull owners. In 1946, she was registered in Grimsby as *Stella Carina* GY279. In 1946, she was renamed *Kopanes*, and in 1949, she was bought by H. Coft Baker who renamed her *Daniel Quare*. She was 440 tons gross, 156 feet long, 26.1 feet in beam and 14.1 feet in depth. She sailed from Grimsby for a fishing trip to Iceland under the command of Skipper Charles Sleeth and a crew of nineteen hands all told. On 9 September 1955, she ran aground in poor visibility 7 miles WNW of Langanes Point and started to make water. Her distress call was answered by the Hull trawlers *Camilla* and *Loch Moidart*, and the Icelandic gunboat *Thor*. These ships were on the scene in about two and a half hours. *Thor* put pumps aboard her, and *Camilla* made unsuccessful attempts to tow her off. Eventually, Skipper Sleeth decided to abandon her and the crew were ferried off in the *Thor*'s launch. There was no loss of life.

*B*arry Castle SA33, although registered at Swansea, was working from Grimsby under the ownership of Consolidated Fisheries. She was launched on 4 March 1942 as the *Grayling* T243 for the Admiralty at Cochrane's yard at Selby. She was a single-screw steel side trawler with a gross tonnage of 380 tons. She was 162.1 feet long overall, 25.1 feet in beam and 13.2 feet in depth. In April 1946, she was bought by Consolidated Fisheries for £45,666 and renamed *Barry Castle*.

On 1 November 1955, she sank off Iceland with the loss of four of her crew. She sailed from Grimsby bound for the Icelandic fishing grounds with a crew of eighteen hands all told under the command of Skipper Walter Oxer. *Barry Castle* was dodging in heavy weather off Vestfjordur when she sprang a leak in a wing bunker. A hole was found in one of the bunker lids and was plugged with fish room boards and tarpaulins. Finding the pumps unable to cope with the rising water, Skipper Oxer called for assistance, and several trawlers in the vicinity answered the call. In a north-east Force 10 gale, the Hull trawler *Princess Elizabeth* secured a tow-line and proceeded to attempt to tow her into sheltered water in Isafjord. The tow rope parted and it took nearly four hours to rig up another tow-line. During this time, the *Barry Castle* sustained further damage, and two of the pumps were choked with coal dust. A bucket chain was formed to attempt to clear three feet of water in the engine room, and the rising water put out her fires. The tow parted a second time and was renewed, and the tow continued. With the vessel now in more sheltered water, and with the water gaining, Skipper Oxer decided there was no hope of saving the vessel and decided to abandon ship. The skipper of the Grimsby trawler *Viviana*, Jim Gamble, performing an incredible feat of ship handling and seamanship, backed the stern of his ship up to the bows of the *Barry Castle*, and ten of her crew were able to jump from one ship to the other. Two other men were picked up by the Grimsby trawler *Stafnes*, and two more by the Hull trawler *Cape Portland*. Four men were lost, the chief and second engineers, the bosun and a deckhand. Skipper Oxer was the last man to leave the ill-fated trawler, and by then, she had settled so low in the water that he simply

Roderigo. (*Hull Daily Mail*)

Lorella. (C. O'Neill)

stepped from the bridge into the sea. But for the efforts of the *Princess Elizabeth* in succeeding in towing the stricken vessel into relatively sheltered waters, it is doubtful if any of the men could have been rescued. Shortly after the rescue, the *Barry Castle* slid beneath the waves.

The loss of the *Lorella* and the *Roderigo* was the biggest disaster to hit the Hessle Road fishing community in postwar years. The *Lorella* was a steel, single-screw steam trawler of 559 tons gross, was 171 feet long, and 29 feet wide. She was owned by the City Steam Fishing Company Ltd, Hull, and commanded by Skipper Steve Blackshaw. The *Roderigo* was a steel, single-screw steam trawler of 810 tons gross, was 189 feet long, and 32 feet beam. She was owned by Hellyer Brothers Ltd, Hull, and commanded by Skipper George Coverdale.

Both vessels were fitted with modern navigation equipment and all safety appliances required by the regulations, and in addition, the *Roderigo* carried an inflatable rubber dinghy. Both vessels were classed at Lloyd's, and on sailing on their last voyage were seaworthy in every respect. The *Roderigo* and the *Lorella* sailed from Hull on 12 and 14 January 1955 respectively on a fishing voyage to Icelandic waters and, on the morning of 23 January, were fishing in the company of the Grimsby trawler *York City* about 22 miles N by E of North Cape, Iceland. It was blowing an ESE gale and freezing hard, and as a consequence, all three vessels pulled the gear aboard and began to run in to the land.

The *York City* proceeded to Isafjord where she anchored under Ritur Huk, but when the *Lorella* and the *Roderigo* got four miles from the land, they decided to lay for a while and wait to see what the weather would do. The weather got worse. At about 8 p.m. that evening, the *Roderigo* spoke to the *York City* on the radio and told her that she and the *Lorella* were proceeding to try to find the *Kingston Garnet*, believed to be about 40 miles north of Ritur Huk with her propeller fouled by a wire. In fact, the *Kingston Garnet* had cleared her propeller at about 1600 hours on the 24th and had broadcast that on her emergency radio, as her main aerial had been brought down by weight of ice. The *Roderigo* and the *Lorella* probably never received this message.

On 23 January, the Grimsby trawler *Stafnes* was about 50 miles NE of North Cape and had to stop fishing on account of a full easterly gale. She made an unsuccessful attempt to run for shelter, and then proceeded to dodge. On the morning of 25 January, she estimated her position to be 90 miles NE of the Cape, and in that position, she observed the *Roderigo* not far from her, but did not see the *Lorella*. The *Roderigo* appeared to be in no difficulty, and icing conditions were very slight with *Stafnes*, who then dodged away to the ENE and, after many hours, found better weather. On the 25th, at 0900 hours, the *Roderigo* reported to the *Lancella*: 'Been blowing a hurricane all night and still blowing very hard. Wind east and not freezing so much now. Last bearing of the Cape SW by S at 0815 hours. 300 fathoms.' At 1650 hours. the *Lorella* reported to the *Lancella* 'Wind east Force 10 since breakfast time. About same position as yesterday. We dodged back a bit early this morning when it fined a bit. Now it is blowing very hard with continuous snow.' At 2115 hours, the *Roderigo* reported, 'Still dodging ENE gale Force 10.' The next report from the *Lorella* was at 0900 hours on the 26th to the *Lancella*: 'Weather still very bad and we are badly iced up top so can't get much joy out of set. Position not known as we had to dodge full speed yesterday.' At 0910 hours, the *Roderigo* reported, 'Been dodging full speed and half speed in night to keep her up. Been trying to get round but no go. Wind freshening again.' Five minutes later, the *Lorella* spoke to the *Roderigo*: 'Boat deck solid with frozen snow. Lads been digging it out since breakfast. Terrible lot on bridge top and they are going up there at daylight if possible.' The *Roderigo* replied, 'Same here,

George, and the whaleback is a solid block.' The only other message heard from the *Lorella* was a Mayday call at 1435 hours heard faintly, and getting fainter, so that the last part was unheard: 'Heeling right over and can't get her back.'

At 1505 hours, the *Roderigo* told the *Lancella*, 'Wind ENE 11 to 12 estimate NE of Cape well off. Think *Lorella* was astern of us somewhere,' and at 1531 hours said '... are taking heavy water now, and the aerials are iced up again.' The following are the last communications from the *Roderigo*. At 1633 hours: 'Manoeuvring with difficulty.' 1650 hours: 'We are listing badly to starboard and would like you to come to us.' 1705 hours: 'She's going over and can't get her back.' 1710 hours: 'Mayday. Heeling right over heeling right over. Heeling right over, please acknowledge.' For some minutes, she repeated, 'Going over, going over.' Then, at 1712 hours, all communications ceased. On 29 January, an Icelandic trawler picked up the *Roderigo*'s inflatable rubber dinghy about 95 miles west of where the *Roderigo* was presumed to have been lost. No other trace of the two ships and their forty crewmen has ever been found.

The *Prince Charles* was a single-screw diesel-engined trawler built at Selby in 1953 for Boston DSF Company. She was 161.1 feet long, 29.2 feet in beam and had a gross tonnage of 514 tons. She registered as H249, but at the time of her stranding, she was working out of Grimsby.

Prince Charles (P. Whiting)

Picture of *Prince Charles* salvage operation. (W. Taylor)

The *Prince Charles* sailed from Grimsby on 3 December 1955 bound for the Barents Sea fishing grounds with a crew of twenty-one men all told under the command of Skipper Tommy H. Baskomb. She finished fishing on 22 December and set course for home with a good trip of fish on board, intending to arrive at Grimsby on the 28th and spend the New Year at home. About noon on the 23rd, she stopped at Honningsvaag, where she embarked two pilots for the passage through the Norwegian fjords.

Late that night, she struck the rocks off the island of Soeroeya, about sixty miles west of Hammerfest, in a snowstorm. The crew abandoned ship and tried to swim ashore. Not all of them made it. The survivors climbed up onto a rocky islet from where they were picked up two hours later by the Norwegian ship *Ingoey*. Skipper Bascombe was the last man to leave the ship. He rescued two men from the water but perished while trying to save a third man. The *Ingoey* then proceeded to Hammerfest, where she landed twelve survivors and two bodies. Eight of the survivors were taken to hospital to be treated for severe frostbite. A Norwegian naval frigate, and the Hull trawler *Kingston Topaz*, stood by the wreck all night searching for possible survivors still in the water, but found nothing. The search was called off at 0700 hours on the 24th. The *Kingston Topaz* sent the following report: 'Thirteen men picked up including one pilot. Also two bodies. Believed no hope of further survivors so I am resuming voyage.'

On 29 December 1955, an official inquiry into the cause of the loss was held in Hammerfest where the first engineer on the *Prince Charles*, Mr George Pomonis, gave evidence that one of the pilots had boarded the ship at Honningsvaag drunk. After the trawler had grounded, he had heard Skipper Baskcomb say that the pilot was 'still intoxicated'. Five deckhands, Thomas McGill, Victor Kershaw, Raymond Sumpton, John Haynes and James Smith, repeated the allegations that one of the pilots, Trygve Skarstad, was drunk when he joined the ship, and another deckhand, Stevens, said that the pilot who was drowned behaved so oddly that he asked the bosun to watch the radar for safety's sake.

The Inspector of Pilots at Honningsvaag and the other pilot, Magnus Strang, defended their dead colleague against the charge of being drunk on duty. The inspector stated that he had spoken to the pilot concerned before he had joined the *Prince Charles* and 'if I had the slightest reason to suppose the pilot had been drinking, another pilot would have been allocated to the job'. Pilot Strang denied the pilot on duty was drunk when he went on board. He told the court that he and Skarstad, with six other pilots, had shared two bottles of brandy at a party the night before. Skarstad had complained of 'flu symptoms during a trip in the German trawler *Stalinstadt* the day before, and Strang said that he had offered to take Skarstad's watch for him but the offer had been refused. He said that the trawler grounded at the moment the course would normally be changed and that the trawler's radar did not function satisfactorily at distances less than ten miles.

Subsequently, the *Prince Charles* was salvaged, bought by the Lord Line, Hull, and renamed *Lord Melford*. In 1965, she was sold to Fleetwood owners and re-registered as FD228, and her name was changed to *Wyre Captain*. She was finally broken up at the Porthleven Shipyard, Hayle, Cornwall, in June 1966.

The *Stella Orion* was owned by Derwent Trawlers Ltd, Grimsby, and managed by Charleston-Smith Trawlers Ltd of Hull. She was built by Cook, Welton & Gemmell at Beverley in 1943 and, in 1948, was converted from coal to oil burning. A steel, single-screw steam trawler of 574.73 gross tons, she was 178.1 feet long and 30.05 feet beam. Classed +100 A1 at Lloyd's, her insured value was £80,000. She was equipped with Marconi radio transmitters – Oceanspan and Transarctic II – and two marine receivers, Lodestone and Seapilot/Guardian direction finders, all serviced by Marconi International Marine on 3 November 1955. A Kelvin-Hughes Type 2C radar was fitted and was serviced on 2 November 1955. She had two echo-sounders, a Marconi Seagraph II and a Kelvin-Hughes type MS 24A, both serviced 2-3 November 1955. She also carried hand leadlines. Her life-saving equipment met mandatory requirements and successfully passed survey on 7 July 1955.

The *Stella Orion* left Hull for a voyage to the White Sea fishing grounds at 8.30 a.m. on 4 November 1955 with a crew of nineteen hands all told under the command of Skipper Harry Claxton. Although a very experienced trawlerman, this was Skipper Claxton's first trip in the *Stella Orion*. On the outward passage, weather conditions were normal for the time of the year, and about noon on 7 November, she was approaching the entrance to West Fjord on a course of NE by E Skonvoer Light, on the southern tip of the Lotofen Islands was abeam to port 6 miles off at 1.15 p.m., and Skipper Claxton altered course to ENE. This was a dangerous course to steer because, if continued, it would take the vessel directly to the Maloy Skarholmen shoals. The ship continued to steer ENE until 6 p.m., when the bosun, who was on watch, was told by the skipper, 'You might see a light on your starboard beam.' Shortly afterwards, the bosun did see a light on that bearing, which he reported to the skipper. The skipper came out, looked in the direction of the light, and said, 'That is Maloy Sharl Light. Alter course half a point to port. Look out for a light on the port bow.' Presumably, the light he was expecting to show on the port bow was Skraaven, but in fact, the light on the starboard beam, which he thought was Maloy, must have been Eggeloysa, seen at its extreme range of 17 miles. The skipper took no precautions to verify his position, or to identify the light seen by its characteristics. The skipper then returned to his day room, and shortly afterwards, the bosun saw a light on the port bow. At 6.30 p.m., the bosun was relieved by the third hand, and it is not clear if the light on the port bow was reported to the skipper. Shortly after taking over the watch, the third hand saw the light on the port bow change to red and promptly informed the skipper. The skipper came to the bridge, but between five and ten minutes later, the ship grounded. She had struck the rocks 2 miles east of Maloy Skarholmen Light about fifteen minutes after the third hand saw the light change to red. She quickly took a list of about twenty-five degrees to starboard, and a distress call was sent out and rockets fired. Two Norwegian lifeboats were quickly on the scene, and they rescued the entire crew, but despite attempts to salvage her, the *Stella Orion* became a total loss. The lifeboats took the survivors to Bodo, where they were billeted at the hotel, given clothes and well looked after. After staying in Bodo for about five days, they were transported by steamer to Lodigen, from where they were given passage to Hull on homeward-bound trawlers.

The Court of Inquiry concluded that Skipper Claxton displayed shocking negligence. He had set a wrong course at the outset, he failed to identify the light on the starboard beam, and he improperly altered course an insufficient amount being falsely confident of his position. On seeing the light turn to red, which should have indicated to him at once that he was in a position of extreme danger, he did not take the immediate, urgent action that was called for. In his favour, the skipper had acknowledged the mistakes he had made and did not try to place the blame on anyone but himself. In the circumstances, the court recommended that his certificate as skipper be suspended for a period of eighteen months from the date of the stranding.

Euclase. (P. Whiting)

Euclase was built by Cook, Welton & Gemmell at Beverley in 1931 for Kingston S. T. Co. Ltd, Hull, and registered as H384. She was a single-screw steel steam side trawler of 295 gross tonnes, 129 feet long, 24 feet in beam and 12.9 feet in depth. In February 1940, she was taken over by the Admiralty and served as a minesweeper, flying pennant FY1636, until April 1946, when she was returned to Kingston to fish from Hull. She was sold to Lothian Trawling Co., Leith, in 1948 and registered at Granton as GN51. At 7.17 on the morning of 22 September 1955, she ran aground on Baxter Rock south of Stacks of Duncansby in dense fog. She was holed for'ard and immediately sent out a distress call on the radio, but mistakenly gave her position as at Noss Head, about 15 miles south of the position she had actually grounded. This resulted in a delay in finding her. When eventually Wick Lifeboat did find her, there were already two seiners and a trawler standing by. By 10.15, the fog was lifting and a SE wind had freshened to the extent that the life-saving crew assembled ashore deemed it prudent to fire a line to the *Euclase*. However, with the rising tide, the lifeboat was able to get alongside the wreck and eleven of the thirteen-man crew were taken off, leaving just the skipper and mate on the stranded vessel. A salvage tug, the *Salveda*, left Scapa Flow and arrived in the early afternoon. By this time, there was a very fresh wind, and the salvage attempt was abandoned. Wick Lifeboat took off the skipper and mate and landed them at Wick at 4 p.m. The incoming tide gradually filled the vessel and she took a 45-degree list to starboard. No further attempt was made to salvage her, and she was declared a total loss. Fortunately, there was no loss of life.

1956

Four ships lost during 1956.

Aberdeen	*Northman* A652	199 tons	11 December 1956
Grimsby	*Osako* GY100	260 tons	21 April 1956
	Northern Crown GY284	803 tons	11 October 1956
Hull	*St Celestin* H233	790 tons	27 May 1956

The *Northman* was built in 1911 at Aberdeen by Hall Russell for Standard Fishing Company. She was a single-screw side trawler of 199 tons gross. 115.2 feet long, 22 feet in beam and 12.1 feet in depth. She was on Admiralty service in both world wars and returned to fishing in 1946 under the ownership of the Stephen Fishing Company, Aberdeen, and registered as A414.

At about 8 p.m. on 5 February 1948, while homeward bound from the Faroes, she ran aground on Belhelvie Sands in stormy weather. Her twelve-man crew was brought ashore by breeches buoy, but *Northman* was abandoned as a constructive total loss and removed from the register in March 1948. However, the wreck was bought by A. J. & R. Mitchell, Engineers of Peterhead, and later that year, they succeeded in refloating her. After an extensive refit, she was re-registered as A652 in February 1950.

She sailed from Aberdeen on 11 December 1956 bound for the Shetland fishing grounds with a crew of thirteen men under the command of Skipper Edward J. Slater. Shortly after leaving Aberdeen, she struck the rocks at South Head, Peterhead. In response to blasts on her whistle, Peterhead Lifeboat was launched and succeeded in taking off all thirteen of her crew, but *Northman* was a total loss.

The *Osako* GY100 was a single-screw steel trawler built in 1918 by Cook, Welton & Gemmell, Beverley. She was a non-standard Castle-class vessel and first named *John Brennan*, and later *Iolite*, and was registered at Hull and worked from that port. In 1934, she was bought by the Diamonds Steam Fishing Company, Grimsby, and registered at Grimsby being renamed *Osako*. Her gross registered tonnage was 260, and she was 125.4 feet long, 22.7 feet beam, and 12.2 feet deep.

In April 1956, she sailed from Grimsby for a fishing voyage to the Faroes under the command of Skipper Harold Gladwell, with a crew of thirteen men all told. On 21 April, while on the Faroe fishing grounds, she sprang a leak. On finding that her pumps were unable to cope with the ingress of water, Skipper Gladwell put out a call for help on the radio. Skipper Harry Ellis, in the Grimsby trawler *Thessalonian*, answered the call and was soon on the scene. The weather was bad at the time, and when it became apparent that *Osako* could not be saved, her skipper decided to abandon ship. The *Thessalonian* was a nearly new ship (she was built in 1955) and fortunately was one of the few vessels at that time that was equipped with an inflatable raft. This raft

Osako. (Fishing Heritage Centre)

was floated down to the *Osako* and all thirteen men of her crew were ferried across to the *Thessalonian*. Shortly after the last man was taken off, *Osako* foundered and *Thessalonian* proceeded to Thorshaven to land the survivors.

The *Northern Crown* was built by Cochrane & Sons at Selby in 1953 for Northern Trawlers. She was a steel, single-screw side trawler of 803.73 tons gross, 183 feet in length, 32 feet in beam and 16 feet in depth. Her life-saving appliances included two wood lifeboats each to carry thirty-two persons, two ten-man inflatable liferafts, eight lifebuoys and twenty-two lifejackets. She was equipped with a radio transmitter, two radio receivers, two direction finders, two radar sets, three echo-sounders, three logs and two lead lines. She was classed 100 A1 at Lloyd's and was last dry-docked in July 1956, her life-saving appliances had been inspected in July, her navigation aids had been inspected on 4 October, and her compasses adjusted on 6 October. *Northern Crown's* regular skipper was Agust Ebernesersson, but when she sailed on her last voyage, Agust was on holiday, and she was under the command of the mate, Skipper Colin Newton. She sailed from Grimsby on 6 October 1956 bound for the fishing grounds on the west coast of Greenland with a crew of twenty hands all told. At the time she sailed, she was seaworthy in every respect.

She passed Cape Wrath some time on 7 October, 10 miles off, and a compass course of 297 degrees was set to take her to a position off Cape Farewell, the skipper allowing a mean variation of 25 degrees west. In fact, the variation at Cape Wrath is about 12 W and at Farewell is about 36 W. Had she continued to steer this course, she would have arrived at her intended position off Cape Farewell, but for the first half of the passage, she would have been making to the northward of the line, joining her point of departure to her point of arrival. By coincidence, this common practice of taking the mean variation on this passage means that the ship sails very close to the great circle track.

In the afternoon of 10 October, Skipper Newton received reports of bad weather and poor fishing at Greenland and decided to alter course for the fishing grounds at

Northern Crown. (Fishing Heritage Centre)

Northern Crown aground. (W. Taylor)

Northern Crown aground. (W. Taylor)

Iceland. Since being abeam of Cape Wrath, the vessel's position had not been checked. At 1230 GMT, the skipper and mate each took a sight and proceeded to work out a meridian altitude. In the longitude the ship was in at this time, the sun would still be over an hour from the meridian, and the position obtained could not have been remotely correct. The ship must have been further north than this calculated position. At 1230 hours on 10 October, a compass course of 061 degrees was set to make for the Westmann Islands, and after running 81 miles, course was altered to 055 degrees to allow for a supposed fetch to starboard. From 0300 hours on 11 October, the duty watch on the bridge consisted of the second hand, Mr R. Macdonald, a deckhand and the decky learner. At about 0400 hours, the second hand left the bridge to go to the toilet, and while he was away, the two men on the bridge saw lights that they took to be a trawler fishing a little forward of the port beam, which the deckhand estimated to be 4 to 6 miles away. When the second hand returned to the bridge, he was informed of the lights of the fishing vessel that had been seen, but told the inquiry that he was then unable to see any lights. He started two of the echo-sounders but neither machine recorded the bottom. He assumed that the water was too deep for a trawler to be fishing, and told his watchmates so. The court expressed doubt as to whether the sounders had been used because, at that time, the depth of water must have been less than 360 fathoms. It would also appear that either the second hand was away from the bridge longer than he stated or that visibility was not good, otherwise he would have seen the lights of the fishing vessel. About 0520 hours, the second hand again left the bridge to work out some mathematical problems, he said, and remained below until about 0635 hours. The wind was south-westerly about Force 6, with a moderate to rough sea and swell, with some rain about. Visibility was under eight miles and it was a dark night. The *Northern Crown* was making a speed of about thirteen knots. At about 0650 hours, what was described as a 'white spume' was seen, estimated as about a couple of ship's lengths ahead, and almost immediately, the ship took a heavy lurch to port, back to starboard, then righted herself, and she began to take water in the engine room. Very shortly after the lurch, Gant Rock was seen close by, some 70 miles west of the Westmann Islands. A radar bearing showed that the ship was about eight miles from Reykjanes, and there is little doubt that the vessel had run on to the 'Grenadiers' reef at Eldey. An SOS was sent out and answered by the Icelandic gunboat *Thor*, who immediately proceeded to the wreck. The port lifeboat was smashed when the vessel struck, and the starboard boat was damaged later when part lowered. The crew abandoned ship in the two liferafts, ten men in each. The *Thor* arrived on the scene about 1000 hours and picked up the whole crew, and about the same time, *Northern Crown* sank by the stern.

The court suspended Skipper Newton for twelve months, and it was stated that he had already appeared at an inquiry held by the Reinsurance Association and been banned from sailing as skipper for eighteen months. It seems unfortunate that a man should be tried twice for the same offence. In the case of Macdonald, the court found him negligent in not making proper use of the navigation aids at his disposal. Had he done so, he must have ascertained that something was wrong with the navigation. His absence from the bridge for well over an hour was a grave dereliction of duty. His certificate was not suspended, probably because he had not been informed of this possibility, thus he had not been given time to prepare a defence. To have dealt with his certificate, another inquiry would have to have been held, and the court decided this would have been unproductive.

The *St Celestin* was built in 1952 by Cook, Welton & Gemmell at Beverley for Thomas Hamling & Company, Hull. She was a steel, single-screw steam trawler of 789.95 tons gross, was 188.5 feet long and 32.1 feet in beam. She was fitted with a triple-expansion reciprocating steam engine, and was adequately equipped with navigational aids and life-saving appliances. *St Celestin* was commanded by Skipper Percival James May and Skipper Robert Gray commanded *Arctic Viking* (for a description of this vessel refer to the chapter on 1961 – *Arctic Viking*).

Both ships were fishing on the Bear Island fishing grounds, and on the afternoon of 27 May 1956, the weather was fine with a light southerly wind, Force 3 to 4, a moderate sea and good visibility. Shortly before the collision, *St Celestin* was proceeding at half speed, making about seven knots, on a southerly course. Her skipper was alone on the bridge and was heading for a 160-fathom patch where he intended to shoot the trawl. He had no lookout posted. He observed several trawlers in the vicinity, and particularly noticed one, which later proved to be the *Arctic Viking*, about 1 ½ miles away, and bearing a point and a half on his starboard bow. The *Arctic Viking* appeared to be heading on a northerly course. He kept his course and speed, expecting the two ships to pass starboard to starboard. When the two ships were about a mile apart, he could see the *Arctic Viking*'s warps, so knew she was fishing. Shortly afterwards, he saw her swinging to port about four cables away, and about four points on his starboard bow. He realised he should give the *Arctic Viking* a good clearance but took no action at that stage. A little later, when *Arctic Viking* was about two cables away and a little forward of his beam, he observed she was still swinging to port and making a bow wave. He then ported the wheel 10 degrees and sounded two blasts on the whistle. At a very late stage, about 45 seconds before the collision, he rang 'full speed astern' on the telegraph and gave three blasts on the whistle. The stem of the *Arctic Viking* struck his starboard side about eight feet abaft the bridge.

St Celestin. (P. Whiting)

The skipper of *Arctic Viking* was also alone on the bridge. He intended to take a turn out of the gear, a manoeuvre that requires a considerable amount of sea room. When he first sighted *St Celestin*, she was about six miles away and heading towards him. He put the helm hard over to port and the engines to 'full ahead'. He next observed *St Celestin* when his head had swung round to SSE. His speed was then 7 to 8 knots and increasing. *St Celestin* was then about one mile away, about four points on his port bow, and still on a southerly heading. He sounded two short blasts on the whistle and continued at full speed under hard port helm. He realised that *St Celestin* would have to take some action to get out of the way. When the distance had closed to about three cables, and *St Celestin* had not seemed to alter course, he rang 'stop engines' and immediately afterwards 'full astern', and sounded three short blasts. He estimated that, at the moment of impact, *Arctic Viking*'s speed had been reduced to 4 or 5 knots. *St Celestin* sank shortly after the collision, and it was not possible for the crew to launch either of her lifeboats. They did manage to launch and board her two liferafts. All except her skipper were picked up by *Arctic Viking*. Skipper May was picked up by the Grimsby trawler *Thomas Tompion* and later transferred to *Arctic Viking*.

The Court of Inquiry into the casualty found that the cause of the sinking of *St Celestin* was due to the fault or default of Skippers May and Gray and suspended the certificates of both men for a period of twelve months.

1957

Three ships and twelve men were lost this year.

Aberdeen	*Robert Limbrick* A283	273 tons	5 February 1957
	Carency A129	233 tons	28 June 1957
Hull	*Andradite* H26	313 tons	7 March 1957

*C*arency was built at Beverley by Cook, Welton & Gemmell in 1916 for the Earl Steam Fishing Company, Grimsby, and registered as GY956, but was taken over by the Admiralty for minesweeping. Released in March 1918, she was bought by Hull owners and worked from Hull until September 1924, when she returned to Grimsby and Earl SF Co. and registered as GY46. In 1938, she moved to Dublin and fished from that port until May 1940, when she again moved back to Grimsby, taking the port number GY277. September that year found her again in the navy on anti-submarine duties. Released in June 1946, she was bought by William and John Wood, Aberdeen, registering as A129. At the time of her loss, she was owned by William Wood & Sons. *Carency* was a single-screw, steel, coal-burning steam trawler with one deck. Her gross tonnage was 233.12 tons, and she was 117 feet long, 23 feet in beam, and 12.75 feet deep. Her steering gear was the hand-operated rod and chain type and was in satisfactory working order. The vessel was fitted with Decca Navigator, echo-sounder, direction finder, Walker's Log, radio telephone, leads and lead lines. All this equipment was in satisfactory working order.

The *Carency* sailed from Aberdeen for the West Coast fishing grounds about noon on 28 June 1957, with a crew of thirteen hands all told, under the command of Skipper David Baxter Wood, a part owner of the vessel. At the Court of Inquiry into her loss, it was established that at the time she sailed, she was not seaworthy in all respects for the following reasons:

a) Her compass, last adjusted on 11 June 1956 was not in good working order.
b) She did not carry the life-saving appliances required by law.
c) She did not have a certificated Second Hand as required by law.

Proceeding to sea, Rattray Head was abeam, 2 miles off, at 1700 hours on 28 June. At that time, the weather was fine and clear. She crossed the Moray Firth at full speed, about 8.65 knots. From 1830 until 2230, an uncertificated man, R. W. Buchan – the second fisherman, was in charge of the watch. The skipper came up to the bridge at 2230, when visibility had started to deteriorate, and by 2330, it had completely closed in and there was dense fog. The vessel continued to proceed at full speed, and no attempt was made to establish her position with the navigational aids available. At 0110 hours on 29 June, she grounded at Greenigoe, about a mile north of Wick. The

Andradite. (W. Dodds)

skipper called Wick Radio, and Wick Lifeboat and another vessel, the *Gilmar*, made unsuccessful attempts to refloat her. At 1500 hours on the 29th, the lifeboat took the crew off. There was no loss of life, but at 1700 hours that day, she heeled over on to her beam ends and was a total loss.

The verdict of the court was that the loss was caused by the skipper's failure to maintain a proper course after passing Rattray Head and to use the navigational aids with which the vessel was equipped. Skipper Wood's certificate was suspended for six months, and he was ordered to pay £200 towards the cost of the inquiry.

*A*ndradite was built at Beverley by Cook, Welton & Gemmell, for Kingston Steam Fishing Company, Hull, in 1934 and registered as H26. She was bought by J. Marr & Son and transferred to Fleetwood in 1949, and at the time of her loss was under the command of Skipper J. Bradshaw. *Andradite* was a steel, single-screw, coal-burning steam trawler, classed 100 A1 (Trawler) at Lloyd's. She had a gross tonnage of 313 tons, was 131 feet long, 24.6 feet in beam and 13.0 feet in depth.

On 7 March 1957, she ran aground on Barra at the southern end of the Hebrides, suffering severe damage to her bottom. Her fifteen-man crew were taken off by Castlebay Lifeboat but the vessel was a total loss.

*T*he *Robert Limbrick* was built by Hall Russell at Aberdeen in 1942 for the Admiralty. She was one of eight Round Table-class ships built at Aberdeen and called after knights of Arthur's Round Table. Originally named *Sir Galahad*, her gross tonnage was 273 tons, 126.2 feet in length with 23.6 feet beam. After the war, she was sold to Walker Steam Trawling & Fishing Company and registered in Aberdeen as A283 and her name changed to *Star of Freedom* in February 1947. She was sold to Milford Fisheries in March 1956 and renamed *Robert Limbrick* but retained her Aberdeen registration.

On 5 February, what was described as the worst storm in living memory hit the west coast of Scotland with hurricane-force winds gusting up to 120 miles per hour reported. Two trawlers from Milford Haven, the *Westcar* and the *Robert Limbrick*,

Star of Freedom renamed *Robert Limbrick*. (G. Coull)

were caught off the west side of Mull. The two skippers were talking to each other periodically throughout the night, and both considered it too dangerous to attempt to enter Mull Sound for shelter in the dark hours and decided to weather the storm out offshore until daylight. Late that night, Skipper Bill Robson on the *Westcar* heard a distress call from *Robert Limbrick*: 'Mayday Mayday Mayday Robert Limbrick hard aground.' This was followed by an order to launch the rubber liferaft. Then silence. At 6 a.m., distress flares were sighted by several trawlers in the area, and one trawler, the *Ocean Harvest*, reported sighting her ashore at Quinish Point. The next morning, two local men who had heard the distress call on the radio, found the smashed wreck of the trawler aground on the rocks off Quinish Point. There was no sign of her crew. All twelve men perished, their bodies being washed ashore on West Mull during the next few days. Her lifeboat was washed ashore with its cover still on, and an empty liferaft was also found.

The vessel was a total loss, and there is no evidence to explain how she ran ashore. When the wreck was examined, it was found that her propeller blades were stripped from the shaft and the bridge telegraph was in the stopped position, but no mechanical defect was found. It can only be concluded that the loss was due entirely to the terrible weather conditions that prevailed that night. *Robert Limbrick* was commanded by Skipper W. Burgoyne of Milford Haven.

1958

This was a good year. Losses were very light.

Aberdeen	*Jean Stephen* A420	212 tons	18 January 1958
	George H. Hastie A27	229 tons	9 December 1958
	Luffness GN57	271 tons	2 February 1958

Jean Stephen was built by Alexander Hall, Aberdeen, as the *Savitri* in 1917. She first registered in Grimsby as GY1028 under the ownership of the South Western Steam Fishing Company, but was requisitioned by the Admiralty for minesweeping duties immediately. Released from the navy in April 1918, she fished from Whitby until 1928, when she was sold to Granton owners, registering as GN9. In October 1936, he was bought by the Stephen Fishing Company Ltd, Aberdeen, and registered as *Jean Stephen* A420. She was a single-screw, steel, coal-burning steam trawler of 212 tons gross, was 115.5 feet long, 22.1 feet in beam and 11.9 feet deep. She was fitted with two compasses and was steered by a rod-and-chain-type hand-operated steering gear. Her compass was last adjusted in February 1958 and was in working order at the time she stranded. Her navigational aids comprised an echo-sounder, Walker's Log, leads and lead lines, a direction finder, radio telephone and a Decca Navigator.

Jean Stephen left Aberdeen on 16 January 1958 for the fishing grounds in the northern North Sea with a crew of thirteen hands all told, under the command of Skipper John Cowie. She was fit for the intended voyage in all aspects but one – her life-saving appliances did not meet with mandatory requirements. She carried one lifeboat for twelve persons, and one liferaft for twelve persons. To comply with the Merchant Shipping Life-saving Appliances Rules, she should have carried a lifeboat capable of holding at least thirteen persons, and two inflatable liferafts each capable of holding thirteen persons. Strictly speaking, this deficiency meant that she could not be described as 'seaworthy in all respects.'

Skipper Cowie commenced fishing 17 miles E by S of Noss Head on 16 January and continued to fish until the morning of the 18th, when, as the weather was deteriorating, he pulled the gear aboard and proceeded into Sinclair Bay for shelter. He anchored with Noss Head bearing approximately SE by S, in about seven fathoms, between half and three-quarters of a mile off the shore. The vessel's draft at this time was 8 feet forward and 13.5 feet aft. A number of other trawlers came in and anchored nearby. At about 8.45 p.m., the skipper ordered the anchor to be lifted. The wind having moved to north, and with the tide setting south, he was on a lee shore and not in deep water. When the anchor was raised, the mate joined the skipper on the bridge, and immediately, the skipper handed over the ship to him and left the bridge to talk to another trawler on the radio. Before leaving, the skipper ordered the mate to 'bring her round to ESE and keep her there till I come back.' Already the skipper had put the helm hard over to port, and rang the engines slow ahead. At the time, there was a snow squall reducing visibility almost to zero. Before the vessel could complete the turn, she grounded. It seems obvious that during the time the anchor was being raised, the vessel was set towards the beach, and when the engines were started, she had insufficient sea room to make a turn either to port or starboard. At no time during the interval between heaving up the anchor and stranding was any attempt made to fix the vessel's position, nor was any use made of her navigational aids. *Jean Stephen* stranded two miles south of Keiss Harbour, and at 3 a.m on 19 January, the crew were taken off by means of a rope from the bow. She was abandoned and became a total loss.

A formal investigation into the stranding and subsequent loss of *Jean Stephen* was held in Aberdeen, and it was found that the loss was due to fault by both the skipper and mate, and the skipper was suspended for twelve months, and the mate for six months. In addition to the suspensions, both men had to pay a contribution towards the costs of the inquiry. Although the owners were guilty of an offence in allowing the ship to sail short of LSA equipment in contravention of the regulations, owing to special circumstances, the court decided to take no action against them. What happened was that a man had signed off the vessel, and because men frequently did not turn up at sailing time, two men were signed on. In this case, both men did turn up, so the vessel sailed with thirteen men instead of the twelve she usually carried.

The *George H. Hastie* was built by Alexander Hall at Aberdeen in 1916 for R. Hastie & Sons of North Shields, who operated their ships from Aberdeen. She was 228.91 gross tons, 117 feet long, and 13.87 feet in beam. She was a steel, single-screw, coal-fired steam trawler fitted with a triple-expansion engine, which gave her a speed of about eight knots. She was taken over by the Admiralty for minesweeping and demobbed in 1918. In 1957, she was bought by North Eastern Fisheries, Aberdeen at a cost of £2,800 and registered as A27. Later, she was sold for scrap to a German company for £2,061 with delivery at Hamburg not later than 31 December 1958. She was insured for £7,000. Before being laid up, all her gear was stripped off her, including her life-saving apparatus, and when she was sold, in preparing her for the voyage, the owners replaced the LSAs but left the skipper to see what was required by way of navigation equipment.

George H. Hastie left Aberdeen at 0915 GMT on 5 December 1958 bound for the scrapyard at Hamburg with a crew of seven hands all told under the command of Skipper Alexander Montador. She had a patent log, but the only publications the skipper had purchased were a Blue Back Consul Fishermans Chart of the southern portion of the North Sea, and a copy of Brown's Nautical Almanac for 1958. On 6 December, the vessel put into the Tyne to effect repairs to a leaking boiler tube, and after repairs were carried out, she set sail for Hamburg at about 2100 GMT. The log was set at Souter Point and a course of S 79 E steered to make the Elbe Light Vessel. This course was not taken from the chart or laid off on the chart. It was read from the Brown's Almanac, in error, being the course given for Flamborough Head to the Elbe, with a distance of 294 miles. This course would take the vessel well to the north of the Elbe. On 8 December at 11 a.m., the log was reading at least 292 miles but nothing could be seen, so the vessel continued on the same course. At 6.30 p.m., the vessel stranded on the Shoals of Amrum Island, 35 miles north of the entrance to the Elbe. By working the engines and helm, the skipper was able to refloat the ship, but she was making water, and at about 9.30 p.m., the crew abandoned ship, taking to the inflatable liferaft. At the time, there was a SW gale with poor visibility. When in the raft, hand flares were fired, but it was not until about 10 a.m. on 9 December that the raft was sighted by the *Rickmer Bock*, a lighthouse tender from Amrum Island, who picked the men up. There were no casualties, but *George H. Hastie* sank and was a total loss.

At the inquiry into the loss, it was found that the cause was negligence by her skipper, and his certificate was suspended for two years.

*L*uffness was built in 1935 by J. Lewis at Aberdeen as the *White Pioneer* for a Newcastle owner. Later, her name was changed to *Mary White*. During the Second World War, she was on Admiralty service flying the pennant Z147. From January 1940 to February 1946, she was employed as a boom defence vessel at Greenock. In March 1947, she was acquired by Shire Trawlers Grimsby and registered as GY465, but in December 1948, she moved to Granton and registered as *Luffness* GN57 under the ownership of Newhaven Trawling Company. She was a single-screw steel side trawler of 271 tons gross, 126.3 feet long, 23.2 feet in beam and 12.6 feet deep.

While entering Aberdeen harbour, she ran aground on the rocky apron at the base of North Pier on 21 January 1858. Bad weather foiled salvage attempts, and when insurance officials boarded her, they found she was badly holed and the engine room and cabins full of water. She was declared a total loss and scrapped.

1959

Eight ships and thirty-six men lost this year

Aberdeen	Strathcoe A6	215 tons	4 February 1959
	River Ayr A337	202 tons	16 April 1959
	George Robb A406	217 tons	6 December 1959
Grimsby	Revello GY373	230 tons	7 December 1959
Hull	Staxton Wyke H479	472 tons	23 August 1959
	Stella Carina H573	555 tons	11 March 1959
Fleetwood	Red Falcon LO4	449 tons	14 December 1959
Granton	Thomas L. Devlin GN58	211 tons	20 December 1959

Strathcoe had an unusual career for a fishing vessel. She was built in 1916 by Hall Russell at Aberdeen for the Aberdeen Steam Trawling Company and was immediately taken over by the Admiralty for minesweeping. At the end of the war, when all the trawlers were returned to fishing, she was retained by the navy and continued to fly the White Ensign until the end of the Second World War, the only trawler to have this distinction. She was released from naval service in 1946 and bought by a Granton company and registered as GN21, but in February 1955, she returned home to Aberdeen, registering as A6 with Bruces Stores Ltd as owners. They continued to operate her until she was lost in 1959. She was a single-screw, steel, coal-burning side trawler of 214.87 tons gross, 117.75 feet long, 22.1 feet in beam and 13.5 feet deep. She had one overhead compass fitted in the wheelhouse and a spare lifeboat compass. They were adjusted on 12 November 1957 and were in satisfactory working order when she sailed on her last voyage. Her navigational aids comprised a Decca Navigator, echo-sounder, direction finder, radio telephone and hand leadlines. All these aids were in working order on the day she stranded. She carried life-saving appliances sufficient to comply with the regulations for a crew of twelve men, her usual complement, but on her last voyage, she had fourteen hands on board. The reason given for signing on the two extra hands was that there was a 'flu epidemic, and it was expected that some crew members would be missing at sailing time. In fact, all the men did turn up.

The *Strathcoe* sailed from Aberdeen on 27 January 1959, bound for the fishing grounds north of Latitude 61 North, with a crew of fourteen hands all told, under the command of Skipper James Hird. Apart from the deficiency in her life-saving appliances mentioned above, she was seaworthy in every respect. She proceeded to trawl off Whiten Head, north of Loch Eriboll, until 10.30 p.m. on the evening of 3 February, when the skipper decided to pull the gear aboard and steam to the east side of the Orkneys. The ship was then about 32 miles WNW of Tor Ness Light. He set off at full speed, about 8 ½ knots, and set a course of ESE to take her into the Pentland

Firth about 30 miles away. He then called the apprentice, Gordon Duff, a fifteen-year-old lad, up to the wheelhouse to steer the boat. Gordon had started his first trip on 8 November 1958 and had steered the boat before, sometimes supervised by the mate or skipper, sometimes without supervision. Having seen the ship's head was on ESE, a proper course to take the ship into the Firth if it was maintained, the skipper left the wheelhouse and turned in. At this time, the mate and the rest of the deck crew were working on the deck, and the skipper did not set a watch, nor did he tell the mate he was turning in. It was a fine clear night with good visibility and little or no wind. Hence the situation was that *Strathcoe* was steaming at full speed towards the Pentland Firth with the only man on the bridge in charge of her a fifteen-year-old inexperienced lad. At 11.30 p.m., Duff was relieved for supper by a deckhand and returned to the bridge at about twelve o'clock. The mate and crew were still working on deck. At 2 a.m., the deck work was finished and the mate set a watch. A deckhand, an eighteen-year-old youth called Winter, came up to the wheelhouse to take the wheel. About ten minutes later, he saw breaking water close on the port bow and realised the ship was in danger. He stopped the engine and started to put the helm hard a-starboard, but before either could take effect, the vessel struck the rocks, stripping the blades off the propeller. The skipper and mate came up to the bridge immediately , and inspection showed that the vessel was making water. The skipper put out a Mayday call, initially giving the position as 'ashore near Dunnet Head', but a check with the Decca Navigator showed that she had grounded off Santoo Head, 7 ½ miles north of where the ship would have been had the ESE course been maintained. After grounding, the vessel listed from port to starboard and was pounding under a heavy ground swell. She was badly holed and her liferaft and lifeboat were carried away by the sea. The crew were forced to group in the wheelhouse to avoid being washed away. Attempts were made to fire distress rockets, but two lifeboat parachute flares failed to ignite. The mate then brought the ship's distress rockets on deck but the container holding them was washed away by the sea. Eventually, Longhope Lifeboat arrived on the scene and, with great difficulty, managed to take the entire crew off by breeches buoy.

At the Court of Inquiry, it was found that Skipper Herd was at fault in leaving the bridge in the sole charge of a young, inexperienced boy, expecting him to keep a lookout and steer a course he was incapable of maintaining. The court suspended his certificate for two years.

The *River Ayr* was a Strath-class Admiralty trawler built in 1917 by Montrose Shipbuilding Company for minesweeping and named *Charles Carrol*. In 1919, she was bought by Montrose Fishing Company and registered as ME79, and her name changed to *River Ayr*. In May 1923, she was sold to Consolidated Fisheries, Grimsby, and registered as GY278. The year 1935 found her in Aberdeen as A337, and she had several owners while working from that port up to the time of her loss, when she was owned by W. H. Dodds & Co. Ltd. She was a steel, single-screw side trawler of 202 gross tons, 115.1 feet long, 22.1 feet in beam and 12.1 feet deep.

She left Aberdeen on a fishing trip to the Shetlands with a crew of eleven hands all told under the command of Skipper David Simpson. She sprang a leak about sixteen miles south-east of Bard Head and the engine room quickly flooded. As the water put the fires out, the pumps and lights were out of action. In response to her radio call for help, two other Aberdeen trawlers, the *Braconbrae* and the *Kosmos* raced to the stricken vessel. *Braconbrae* arrived first and took the *River Ayr* in tow. But after being towed for 5 miles towards Lerwick, with the water gaining rapidly, Skipper Simpson decided the situation was hopeless and gave the order to abandon ship. The crew took to the liferaft and after being 15 minutes adrift, they were picked up by the *Kosmos*. *River Ayr* sank a few minutes later 16 miles south-east of Lerwick on 16 April 1959.

George Robb was built by Hall Russell at Aberdeen in 1930 for the Carnie family and named *Elise I. Carnie*, and registered at Granton as GN24. In 1936, she was sold to George Robb & Sons, Aberdeen, her name was changed to *George Robb* and she was registered as A406 . She was requisitioned by the Admiralty in August 1939 and was employed as a minesweeper until her release in 1946. In 1959, she had a major refit and was converted to diesel power at Lowestoft. The work was completed in October 1959, and she returned to Aberdeen. It was only her second trip after the conversion when she sailed from Aberdeen at about 11 a.m. Sunday 6 December 1959, bound for the fishing grounds with a crew of twelve men all told under the command of Skipper Marshal Ryles. Late that night, in storm-force winds, *George Robb* was driven on to the rocks at the foot of Duncansby Head. A local farmer, Mr Ham, was listening to the trawler band on his radio when he heard the distress call: 'Ashore south of Duncansby. Making water. Immediate assistance required.' Taking his wife, he drove to Duncansby, gathered a party, and they set out to search the cliffs. They found the trawler on the Stacks of Duncansby, a reef at the foot of the cliffs. Men aboard the wreck were still alive at that time, because they heard the sound of the vessel's siren. They drove back to Duncansby Lighthouse, where they found the rescue teams from Wick and Skarfskerry already gathering and led them back to the scene of the wreck. There was no sign of life on board, and the ship was being battered by huge waves. Even had they been able to get a line to the ship, it would have been impossible for anyone on board to have recovered it and made it fast. They could see the Longhope Lifeboat standing by just offshore, but it was impossible for her to render any assistance. Some members of the shore party climbed down the cliff and searched for survivors. One body was found but all twelve men aboard the ill-fated vessel perished that wild night. Nine women were made widows and thirty-four

Revello. (Fishing Heritage Centre)

children fatherless. In addition, one of the rescue party, Station Officer Eric Campbell of Wick, died in the terrible weather conditions.

*R*evello was a steel, single-screw trawler built in 1908 by Cook, Welton & Gemmell for G. F. Sleight, Grimsby, and registered as GY373. She was 230 tons gross, 117 feet long, 22 feet wide and 11.7 feet deep.

She left Grimsby for a fishing voyage in the North Sea under the command of Skipper Robinson. She had been at sea a week, and was presumably bound home, when, on 7 December, she sprang a leak when 10 miles off Spurn Light Vessel. Finding that the pumps were unable to cope, and with the water level rising rapidly, the crew abandoned ship, taking to the liferaft. The Newcastle steamer *Baluchistan* was in the vicinity and heard the *Revello*'s call for assistance. She was soon alongside *Revello* and picked up the men in the liferaft. There were no casualties. 3 ½ hours after being abandoned, *Revello* disappeared beneath the waves.

*T*he *Staxton Wyke* was built at Beverley by Cook, Welton & Gemmell in 1937 as the *Lady Hogarth*. In 1946, her name was changed to *Kingston Emerald* and, in 1951, to *Staxton Wyke*. At the time of her loss, she was owned by the West Dock Steam Fishing Company, Hull. She was a steel, single-screw steam trawler of 472 tons gross, 163.5 feet long and 27.2 feet in beam. She was fitted with a reciprocating steam triple-expansion direct-acting inverted-cylinder engine of 750 ihp, which gave her a full speed of about twelve knots. Her life-saving appliances included two inflatable liferafts, and she was fitted with a Decca type 45 radar. She left Hull for a voyage to the Icelandic fishing grounds on 5 August 1959 with a crew of twenty-one hands all told under the command of Skipper Andrew Christopher Whitely. She finished fishing on 17 August and commenced her return passage to Hull with about 1,000 kits of fish on board.

The *Dalhanna* was built at Port Glasgow in 1958 by Lithgows Limited and was owned by Northern Mercantile & Investment Corporation Ltd, London. She was a steel, single-screw motor vessel of 11,452 tons, 486 feet in length, and powered by a Rowan Doxford opposed-piston oil engine of 5,150 ihp. She was fitted with a Decca model TM 46 true motion radar. At the time of the collision, she was on passage from Immingham to Middlesbrough with a part cargo of 8,826 tons of iron ore. She was commanded by Captain John Evans and had a crew of forty-five persons all told.

The collision happened in dense fog at about 0130 GMT on 23 August 1959, in a position about 12 miles, 138 degrees true, from Flamborough Head. The stem of *Dalhanna* struck the starboard side of *Staxton Wyke* about amidships at about a right angle. As a result, the trawler sank within 1 ½ minutes with the loss of five of her crew. The remaining members of her crew were able to launch and board her liferafts and were picked up by the *Dalhanna*.

This disaster was brought about mainly because, in an area where a lot of shipping was to be expected, two vessels were navigated at full speed in dense fog in flagrant disregard of the Collision Regulations. The Court of Inquiry suspended the certificates of Skipper Whitely and Captain Evans for a period of two years, and the certificate of Walter Allison, mate of *Staxton Wyke*, for a period of eighteen months.

*T*he *Stella Carina* was built in 1948 at Selby by Cochrane for the Boston Company and named *St Christopher*. Later bought by Charleson Smith Trawlers, Hull, her name was changed to *Stella Carina*.

She left Hull on 11 March 1959 for a fishing voyage to the Norway Coast grounds under the command of Skipper Fred Sullivan. Shortly after leaving the lock pits, she

Stella Carina in St Andrews Dock. (P. Whiting)

Stella Carina aground showing collision damage. (P. Whiting)

was in collision with the collier *Mendip* and sustained a gash 22 feet long and 3 feet wide along her port side. Almost immediately, she began to settle by the stern, and with Chief Engineer George Roberts working waist deep in water, Skipper Sullivan drove her up on the stones between Victoria Dock and Earle's Yard. The crew launched and boarded the rubber dinghies and were picked up by the Humber pilot cutter. There were no casualties.

In May 1959, she was salvaged and towed to Immingham, where she was repaired and returned to fishing. Later taken over by the Ross Group, her name was changed to *Ross Carina*. She was finally scrapped in 1967.

R*ed Falcon* was built by Cochrane at Beverley in 1936 as the *Davy* for F. & T. Ross Limited. In August 1939, she was bought by the Admiralty and served throughout the war as FY147. She returned to Hull for fishing in 1945 under the ownership of Hull Ice Company Ltd and, in 1951, was bought by Hudson Bros Trawlers Ltd, who registered her as H213 and changed her name to *Cape Barfleur*. In 1954, she was bought by Iago Steam Fishing Company and transferred to Fleetwood, where her name was changed to *Red Falcon* with a London registration – LO4. She was a steel, single-screw, coal-burning steam trawler. Her gross tonnage was 449 tons and she was 161.3 feet long, 27.2 feet beam and 14.2 feet deep. Her life-saving appliances included an 18-foot wood lifeboat, four inflatable liferafts, twenty-eight lifejackets and six circular cork lifebuoys. Navigational aids included a direction finder, a Decca 45 marine radar, and two echo-sounders. Her wireless communications equipment could cope with telephony or telegraphy. She was classed +100 A1 (Trawler) with Lloyd's, and when she sailed from Fleetwood on her last voyage, she was seaworthy in every respect.

Red Falcon left Fleetwood at 0630 hours on 25 November 1959 bound for the Icelandic fishing grounds manned by a crew of nineteen hands all told under the command of Skipper A. Hardy. She finished fishing on the Kidney Bank at 1530 hours on 11 December and set course for home. She reported a catch of 500 boxes of fish. During her passage, she maintained radio contact with other trawlers who were also bound for Fleetwood, and the skippers of these vessels exchanged information about the weather conditions they were experiencing. At 0715 hours on 14 December 1959, the skipper of *Red Falcon* told the skipper of *Red Knight* that he was abeam of Skerryvore Light and approximately twelve miles off. He went on to say that the weather was very bad from the west or west-south-west with a very confused sea, and that he proposed to steer for Inishtrahull and get a lee from the Irish coast. He added that *Red Falcon* would behave better closer to the wind than when broadside to the heavy seas. That was the last that was ever heard from *Red Falcon*, and it must be presumed that she was lost with all hands shortly after that conversation. At 1830 hours, the skipper of *Red Knight* called *Red Falcon* on the radio but received no reply, and the skipper of the *Red Sabre* called the *Red Falcon* several times during 14 December also without reply.

The *Red Knight* arrived in Fleetwood on the midday tide on 15 December 1959, and when *Red Falcon* didn't arrive, the alarm bells started to ring. At 1220 hours on the 16th, the Northern Rescue Co-ordination Centre at Pitreavie was informed by the Coastgaurd Station at Formby that *Red Falcon* was twenty-four hours overdue and assistance in searching for her was required. Due to the adverse weather conditions prevailing at the time and the early onset of darkness, an air search was not started until first light on 17 December using a Shackleton aircraft. Three sorties were made by the aircraft, the search being called off at 1632 hours on 18 December. Nothing was found. Later, an inflatable liferaft was washed ashore on the Island of Mull and three lifebuoys, sixteen deck pound boards and a lifeboat cover came ashore on the

Thomas L. Devlin. (P. Whiting)

Island of Tiree. It was presumed that *Red Falcon* went down somewhere between Stanton Bank and Skerryvore, probably to the south-west'ard of Skerryvore. Nineteen men were lost – there were no survivors.

The *Thomas L. Devlin* was built at Aberdeen in 1915 by Alexander Hall & Co. and, at the time of her loss, was owned by Thomas L. Devlin & Sons Ltd, Edinburgh. She was a single-screw, steel, steam side trawler of 211.16 gross tons, 115.7 feet in length, 22.6 feet in beam and 13.9 feet in depth. She had a triple-expansion engine, which gave her a speed of about nine knots.

She left Granton on 12 December 1959, bound for fishing grounds in the North Sea, with a crew of thirteen hands all told under the command of Skipper James Anderson Glasgow. She was well fitted with navigational aids and was seaworthy in every respect when she left Granton on her last voyage.

She completed fishing on 20 December and set a course for Granton. At 1745 hours, the second fisherman, James Dick, took over the watch from the skipper. He did not hold a certificate. At 1930 hours, Bell Rock Light was about three miles off to starboard, and at 1950 hours, May Island Light was sighted. The skipper altered course to SW to stem the light, and at 2050 hours, an echometer reading of 26 fathoms was reported to the skipper. The skipper came to the bridge and gave a course alteration to WSW, a course that would have taken the vessel safely up the Firth of Forth and well clear of May Island if it was kept to. The skipper then went below. At about 2110 hours, the second fisherman sent the deckhand below to call the watch. As he was returning along the foredeck some minutes later, the deckhand saw that May Island Light was too close. He went up to the wheelhouse and warned the second fisherman, and although Dick immediately put the helm hard over, it was too late. The vessel grounded on Norman Rock, the northernmost point of the May Island group, at about 2115 hours. The chief engineer stopped the engines and reported to the skipper that the vessel was making a lot of water. It was then found that it was not possible to restart the engines owing to the propeller being fouled. The skipper put out a Mayday call, which was acknowledged by Stonehaven Radio, and gave the order to abandon ship. The crew took to the liferafts and were picked up shortly afterwards by Anstruther Lifeboat. There was no loss of life, but later the vessel slid off the rocks and sank. She was a total loss.

The subsequent Court of Inquiry found that the loss was caused by the negligence of the skipper in that he went below in the near vicinity of May Island, leaving the vessel in charge of an uncertificated man who was not capable of keeping the vessel on a proper course, or of realising when she went off her course. Skipper Glasgow's certificate was suspended for two years.

1960

Two ships and four men lost.

Hull	*St Hubert* H104	568 tons	29 August 1960
Grimsby	*Vindelecia* GY954	248 tons	4 December 1960

The *St Hubert* was built at Kiel in 1950 for the Boston DSF Company and worked from Hull registering as H104. She was a steel, oil-fired steam side trawler. She had a gross tonnage of 568 tons and was 178.1 feet long with a beam of 28.7 feet. While fishing off the Norwegian coast, she picked up a mysterious cylindrical object in the trawl, which the crew heaved for'ard and lashed up secure. Three days after being brought on board, on 29 August 1960, it started to tick and exploded, killing three of the crew. Skipper Ness, although badly injured, strived to keep *St Hubert* afloat in gale-force winds for six hours, but eventually, she had to be abandoned, and sank off Vardo. The Hull trawler *Prince Charles*, who had been standing by the stricken ship, picked up her remaining crewmen but sadly, Skipper Ness died of his injuries.

St Hubert. (P. Whiting)

St Hubert abandoned and sinking. (P. Whiting)

The *Vindelecia* was a steel, coal-burning steam side trawler built by Cook, Welton & Gemmell in 1913 for Gt. Grimsby & East Coast Steam Fishing Company and was registered as GY954. In February 1937, she was bought by Hopwood & Taylor, Grimsby, but, in June of that year, was transferred to Japan Steam Company, who were her registered owners at the time of her loss. She had a gross tonnage of 248 tons, was 120 feet in length, 22.5 feet in beam and 11.9 feet deep.

On 4 December 1960, while on a North Sea fishing trip under the command of Skipper Stanley Nicholls, she sprang a leak when 90 miles off the Humber. Finding that the pumps were unable to cope with the ingress of water, Skipper Nicholls put out a distress call on the radio. The Grimsby trawler *Taipo*, Skipper A. Gill, was about 20 miles away and proceeded to her. There was a gale blowing at the time, and Skipper Gill had some difficulty in manoeuvring *Taipo* alongside the stricken vessel. A tow-line was eventually rigged and towing started. After about ninety minutes, the tow-line parted and Skipper Nicholls reported that the situation was getting worse and water was coming in faster. After taking off half the *Vindelicia*'s crew, it was decided to lie to until daylight before attempting to rig a new tow-line, but soon afterwards, Nicholls decided to abandon ship. When he left the vessel, her decks were awash, and she sank beneath the waves shortly afterwards. *Taipo* then proceeded to Grimsby to land the survivors. Fortunately, there was no loss of life.

Vindelecia. (Fishing Heritage Centre)

1961

Four ships and five men were lost this year.

Aberdeen	*D. W. Fitzgerald* A629	235 tons	13 June 1961
Grimsby	*Invertay* GY287	230 tons	10 March 1961
Fleetwood	*Ssafa* FD155	426 tons	17 January 1961
Hull	*Arctic Viking* H452	533 tons	18 October 1961

D. W. Fitzgerald was built by Hall Russell & Co. at Aberdeen for Richard Irvin & Sons Ltd. She served as a minesweeper in both world wars and was released to return to fishing in late 1945 registering as A629. She was sold for scrap and, on 13 June 1961, was being towed from Aberdeen to the scrapyard by the Aberdeen trawler *Cadorna*. She was unmanned at the time, and secured alongside the *Cadorna* with chains. Heavy swell across the harbour bar caused the chains to part, and she was driven by the tide onto the ledge at the foot of Girdleness Lighthouse. An attempt was made to break her up in situ, but one night, she rolled off the ledge and sank.

The *Arctic Viking* was built in 1937 as the *Arctic Pioneer* at Selby by Cochrane & Sons, and at the time of her loss, she was owned by Boyd Line Ltd, Hull. She sank during the war while on Admiralty service but was raised and rebuilt in 1947 at West Hartlepool, and at the same time, she was converted from coal-burning to oil-fired. She was a single-screw steel steam trawler of 532.56 tons gross, and was 165 feet long, 27.5 feet in beam and her moulded depth midships was 15 feet. Her designed speed was 12 knots.

Arctic Viking left Hull on 27 September 1961, bound for the fishing grounds off the north coast of Norway with a crew of nineteen men all told under the command of Skipper Philip William Garner. She left the fishing grounds on 12 October 1961 and set course for Hull with about 1,500 kits of fish on board. In the early hours of 18 October when approaching Flamborough Head, she was running before a Force 7 wind with a heavy sea. She took a heavy roll to port, which filled the port side with water, giving her a list of about twenty degrees. Speed was eased and corrective helm action taken, and she cleared the water almost immediately. Subsequently, she laid over to port a couple of times between four and eight o'clock that morning. Shortly after 8.30 a.m., a very heavy sea rolled over the port quarter, filling the port side and the foredeck. The vessel heeled heavily to port, and then she turned right over and floated bottom upwards. *Arctic Viking* carried two liferafts, one on each side of the vessel. The one on the port side was inaccessible, but some of the crew managed to launch the raft on the starboard side, and fourteen men were able to board it. Skipper Ryszard Sleska of the Polish trawler *Derkacz* was fortunately in the vicinity and picked up the men from the raft. Five men were lost, presumably by drowning.

D. W. Fitzgerald. (J. Worthington)

Arctic Viking (P. Whiting)

Invertay. (Fishing Heritage Centre)

The official inquiry into the loss decided that 'a coincidence of wave formations of unpredictable and unascertainable proportions overcame the stability of the vessel in her then trim'.

The *Invertay* was built by Goole Shipbuilding Company at Goole in 1916 for the Grimsby and North Sea Fishing Company and was registered at Grimsby as the *Cancer* GY918. In August 1921, she was sold to Lindsey Steam Fishing Company, Grimsby, who operated her until September 1929, when she was acquired by Granton owners who changed her name to *Invertay*. In June 1946, she returned to Grimsby registering as GY287 with a St Annes owner, and in September 1950, she was bought by Sir Thomas Robinson, Grimsby, who operated her until her loss. *Invertay* was a steel, single-screw steam trawler of 230 tons gross, 120.2 feet long, 22 feet in beam and 12.1 feet in depth.

She sailed from Grimsby in early March 1961 with a ten-man crew under the command of Skipper A. Osborne. At 1.20 a.m. on 10 March, in a position 190 miles off the Humber, she collided with the German trawler *Franz Schau* in thick fog. The crew had just time to launch the liferaft and abandon ship before *Invertay* sank. The *Franz Schau* was unable to locate the liferaft despite searching for it, but fortunately, it was found by another German trawler, the *Grundmann*, who picked up the castaways. She later transferred the men to the *Saxon Progress*, a brand-new Grimsby trawler making her maiden voyage, which landed them at Grimsby the next day. Fortunately, there was no loss of life.

The *Ssafa* was a steel motor side trawler built in 1958 by Goole Shipbuilding Company and owned by Boston Deep Sea Fishing Company and registered as FD155. She was 138.7 feet long, 28.5 feet in beam with a net tonnage of 139 tons. She left Fleetwood with a crew of sixteen men under the command of Skipper Harry Pook for a fishing trip off the west Scottish coast. On the morning of Tuesday 17 January 1961, there was a gale of wind blowing when she took the ground in Friesland Bay on

Ssafa. (Fishing Heritage Centre)

the island of Coll while she was trying to navigate the narrow channel between Coll and Tiree on her outward passage to the fishing grounds.

Oban Radio picked up, and relayed her distress call at 0636 hours that morning, and several trawlers in the vicinity headed for her position. However, Skipper Pook cancelled the Mayday at about 0730 hours when it was evident that the crew were in no immediate danger. Another Boston trawler, *Princess Ann*, and Mallaig Lifeboat stood by the stranded vessel while she waited for high tide, hoping to refloat, but in the rising tide, *Ssafa* took a heavy list to port. Twelve of the crew were pulled ashore by the Coll Rescue Team using the ship's liferaft, leaving the skipper and three other men aboard the wreck. Later, when it became obvious that the vessel was not going to float clear, they abandoned her and reached the shore by jumping from rock to rock. There were no casualties. Next day, the 18th, weather conditions of wind and sea were very severe and huge waves were battering the wreck, preventing any attempt to salvage her. *Ssafa* was eventually refloated on 18 April 1961 and towed to Tobermory for temporary repairs before being taken to Port Glasgow. In 1971, she was sold to Heward Trawlers, Fleetwood, and in 1976, she was acquired by Huxley Fishing Company, Lowestoft, a Colne subsidiary. After a brief spell fishing from Lowestoft, she was transferred to oil rig standby work. She was finally scrapped at Barking in 1986.

1962

A good year. Four ships were lost and seven men.

Grimsby	*Ross Kenilworth* GY2	442 tons	May 1962
Fleetwood	*Ella Hewett* LO47	595 tons	6 November 1962
Hull	*Stella Rigel* H170	568 tons	21 December 1962
Milford Haven	*Boston Heron* FD48	314 tons	3 December 1962

The *Ross Kenilworth* was built in 1955 by Cochrane at Selby. First registered at Grimsby as the *Joseph Knibb*, her name was changed to *Kenilworth* in 1960, and to *Ross Kenilworth* in January 1962. At the time she was lost, her registered owners were Richardson Trawlers Ltd, Grimsby. She was a single-screw, steel steam trawler of 442 gross tons. 139.6 feet long, 28.3 feet wide and 14.1 feet deep.

She sailed from Grimsby, bound for Iceland, in May 1962, under the command of Skipper Jack Simpson, with a crew of seventeen men. She was 20 miles off the south-west coast of Iceland when it was discovered that she was leaking badly. Two vessels, the Grimsby trawler *Rodney*, Skipper Jock Kerr, and the Icelandic gunboat *Thor* answered her call for assistance. Initially, the *Rodney* took off eleven of her crew, and the *Thor* put a salvage pump aboard her. *Rodney* then attempted to tow her to land to beach her, but when it became evident that the pumps could not cope with the rising water, the *Thor* took off the remaining seven crew members and her pump, and *Rodney* cast off the tow-line. Shortly after this, *Ross Kenilworth* sank. *Rodney* then transferred the survivors she had on board to the *Thor* for conveyance to Reykjavik and resumed fishing.

The *Ella Hewett* was built at Beverley by Cook, Welton & Gemmell in 1953 and owned by Heward Trawlers Ltd. She was a single-screw, steel steam trawler of 594.52 gross tons, 170.1 feet long. 29.2 feet in beam, and 14.5 feet deep. Her hull was constructed with eight watertight bulkheads, and she was fitted with a triple-expansion engine and a multitubular boiler, both made in 1953 by Charles D. Holmes, Hull. She was classed 100 A1 (Trawler) with Lloyd's and the last survey to maintain class was made on 20 August 1962. The vessel was provided with two 21-foot wooden lifeboats, each for twenty-six persons; two inflatable liferafts, each for ten persons; four circular cork lifebuoys; nineteen standard MOT lifejackets; a Schermuly Supreme line throwing appliance and twelve parachute distress flares. These life-saving appliances were last inspected by a MOT surveyor on 13 February 1962, and found to be satisfactory. Communications equipment fitted comprised a Marconi Transarctic II transmitter with type 993 receiver, two Marconi receivers types CR 300/2 and 1060D with DF Loop type 542A, a Redifon VHF transmitter and receiver type GR 286, and an Eddystone VHF receiver type 770 R. Her navigational aids comprised two radars,

Ross Kenilworth. (P. Whiting)

Ross Kenilworth – Rodney in the background. (W. Taylor)

a Decca type 12 and a Decca type 404; two echo-sounders, a Marconi Seagraph II and a Kelvin-Hughes type MS 29 F; a Walker's electric log and two hand leads with lines. When the vessel left Fleetwood on her last voyage, she was completely seaworthy and fit for the proposed voyage in every way.

Ella Hewett left Fleetwood at 0145 hours on the early morning of 2 November 1962 for a fishing trip to Iceland, with a crew of nineteen men all told, under the command of Skipper William Storm 'Bluey' Gregson. Shortly afterwards, she put in to Heysham to take bunkers. While at Heysham, the cook fell down an open grating, injuring himself, but received no medical attention. The vessel left Heysham at 0530 hours and a course was set for Rathlin Island with the intention of entering Church Bay to put the cook ashore. At 1830 on 2 November, *Ella Hewett* was just off Rue Point. The second hand, James Rixon, was in charge of the watch, and had been ordered by the skipper to take the ship to the anchorage in Church Bay. Shortly after 1830, she stranded on the wreck of HMS *Drake*. The buoy marking the wreck was in its charted position, and had been seen on the radar, and visually, when illuminated by the vessel's searchlight. Church Bay is well lit, and entering it should provide no difficulty for a navigator if normal precautions are taken. As soon as the vessel struck, the skipper rushed to the bridge, but apart from running the engines astern, nothing useful was done to try and free the vessel. At 2210 hours, it was found that the ship was making water in substantial quantities, and Skipper Gregson made the first call to the outside world in the form of a link call to the owner's agents in Belfast requesting a tug. The situation got worse, and at about 2230, the chief engineer found oil on the surface of the water in the stokehold and decided, in the interests of safety, to draw the fires. At 0052 hours on 3 November, pumping ceased because there was insufficient steam to run the pumps. A Mayday call was sent out asking for immediate assistance, and Portrush Lifeboat was quickly on the scene. At 1100 hours, the vessel had taken a starboard list to an extent that it was thought wise to take thirteen crew members off onto the lifeboat. The lifeboat took these men to Ballycastle and returned to the wreck shortly afterwards. At 2115 hours, the remaining men were taken off by the lifeboat, and *Ella Hewett* heeled over on her beam ends and sank.

At the subsequent inquiry into the loss, the court found the casualty was due to wrongful acts or defaults of both skipper and mate. Skipper Gregson's certificate was suspended for three years, and Second Hand Rixon had his skipper's certificate cancelled, but it was recommended he be granted a second hand's certificate.

The *Stella Rigel* was built at Beverley in 1949 by Cook, Welton & Gemmell for Boston DSF Company, and named *Prince Philip*. In July 1955, she was sold to Derwent Trawlers, Grimsby, and registered as GY7 and her name was changed to *Hargood*. July 1958 found her back in Hull as H170 under the ownership of Charleson-Smith Trawlers, who changed her name to *Stella Rigel*. At the time of her loss, her registered owners were Ross Trawlers, Grimsby. *Stella Rigel* was a single-screw, oil-fired steam trawler of 567.88 gross tons, 170.5 feet in length. 29.2 feet in beam and 14.45 feet deep. Her life-saving appliances were last inspected by an MOT Surveyor on 23 November 1962 and found to be satisfactory and in compliance with the regulations. She was equipped with three radio transmitters and receivers, two direction finders, three echo-sounders and a marine radar. All this equipment was checked and serviced by the maintenance company on 14 December 1962. She also had a Walker's Electric Log, three Walker's 1,000-mile Logs, and a 120-fathom sounding leadline. The vessel was classed 100 A1 (Trawler) with Lloyd's, and was seaworthy in every respect when she sailed on her final voyage.

The *Stella Rigel* left Hull on 17 December 1962 bound for northern waters with a crew of twenty men all told under the command of Skipper John Gay. After passing

Stella Rigel. (P. Whiting)

Svino, a course of NE by N was set and the vessel proceeded on this course at about twelve knots. At 1535 hours on 20 December, a position 12 miles abeam of Skonvaer was fixed using the D/F for bearing and the radar for distance, and the patent log was set. About 0420 hours on 21 December, she had run 160 miles by patent log, when the skipper altered course to E by N ¼ N intending to round North Cape and proceed to the White Sea fishing grounds. The ship stayed on this course until she stranded. At 1200 hours, the skipper observed land a little forward of the beam and apparently showing at 15 miles on the radar. At 1230 hours, he handed over the watch to the second hand, telling him he was going below for five minutes for a plate of soup and that he would alter course when he returned. At 1235 hours, *Stella Rigel* took the ground on submerged rocks off the Isle of Vannoy. There was moderate wind and sea with moderate visibility and occasional snow showers. The second hand checked the position by radar and found the ship to be 8 miles from the nearest point of Vannoy. That seems to be the only time the position of the vessel was ascertained between the time of being abeam of Skonvaer until the stranding. Shortly after striking the rocks, the vessel took a heavy list to starboard and 'abandon ship' was ordered. All the crew got away safely in the liferafts and were picked up by the Norwegian trawler *Siv* commanded by Skipper Olsen. Skipper Gay decided to remain on board and was later taken off by the Norwegian trawler *Hansnes*, commanded by Skipper Hansen.

At the subsequent inquiry, the court found that the loss was caused by the wrongful act or default of her skipper, John Gay, and suspended his certificate for two years from the date of the stranding.

*B*oston Heron was a steel, single-screw steam trawler built in 1939 by Cochrane & Sons at Selby as the *Akita* and registered at Cardiff as CF4. She was transferred to Fleetwood and re-registered as FD48. In 1950, she was renamed *Boston Heron* and, at some later date, was moved to Milford Haven. She was 314.11 gross tons, 131 feet long, 25 feet in beam and 12 feet in depth. At the time of her loss, she was owned by Merchants (Milford Haven) Limited. A Mr Albert Henry Davies was her designated manager. Her life-saving appliances comprised a 16-foot wood lifeboat for twelve persons, an inflatable liferaft for twelve persons, four lifebuoys, fourteen lifejackets,

Boston Heron aground. (J. Campell)

twelve parachute distress flares and a line-throwing appliance. This equipment complied with the regulations, permission having been obtained under section 48 of the MS Life-saving Appliances Rules 1958 for the vessel to continue fishing, although the lifeboat was not attached to a davit. The vessel had one overhead magnetic steering compass and one magnetic pole compass. They had been adjusted on 29 June 1962 and were both in working order. She was fitted with a radio telephone, a Decca Navigator, two echo-sounders and hand leads and lines. All this equipment had been recently serviced and was in good working order. She was classed 100 A1 with Lloyd's and was subjected to survey on 28 November 1962. When she sailed on her final voyage, she was seaworthy in every respect.

Boston Heron sailed from Milford Haven on 30 November 1962 with a crew of twelve hands under the command of Skipper John William Bean, bound for the North Atlantic fishing grounds. On the afternoon of 3 December, with deteriorating weather conditions and reports of better weather further north, Skipper Bean decided to change ground and proceed northwards to Little Minch. At 1920 hours that evening, Vaterneish was abeam. Glas Eilean Light was visible, and the skipper brought it ahead and set a course of NE ¼ N. At this time, the ship was making full speed of about ten knots. The wind was increasing to Force 7 or 8, and at about 2000 hours, visibility closed down and Glas Eilean Light was obscured. At about 2120 hours, the *Boston Heron* took the ground on what later proved to be the rocks off Stilamair Island, about 1 ½ miles west of Glas Eilean. The vessel took a heavy list to starboard and the seas were breaking over her. Engines were stopped, distress rockets fired and a distress message was sent out. Under orders from the skipper, some of the crew began to prepare to inflate the liferaft, but a sea broke over the starboard side and washed it overboard with the painter still attached. The skipper went to the raft, which was then on the port side of the vessel, with the intention of getting it round to the starboard side. A sea swept the raft right over the vessel with the skipper still hanging on to it, and he was washed into the sea on the starboard side, and he got a severe blow on the head. Somehow, he managed to climb onto the rocks. Meantime, some of the men were trying to launch the lifeboat, but a sea washed it into the scuppers. At the same time, the second and third hands were washed into the sea but managed to reach the rocks and climb ashore. Local inhabitants were quickly on the scene and two men were got ashore by breeches buoy with apparatus brought from Tarbert. The skipper and second and third hands were rescued by a small boat from the fishing vessel *Scalpay Isle*. Of the crew of twelve men, seven were drowned, five of the bodies being recovered.

At the Formal Investigation into the stranding, the court found that the casualty was caused by the wrongful default of the skipper in failing to heed the warning given him by the Decca Navigator and not immediately hauling his vessel out into deeper water and suspended his certificate for three months.

1963

Six ships lost this year.

Fleetwood	*Lord Stanhope* H199	448 tons	7 November 1963
	Achroite H81	314 tons	February 1963
	Margaret Wicks FD265	366 tons	8 December 1963
Grimsby	*Lord Cunningham* GY109	635 tons	20 December 1963
	Northern Spray GY190	655 tons	23 October 1963
Aberdeen	*Aberdeen City* A113	264 tons	16 September 1963

The *Lord Stanhope* was a steel, single-screw steam trawler, built in 1935 at Selby by Cochrane & Sons for the Lord Line, Hull. Originally built as a coal-burner, she was converted to burning oil in 1947. After being on Admiralty service throughout the war, she returned to Hull and was sold to Wyre Trawlers, Fleetwood, in 1963, and worked from the Lancashire port until she was lost. She was 157.35 feet long, 26.15 feet in beam and 14.15 feet in depth, with a gross tonnage of 448.48 tons. Fitted with a steam triple-expansion reciprocating engine built by C. D. Holmes & Company Ltd of Hull, she had a speed of about eleven knots. Steering gear consisted of a steam engine sited abaft the wheelhouse operated by a hand wheel, and connected to the quadrant by a system of rods and chains. The vessel was classed 100 A1 at Lloyd's, and she retained her class up to the time of her loss. The vessel was equipped with one radar set, two echo-sounders, a radio direction finder, a radio telephone transmitter and receiver, two wireless receivers, and VHF. All this equipment was checked at Fleetwood before she sailed, and found to be in good order. She was also supplied with two patent logs and three hand leads and lines. She had two 9-inch liquid magnetic compasses, one fitted in the wheelhouse as a steering compass, the other, the standard compass, fitted on a pole forward of the bridge. They were last adjusted on 21 March 1963. Her life-saving appliances consisted of one wood lifeboat for twenty-three persons, twenty-six lifejackets, six lifebuoys, four inflatable life rafts with a total capacity of forty-four persons, a line-throwing appliance and twelve parachute distress rockets. The inflatable rafts were last inspected at Hull in November 1962 and were due for inspection again when she returned from her final voyage. The rest of the life-saving equipment was inspected at Fleetwood on 10 May 1963 and found to be in order.

A formal investigation into her loss was held at Fleetwood on 15 and 16 September 1964, when it was found that her stranding and subsequent loss was partly caused by default or wrongful acts of the skipper, George Harrison, in the following respects:

1. He set unsafe courses without regard to the probability of the ship being set towards the shore when proceeding at half speed in the conditions of wind and

sea prevailing at the time.

2. Failure to recognise from positions previously obtained that the vessel was in fact being set towards the land.

3. Failure to heed warnings given in the *Arctic Pilot* about the possibility of an inshore set, and the difficulty of ascertaining distances from the shore on account of a low-lying coast backed by high ground.

4. Failure to take heed of the possibility of local magnetic disturbance of the compass, which was clearly marked on the chart and referred to in the *Arctic Pilot*.

5. Failure to give clear orders to the acting bosun as to the course to be steered after he left the bridge.

The court also found that a partial cause of the loss was due to the default of the acting bosun, John James Larkin, in failing to keep a good look out when approaching Ingolfshofdi Light. The skipper's certificate was suspended for twelve months, and he was ordered to pay £100 towards the cost of the inquiry. The acting bosun was censured.

The *Lord Stanhope* sailed from Fleetwood at 0500 hours on 26 October 1963 bound for the fishing grounds at Iceland with a crew of nineteen hands under the command of Skipper George Harrison. Shortly after leaving port, the bosun took ill and was landed at Belfast, and a deckhand, John James Larkin, was promoted acting bosun for the voyage. After leaving Belfast, the vessel proceeded to the fishing grounds off the west coast of Iceland, where she caught about twenty-five tons of fish when the weather deteriorated. On 5 November, Skipper Harrison decided to steam to the east side of Iceland in search of better weather. At 1215 hours on 6 November, Portland Lighthouse was observed on a bearing of north-east, 5.3 miles off. The course being steered was SE and the ship was making 11 knots. At 1445 hours, the wind was E by N force 7, when the skipper calculated the ship's position as 22.4 miles SE by S ½ S from Reynisdrangar. Speed was reduced to half speed and course altered to E ¾ N. At 1830 hours, the second hand took over the watch and steered the same course until 2230 hours when the watch was again changed. The acting bosun was in charge of the new watch accompanied by a deckhand named Martin. Shortly before this change of watch, about 2100 hours, the radar failed. Another trawler, the *Kingston Diamond*, was slightly ahead of *Lord Stanhope* and also proceeding to the east coast grounds and was visible on the port bow. At 2300 hours, the skipper went below but, before leaving the bridge, instructed the acting bosun to keep *Kingston Diamond* on the port bow and to call him when Ingolfshofdi Light was seen or, if not seen, to call him at 0200 hours on 7 November. After the skipper left the bridge, a course of E ½ S was steered with the engines remaining at half speed. No shore lights were seen. At 0200 hours on 7 November, the acting bosun went down to call the skipper, and when the skipper did not appear, called him again about fifteen minutes later. At about 0220 hours, just as the skipper was about to come to the bridge, *Lord Stanhope* took the ground about four miles west of Ingolfshofdi Light.

A distress call was sent out and *Kingston Diamond* located the wreck and alerted the Icelandic Rescue Services. In the prevailing weather, there was nothing more he could do other than stand by. Efforts were made to launch two of the liferafts, but these were damaged by contact with the rocks. A third raft was carried away by the sea, and it was decided to await daylight before making another attempt to leave the ship.

At daylight, a party was seen ashore and a line was fired from the ship. By means of this line, the crew were hauled ashore in two lots in the remaining liferaft. On reaching the shore, the crew of *Lord Stanhope* were escorted to shelter and well looked after by the locals. This stranding provided yet another example of the promptitude and competence of the Icelandic rescue parties, and the care and hospitality the Icelandic people always show to shipwrecked mariners.

Margaret Wicks was built at Beverley by Cook, Welton & Gemmell in 1948 for Clifton SF Co., Fleetwood, and registered as FD265. She was a steel side trawler of 340 tons gross, 136.9 feet long, 26.1 feet beam and 13.3 feet in depth. In 1956, she was bought by Boston DSF Co. Ltd. *Margaret Wicks* left Fleetwood at 0430 hours on 7 December 1963 with a crew of fourteen hands under the command of Skipper Harry Chandler bound for the fishing grounds off the west coast of Scotland. It was twenty-three-year-old Skipper Chandler's first command. He had qualified for his skipper's certificate only two weeks previously and had been given command of the *Margaret Wicks* when her regular skipper, Ben Crendson, had to stay ashore when his wife took ill. Proceeding to Belfast to take on fuel oil, she arrived there at 1655 hours and left at 1930. At 0225 on 8 December, she took the ground on the south-east corner of Mull of Oa, Isle of Islay, about 2 miles from Port Ellen Light. Her crew were taken off by the Islay Rescue Association, the last man being pulled ashore by about 0730. There were no casualties. After several unsuccessful attempts at salvage on 15 December, she was refloated and towed to Port Ellen Bay. On 12 February 1964, she was towed to Ardrossan for examination. She was found to be too badly damaged to repair, and it was decided to scrap her.

Subsequently, the DTI held a preliminary inquiry into the loss, but it went no further. The following account of the stranding is taken from Skipper Chandler's statement to that inquiry.

When we sailed (from Belfast) we took a pilot. We dropped the pilot at the Harbour Entrance and with myself and Bosun Dalton in the wheelhouse, rounded Black Head so as to pass the Maidens 5 miles off. Radar and Decca Navigator were in operation. The Maidens was abeam about 2230 and I told the Bosun to steer NNW which would open Altacarry Head. I stayed in the wheelhouse with the Bosun until 2235 and before leaving I instructed the Bosun to tell the Mate to set a course to pass the east end of Altercarry Head at a distance of 3 miles off and then alter course to NW by N which would bring us 4 miles off Oversay, and to call me when we were 4 miles from being abeam of Oversay. I plotted this course on Admiralty Chart No.46 marked with Decca Lattice. This chart was pinned to the chartroom table and the Mate was aware of this. Radar and Decca Navigator were in operation and both were working perfectly. The weather at this time was SE Force 2, fine, good visibility and fairly smooth sea. Both Mate and Bosun had my standing orders to call me at any time if in doubt. I retired to my berth at 2235 and about 5 minutes later I heard the Mate enter the wheelhouse. At 0225 hours, 8 December, I was awakened by the vessel striking heavily and immediately went to the wheelhouse. I found the Mate and Deckhand Hayway there and the telegraph rung to Astern. I stopped the engines and asked the Mate where we were. He replied, 'I don't know Skipper.' Checking the ship's position by Radar and Decca, which were both working perfectly, I found we were on the SE coast of Mull of Oa. I could see Port Ellen Light on our starboard beam. I then told the Mate where we were and he replied, 'We can't be Skipper as I can see Oversay Light on our starboard beam and it is 4 miles distant which you told me to do.' Plotting Port Ellen Light I found it to be 2 miles off with the ship's head NW by N ½ N. The vessel then started to list and I ordered the crew to launch the two liferafts. The ship had listed to 40 degrees by now and I thought she was going to capsize. The crew had manned the liferafts but one of them had started to sink. The vessel steadied at 40 degrees and I could hear her banging on the bottom, so I ordered the crew back on board and sent out distress signals. Mate and Bosun had sounded the vessel and found no sign of leakage. Soundings on the port side midships gave two fathoms and there was 4 fathoms under the stern. After about two hours a small boat with two men in it approached our stern. The wind was now rising and was about SE Force 5 with heavy ground swell. As the boat closed with our starboard quarter our stern was rising and falling and a heavy sea slewed the small boat under our quarter and the stern smacked down on the boat smashing it up. We managed to get the two men aboard. I was in constant touch with Port Patrick Radio and about 0500 hours HMS *Hampshire* arrived in the vicinity. She laid about 1 ½ miles from us but owing to the heavy seas her boats were unable to approach us. Between 0630 and 0700, a life-saving crew came down the cliffs ahead of us and fired a rocket. Bosun Dalton secured the line and with Lyall to help a breeches buoy was rigged. By this means we were all pulled ashore by 0730. We were all taken to Port Ellen and given accommodation. I later made enquiries from the Mate and his watchmates regarding the stranding. I asked the Mate how far he passed off Rathlin and he replied, 'I don't know.' He did say we were 4 miles abeam of Mull of Kintyre at 0030 hours but after that he had no further information to offer. I also enquired from Deckhand Lyall. He told me the course of NNW had not been altered until we had passed the Mull of Kintyre and then the course was altered to NW by N Lyall also told me that the Mate was asleep in the wireless room at 0150 hours and he had to wake him to tell him that there was land on the radar right ahead. The Mate had then gone in the wheelhouse, looked out of the starboard window, and said 'We are alright. That is Oversay Light there.' He told the helmsman to maintain the course and did not bother to look at the radar.

From the above, it would seem that blame for the stranding and eventual loss must be placed on the shoulders of Mate Maclean. Incidentally, the mate disappeared and did not attend the preliminary inquiry.

*L*ord Cunningham was built by Cochrane & Sons at Selby in 1949 for the Lord Line, Hull, and worked from Hull until April 1963, when she moved to Grimsby and was registered as GY109. At the time of the stranding, she was owned by Northern Trawlers. She was a steel, single-screw steam side trawler of 635 tons gross, 177.9 feet in length, 30.7 feet in beam and 16 feet in depth. Her navigational aids comprised two direction finders, two echo-sounders, two radars, and Loran. All were in good working order except for one of the radars, which was put out of action by bad weather in the North Sea. She was supplied with adequate charts and publications for the voyage.

Lord Cunningham sailed from Grimsby on 16 December 1963 bound for the White Sea fishing grounds with a crew of twenty hands all told under the command of Skipper Frederick Hilton Hankin. During her passage across the North Sea, bad weather was encountered, which caused superficial damage and put one of the radar sets out of action. At 0300 hours on 20 December, she crossed Traen Gully and proceeded up West Fjord towards Lodigen, where it was intended to pick up a pilot for the passage through the northern fjords. The wind was northerly Force 4 with frequent snow showers with visibility about 2 miles between the showers. The vessel was making 12 knots and radar and echo-sounders were in use. The skipper intended to alter course for Lodigen when the south point of Baroy Island came abeam but never reached this position. Vadholm was passed to port 1 ½ miles off, and after that, snow showers became very thick, blotting everything out on the 3-mile range on the radar, although land could be seen on the 6-mile range. Shortly before stranding, the vessel crossed the 100-fathom line. Thereafter, the water shoaled rapidly and the skipper took no action until not more than one minute before stranding, when he rang the telegraph to stop. At 1600 hours, the vessel took the ground while still moving at full speed close to Rotvaer Light. Efforts to refloat the vessel by working the engines astern were unsuccessful, but eventually she was pulled off the rocks by two tugs. The tugs proceeded to tow her to Lodigen, where temporary repairs costing £5,597 were carried out.

The Court of Inquiry found that the stranding was due to negligent navigation by Skipper Hankin and suspended his certificate for twelve months. In 1967, *Lord Cunningham* went to Belgium where she was scrapped.

A chroite, H81, was built by Cook, Welton & Gemmell at Beverley in 1934 for Kingston ST Co. of Hull. She was sold to J. Marr and transferred to Fleetwood in August 1949. In 1959, she was bought by Cevic SF Company, Fleetwood. She was a steel, single-screw, coal-burning side trawler of 314 tons gross, 133.2 feet long, 24.5 feet in beam and 12.9 feet in depth. In February 1963, she was wrecked at Rosslare in severe weather while on passage to Faslane for breaking up by Shipbreaking Industries Ltd.

N orthern Spray was built in Germany in 1936 and was registered in London as LO140. She first worked from Fleetwood under the management of the Iago Steam Fishing Company, but was soon transferred to Grimsby. One of the famous Northern Boats, she was 655 tons gross, 188 feet long, 28 feet in beam and 15.5 feet deep. After performing Admiralty service on convoy escort duties during the war, she returned to fishing in February 1946 and registered as GY190 under the ownership of Northern Trawlers, Grimsby.

On 23 October 1963 at 2115 hours, while seeking shelter in Isafjord, she ran ashore at Ritur Huk, NW Iceland. The Hull trawler *James Barrie*, who was also entering the fjord for shelter, was about a mile away and, hearing the *Spray*'s call for assistance, moved in close to the wrecked vessel and managed to get a line to her. Eight of *Northern Spray*'s crew boarded a liferaft and were pulled across to the *James Barrie*.

Northern Spray. (W. Taylor)

Northern Spray. (W. Taylor)

Northern Spray aground. (Captain Helgi Hallvardsson)

Meantime, the trawler *Oratava* contacted the Icelandic coastguard vessel *Odinn*, who was sheltering in Adlavik Bay and advised him of the situation. *Odinn* immediately weighed anchor and was on the scene in less than an hour. Anchoring about three cables offshore from the wreck, he launched his motorboat. With the mate of the gunboat in charge, the boat proceeded to the *Northern Spray*. A gale was blowing, and with hurricane winds forecast, the wrecked seamen were advised to abandon the vessel. All twelve remaining crewmen boarded the motorboat and were taken to the *Odinn*. They spent the night aboard the *Odinn*, and next morning, the skipper, mate, third hand and chief engineer were taken back to the wreck. They found the fish room full of water. The *Odinn* made unsuccessful attempts to refloat the vessel, and with the wind increasing, she proceeded to Isafjord to land the survivors. Fortunately, there was no loss of life. On 27 October, the wreck was inspected by the underwriter's surveyors, who then decided it was not possible to salvage her, and she was declared a total loss. That fatal trip, *Northern Spray* was under the command of Skipper Peter S. Fenty. In December 1950, while under the command of Skipper E. Sverrir, the *Northern Spray* had grounded in almost exactly the same place.

*A*berdeen City was a diesel-driven single-screw trawler. She was built by Alexander Hall Ltd at Aberdeen in 1957 and was owned by Aberdeen Motor Trawlers Ltd and registered at Aberdeen as A113. She was 115.6 feet in length, 25.5 feet in beam with a gross tonnage of 263.51 tons. Her navigation equipment comprised a Decca type D.606 Radar, Decca Mark V 'Navigator' position fixing device, Decca Track Recorder, Marconi Guardian Direction Finder, Marconi radio telephony installation and two Marconi Fishgraph echo-sounders. All this equipment was in working order except the radar, which broke down at 0050 hours on 16 September. Her life-saving appliances complied with the regulations and had been properly maintained and surveyed. When she left Aberdeen on her final voyage, she was seaworthy in every respect.

Aberdeen City left Aberdeen at 1020 hours on 15 September 1963 bound for the Faroe fishing grounds with a crew of thirteen men all told under the command of

Aberdeen City. (G. Coull Collection)

Skipper William Henderson. It had been intended to proceed there direct up the east side of the Orkneys, but the weather deteriorated, so the skipper decided to reduce speed and come into the shelter of the land off Sanda so that he could round Dennis Ness between 0400 and 0500 hours on the 16th on a flood-tide when, with the wind from the west, the conditions would be more favourable. Shortly after midnight on the 16th, the skipper ordered the mate and the deckhand on watch to go forward to secure gear and make a small repair to the trawl in view of heavy weather expected rounding Dennis Ness, leaving the skipper alone in the wheelhouse. At about 0105, Start Point bore NNW about 1.7 miles off with the vessel stopped in the water. Sometime after midnight, the radar had broken down and the light was on in the wheelhouse while the skipper tried to get it going. At this time, he noticed a sounding of 14 fathoms on the echo-sounder and realised the ship was drifting into danger. At 0122, he put the engine slow ahead and the helm hard a-starboard. At about 0125, the vessel took the ground with Start Point bearing SW by W. There was a strong westerly wind, a confused sea and good visibility. Immediately, the skipper called Wick Radio and requested the services of a lifeboat. Stronsay lifeboat arrived at 0300 hours and took off nine of the crew. She returned at about 0800 hours, and by this time, the stranded vessel had a serious list of about sixty degrees to port. The starboard fuel tank had burst and there was water in the engine room and fish room. It was then decided to abandon her, and the lifeboat then took off the skipper, mate and the other two crew members. The vessel was a total loss, and it seems that no attempt was made to pump her out and try to save her.

At the Court of Inquiry into the casualty, it was found that the cause was the failure of the skipper to keep a lookout while he was preoccupied by investigating the breakdown and repair of the radar instead of attending to the safety of the ship. The court suspended his certificate of competency for six months and ordered him to pay £200 towards the cost of the inquiry.

1964

A good year. Four ships were lost and three men died.

Aberdeen	*Rangor* A288	200 tons	17 January 1964
	Ben Barvas A111	235 tons	3 January 1964
Fleetwood	*Irvana* FD152	317 tons	23 March 1964
Hull	*Arctic Adventurer* H381	565 tons	8 December 1964

The Aberdeen motor trawler *Rangor*, Skipper John Chisholm, was lost in the south approach to Lerwick Harbour on 17 January 1964. Skipper Bill Cowie had taken command of her in September 1959 and had worked her with some success until October 1963, when the vessel was laid up for a major refit. Skipper Cowie then took command of the motor trawler *Coastal Empress* and his young mate, twenty-five-year-old John Chisholm, decided to go to school to study for his skipper's certificate. Just before the New Year, he passed his exams and obtained his skipper's ticket, he got married on New Year's Day, and on 13 January 1964, he took command of the *Rangor*, her long refit completed. He took his first command away from Aberdeen with a crew of thirteen hands all told on 14 January for a fishing trip off the Shetlands. Then things started to go wrong. Soon after leaving port, the radar went on the bum, and on arrival at the fishing grounds, a fault developed on the main engine before fishing started. He had no other option than to proceed to Lerwick for repairs. Repairs to the engine were completed, but the radar remained inoperative because no spares were available. *Rangor* sailed from Lerwick early on 17 January, but she didn't get very far. Two miles south of Lerwick, on the west side of the approach channel, is the Ness of Sound. Foul ground on which lay several skerries and above water rocks extend nearly a cable south-east from the southern extremity of Ness of Sound. Probably due to a combination of lack of radar, poor visibility and inexperience, Skipper Chisholm allowed *Rangor* to get too far to the westward, and she ran aground on these rocks about 150 yards off the Ness. In response to her distress call, Lerwick Lifeboat was quickly on the scene, but could not get close enough to render any assistance on account of the surrounding rocks. The Lerwick Life-saving Crew assembled on shore, and a line was fired to the stranded trawler. A breeches buoy was rigged and all thirteen crew members were got ashore. Just after the rescue, smoke and flames began to pour from the after end of the vessel, the fire believed to have been started by a short circuit in the electrical equipment. The fire brigade were helpless, and Skipper Chisholm could only watch from the rocky shore as his ship turned into a blazing hulk. Gradually, she heeled over and settled on the rocks, her stern high out of the water and her bows below the waves. She was a total loss. The Shipwrecked Mariners Society were there, as always, to help the survivors with new clothes and necessities until they could be transported back to Aberdeen.

Rangor. (G. Coull)

Ben Barvas. (G. Coull)

Every trawler skipper will always remember his first command. John Chisholm will probably remember his for all the wrong reasons.

Rangor was owned by Rangor Fishing Company, Aberdeen, and registered as A288. Built by Mitchel at Peterhead in 1951, she was a motor trawler of 200 tons gross, 126.75 long, and 25.3 feet beam.

The *Ben Barvas* was a modern motor trawler built in 1957 by John Lewis at Aberdeen and was owned by Richard Irvin & Sons, North Shields. She was 125 feet long and had a gross tonnage of 235 tons. Her top speed was about 9.5 knots. She had two liquid magnetic compasses – one overhead in the wheelhouse used for steering, the other in the skipper's cabin. Both were adjusted on 13 November 1963. Her life-saving appliances complied with the regulations, and they had been properly surveyed and maintained. Her communications and navigational equipment comprised a radio telephone, a direction finder, radar, two echo-sounders, Decca Navigator and Decca Track Plotter. All this equipment was in satisfactory working order until the time of her stranding. When she sailed on her final voyage, she was seaworthy in every respect.

Ben Barvas left Aberdeen at 1010 hours on 3 January 1964 bound for the Icelandic fishing grounds with a crew of fourteen men all told under the command of Skipper Joseph Berry. At 1445 hours, she was abeam of Rattray Head, 3 miles off, and the skipper set a course of NNW. At 1830 hours, Skipper Berry took over the watch and had three deckhands on watch with him, Queen, Edgar and Paterson. The weather was fine and clear with little or no wind. Skipper Berry had never been to Iceland as skipper before and, from coming on watch at 1830 hours, was in the wireless room talking to other skippers to obtain information as to the fishing there. He came into the wheelhouse about 2000 hours and, thinking the vessel was setting to the eastward, altered course from NNW to NW, then returned to the wireless room to continue his conversations. About 2130 hours, Deckhand Edgar reported to the Skipper, who was still in the wireless room, that the vessel was coming close to a light that was close on the starboard bow. The skipper came to the wheelhouse and, on seeing the light, altered course to WNW. When he first saw the light, it was estimated to be two miles away, and when the course was altered, it was about one mile off. Shortly after altering course, at 2140 hours, the vessel took the ground. On checking the Decca Navigator, it was found that she had stranded on the Little Skerries about a mile south of the Skerries Light. At first, she remained upright, but with the rising tide, she remained fast, started to list and began to make water. Pumps were started but could not cope. A Mayday call was sent out which was answered by Wick Radio, and a call was also made to the Longhope Lifeboat. A liferaft was launched, but when five crew members had boarded it, the line holding it to the vessel slipped and it drifted away. The second raft was being made ready when water breaking over the vessel washed it away and it was lost. The lifeboat arrived on the scene about an hour after the stranding but was unable to get alongside of the stranded vessel. Standing about 40 yards off, she fired two lines, which the crew of *Ben Barvas* were able to secure. A breeches buoy was rigged, and the remaining crew members were pulled across to the lifeboat. A trawler picked up the five men in the liferaft; thus all the crew were saved, but *Ben Barvas* was a total loss. The wreck can still be seen at low tides.

At the subsequent Court of Inquiry, it was found that the loss was caused by the skipper's failure to pay attention to the navigation of his vessel, and his certificate was suspended for twelve months, and he was ordered him to pay £200 towards the cost of the inquiry.

The *Irvana* was a single-screw steel motor trawler built in 1953 by Cook, Welton & Gemmell at Beverley for J. Marr and registered as FD152. Her original length when built was 128.2 feet, but in 1960, she was lengthened at Hull. At the time of

Irvana. (Fishing Heritage Centre)

the stranding, her registered dimensions were length 135.7 feet, 26.6 feet beam and 12.2 feet depth, with a gross tonnage of 317 tons. *Irvana* was equipped with two compasses, both adjusted on 1 March 1964 and in satisfactory working order at the time she stranded. Her other navigational gear included a Decca 206 Radar, Redifon Loran, two Marconi echo-sounders, Marconi Direction Finder, Walker Log, and hand leads and lines. All this equipment was in efficient working condition up to the time of her grounding. She had adequate charts on board for her intended voyage.

Irvana left Fleetwood at 0930 hours on 23 March 1964 with a crew of seventeen hands all told under the command of Skipper Charles Louis Scott for an intended voyage to the fishing grounds on the west side of Iceland. When she left, she was seaworthy in every respect. Crossing the Irish Sea and proceeding through North Channel, it was reasonably fine with a southerly Force 4 wind, although visibility may have been reduced by continuous rain or drizzle for most of the time. According to Skipper Scott, because he expected bad weather ahead, he decided to proceed into Cushendun Bay, County Antrim, in order to anchor while the crew fixed the gear alongside in comfort. He had been into the bay on four previous occasions to anchor but had never made the approach in darkness before. He attempted to find a good anchorage in an unlighted bay in darkness using only his radar to assist him. No use was made of either the echo-sounder or the hand lead, and when the anchor was dropped, he had no idea how much water was under the vessel. After dropping the anchor, the skipper went to his berth without taking any steps to check whether the anchor was holding. Shortly after the anchor was let go, the vessel was found to be striking the rocks with her after part on the port side. When an attempt was made to put the engines ahead, the propeller struck rock repeatedly until the engine stopped. The crew were ordered to launch the liferafts and all got ashore. There were no casualties.

At the subsequent inquiry, it was revealed that when the crew left the vessel in the liferafts, she was not making any water, and no attempt was made to secure any openings where there could be an ingress of water. A few hours later, she was found to be full of water in all her compartments, and a fish room hatch was found to be in a condition that large quantities of water could enter the vessel through it. The skipper stated that he failed to take any steps to preserve the vessel because he was of the opinion that the ship was about to break up in weather he believed to be deteriorating. In fact, *Irvana* remained grounded until 25 April 1964, when she was refloated and towed to Port Glasgow. After examination on the slipway, she was declared a total loss and sold for scrap.

The Court of Inquiry found that the casualty was caused by the wrongful act or default of Skipper Scott and suspended his certificate for two years. He was also ordered to pay £250 towards the cost of the investigation.

The *Arctic Adventurer* was a steel, single-screw side trawler of 565 tons gross built in 1936 for Thomas Hamlin & Co. of Hull by Cook, Welton & Gemmell at Beverley as the *St Loman*. After service throughout the war on convoy escort duties, she was bought by Boyd Line, Hull, in December 1951 and re-registered as *Arctic Adventurer* H381. She was 172.2 feet long and 29.1 feet in beam.

She sailed from Hull at 0830 hours on 7 December 1964 for a voyage to the Barents Sea fishing grounds. She proceeded down the Humber, rounded Spurn Light Vessel at 1130 hours, and set a NNE course. Watches were set at 12.30 p.m., the second engineer and Fireman Rayworth taking the first engine-room watch. Throughout the watch, there was trouble with the bilges. The watch was changed at 18.30, but the second engineer remained down the engine room to assist the chief engineer with the bilge problem. At about 12.20 a.m. on 8 December, the vessel took a sea and lurched to port. At 12.50 a.m., a noise like 'blowing off' was heard, followed by a rumbling noise, and all the lights going out. The chief engineer was found calling for help from the starboard scuppers and was assisted to the bridge. The second engineer was found moving about in the alleyway leading to the engine room and also assisted to the bridge. A party consisting of skipper, mate, third hand and fireman went down to the engine room to investigate and found Fireman Minns lying in the stokehold alleyway. He was still conscious and was taken to the galley but died shortly afterwards. Fireman Rayworth remained down the engine room to shut off all the fuel oil valves and safety cocks on the furnace fronts. The vessel was battened down and anchored while awaiting assistance. Both engineers were badly scalded and both men died between 7 and 7.30 a.m. on 8 December 1964. The vessel was taken in tow and arrived in Hull at 0730 hours, 10 December 1964.

An official inquiry was held in Hull and the findings published on 13 May 1965. It was agreed that the boiler had exploded in a violent manner caused by overheating due to shortage of water. The boiler was twenty-seven years old, being built by Charles D. Holmes & Co. in 1937. It had originally been installed in the trawler *St Elstan*. In May 1949, it was removed from that vessel and, after retubing, was installed in the *St Loman*. In 1953, the boiler was converted to oil firing and after that date the following important repairs were carried out:

August 1954: boiler was retubed.
February 1959: lower portion of the front end plate removed to eliminate grooving.
April 1960: boiler retubed.
February 1963: all furnaces renewed.

Because the three men in the engine room died from their injuries, it was not possible to establish the precise sequence of events that culminated in the explosion. There is reason to believe that prior to the explosion the boiler was thought to be too full of water and blowing down was resorted to. An empty water gauge glass was probably read as a full one. In view of the extent of the damage and the age of the vessel, her owners decided to scrap the ship, and she never went fishing again.

1965

Three ships and twenty-three men lost.

Hull	*Kingston Turquoise* H50	811 tons	26 January 1965
Aberdeen	*Blue Crusader* A251	274 tons	14 January 1965
Lowestoft	*Boston Pionair* LT432	166 tons	14 February 1965

The *Kingston Turquoise* was built in 1955 by Cook, Welton & Gemmell at Beverley for Kingston Steam Trawling Company, Hull. She was a steel, single-screw steam trawler of 810.7 gross tons, was 189.4 feet long and 32.1 feet in beam. She was classed at Lloyd's for hull and machinery +100 A1 and +LMC respectively, and she retained her class up to the time she was lost. Her hull was divided by nine watertight bulkheads, and she was propelled by a triple-expansion direct-acting steam engine of 1,100 bhp, which gave her a speed of 14 knots. She was fitted with a 9-inch overhead magnetic compass, a 9-inch magnetic pole compass, and carried one spare compass. The overhead and pole compasses were adjusted on 13 August 1964, and there was no deviation on any of the Southerly courses steered before the stranding. Her steering gear comprised a Donkin steam-driven hydraulic steering engine with an emergency electric-driven hydraulic pump, emergency friction hand gear, and emergency control in the steering flat. *Kingston Turquoise* was fitted with navigation aids of a high standard comprising Decca D808 Radar, Loran APN9 manufactured by Redifon, Kelvin-Hughes Echo-Sounder MS 24J, Kelvin Hughes Echo-sounder MS 29F, Mullard Discovery Direction Finder, Electric log, leads and lead lines. Her life-saving appliances met all mandatory requirements and consisted of two 26-foot wood lifeboats under Welin Maclachlan Crescent davits, twenty-four Victory lifejackets, four circular cork lifebuoys, two Elliott ten-man inflatable liferafts, one Schermuly Supreme line-throwing apparatus, twelve Schermuly parachute distress flares.

The *Kingston Turquoise* sailed from Hull for the Icelandic fishing grounds on 6 January 1965, with a crew of twenty men all told, under the command of Skipper Colin Cross. At the time of sailing, she was in a seaworthy condition in every respect, with all the above-listed equipment in efficient working order, except for the radar. The radar had a maximum range of 48 miles, but was not effective beyond the 24-mile range. The radar had been serviced while the ship was in dock and was supposed to be in full working order. The above defect was only discovered after the ship sailed, and the skipper was aware of the defect and of the limitation of the effective use of the radar resulting from it. She completed fishing shortly before noon on 25 January having spent the last two days fishing on the Rising Grounds in depths of around 150 fathoms. When she started for home, the weather was fine with a light north-east breeze, slight sea with moderate swell and good visibility. She had about 1,500 kits of fish on board and her draft was 12 feet 6 inches forward and 17 feet aft. The skipper

Kingston Turquoise. (P. Whiting)

worked out a dead-reckoning position and set a course of SSE calculating he would reach the western entrance to the Pentland Firth at about 1800 hours. At 1300 hours, a D/F bearing was taken of Sule Skerry indicating a bearing of SSW, and using this bearing and the run from the first DR position, a new position was marked on the chart. From this position, the skipper calculated that a course of S ½ E would take him 4 miles west of Rora Head on Hoy Island and set this course at 1305 hours. At 1320 hours, the skipper left the bridge to lie down, leaving the third hand in charge of the watch with orders to keep the course of S ½ E, and to call him at 1530 hours, or when land was sighted, whichever came first. On leaving the bridge, the skipper switched the sounder off but the radar remained on. At 1430, the second hand took over the bridge watch. He was given the course to steer, and the skipper's orders as regards being called. He took no steps to check the vessel's position. Just before 1530 hours, the second hand sighted land ahead and on the port bow and called the skipper. No land was showing on the radar, which was set to its maximum effective range – 24 miles. The skipper and second hand discussed what the land was and decided (wrongly) that the land ahead was Dunnet Head and the land on the port bow was Old Man of Hoy. At about 1635, the second hand observed a light flashing 3-4 points on the port bow with an interval he timed to be 17 seconds and reported this sighting to the skipper. The skipper then went into the day room to try to identify this light but failed to do so. In fact, this light must have been Brough Head. Very soon afterwards, about 1640 hours, the vessel struck the bottom. One of the duty engineers reported that the engine room was filling rapidly, and at the same time, the ship listed heavily to starboard. Just prior to the vessel hitting the bottom, the wireless operator came on to the bridge and looked at the radar. It was showing echoes from the land. Almost immediately after touching bottom, he (the WO) returned to the wireless room and transmitted a distress call to Wick, giving a position as 14-16 miles NNW of Hoy Head and stating that the ship was sinking. He did this on his own initiative without any orders from the skipper, basing his position on the ship's head and his view of the land on the radar. Two inflatable rafts were launched on the starboard side as the ship sank, and nineteen members of the crew were able to board them. One crew member, Denton, jumped overboard from the high side, and although the ship's engines were stopped, she still had some way on. As a result, Denton was separated from the rafts, and although the men on the rafts saw him and heard his calls, they were unable to get to him, and he was lost, presumably drowned. The *Kingston Turquoise* went down stern first within five minutes of striking the bottom. As result of the Mayday signal to Wick Radio, the Stromness Lifeboat was launched and, at 2000 hours, found the liferafts. The nineteen crew members were transferred to the lifeboat and taken safely to Stromness. The lifeboat made a further search for Denton without success.

To conclude, it is obvious that the *Kingston Turquoise* struck the North Shoal. This is a small, almost perpendicular rock, with a depth of 7 feet over it. It is clearly marked on Admiralty Chart No. 1954, which was on board the ship. It is also marked on Imray fishing chart, which was being used, although, on this chart, the depth over it is not given. A trawler fishing at Iceland does not usually shoot the gear on the Rising Ground, and it is probable that the position calculated at 1300 hours was inaccurate, and he was much further to the eastward than the position calculated. In the event, at the Court of Inquiry into the cause of the casualty, the court found that Skipper Cross had not taken proper care to establish his position. Between 1515 and 1615 hours, he should have taken the following precautions:

1. Observed and identified Brough Head and taken bearings and distances from it.
2. Taken D/F bearings of Sule Skerry and North Ronaldsay and laid these bearings off on Admiralty Chart No. 1954.
3. Took successive D/F bearings of Sule Skerry, thus obtaining a running fix.

Had the ship's position been fixed and plotted by any of the above methods, it would have been apparent that the ship was further to the eastward than she should have been and was in danger of passing over North Shoal, or close to it. Running the echo-sounder would have given an additional check. The court suspended Skipper Cross's Certificate for six months.

Author's Note: Despite Colin's failure to follow basic navigation principles, I think he was unlucky. North Shoal covers a very small area, and had *Turquoise* been a dozen yards either side of her actual track, she would probably have missed the pinnacle that did the damage, and she would have sailed on oblivious of its existence.

The *Blue Crusader* of Aberdeen was another trawler that vanished without trace. She was a modern motor trawler built by John Lewis & Sons at Aberdeen in 1958 and owned by Crusader Fishing Company, Aberdeen. A vessel of 274 tons gross, she was 121 feet in length, 25.65 feet in beam and 11.4 feet in depth. She was equipped with radio telephone, direction finder, echo-sounder, Decca Navigator and radar. Her life-saving equipment complied with the regulations and was well maintained. When she sailed on her last voyage, she was seaworthy in every respect.

Blue Crusader sailed from Aberdeen at 0930 hours on 13 January 1965 with a crew of thirteen hands all told under the command of Skipper Fred Baker. At the time of sailing, it was the skipper's intention to fish in the North Sea, but he later changed his mind and decided to proceed to the Faroese fishing grounds. At 2000 hours that evening, Skipper Baker spoke on the radio to the skipper of the *Scottish King* and asked if the *Scottish King* was going to Faroe, and on being told she was, he said he thought he would go there too. Leaving Aberdeen, the wind was SE and backing all

Blue Crusader. (G. Coull)

the time and, at 2200 hours, was blowing from the NE with a falling glass that should not have fallen with a NE wind. During the conversation with the *Scottish King*, it was arranged that they would have another chat after the 0200 hours weather forecast. At 1930 hours, the *Blue Crusader* was about 70 miles north of Rattray Head and *Scottish King* was about three hours behind her. Taking the time *Crusader* left port and her position at 1930 hours, she should have been off North Ronaldsay about midnight. The skipper of *Scottish King* got the 0200 weather report and then called *Blue Crusader* several times but received no reply. At this time, he was sheltering off Stronay, because, by 0130 hours, the wind had backed to north and was blowing Force 8 to 9. He proceeded to Start Point, thinking he might see *Blue Crusader*, but she was not there. He was able to get underway at 1800 hours on 14 January and proceeded to the Faroe grounds and, on arrival, enquired of other vessels there if they had seen or heard *Blue Crusader*. None of them had. By the evening of 16 January, there was still no contact between the *Blue Crusader* and other vessels fishing at Faroe, and although this caused no anxiety, it was strange because Skipper Baker spoke a good deal on the radio. The skipper of *Scottish King* assumed he was maybe fishing on the west side of the Shetlands, catching a lot of fish and keeping quiet about it. Between 2000 and 2030 hours, *Blue Crusader* also spoke to the skipper of *Brancondene*, another Aberdeen trawler, and said he had intended to go to Otter Bank but, in view of the weather, intended to go to Faroe, and that he would clear North Ronaldsay about midnight. This conversation was the last that was seen or heard of *Blue Crusader*. At the time of this conversation, *Brancondene* was fishing, but the weather deteriorated and she pulled the gear aboard and dodged under Noss Head for shelter and remained there until Tuesday evening, 15 January. Not until 27 January was an air search for the trawler begun, but no trace of her was found. On the night of 13/14 January, the weather where *Blue Crusader* was thought to be was very severe, and it is believed that she was overwhelmed by a heavy sea. On 5 and 6 February, a lifebuoy, two hatch covers and other bits of wreckage identified as probably coming from *Blue Crusader* were found strewn along the coast between Auskerry and Start Point. The lifebuoy

Boston Pionair. (J. W. ex Ford Jenkins)

was tested at Aberdeen, and it was found to have been submerged for a long time and had probably broken adrift from the vessel.

The *Boston Pionair* was built at Lowestoft by Richards (Shipbuilders) Ltd in 1956 and was owned by Pegasus Trawling Company, Hull, a subsidiary of the Boston group. First registered at Fleetwood as FD96, she was later transferred to Lowestoft and re-registered as LT432. She was a single-screw steel motor trawler of riveted construction with a gross tonnage of 165.85. Her registered dimensions were 103 x 22.1 x 10 feet. Her life-saving equipment included a 17-foot wood lifeboat for sixteen persons, two inflatable twelve-man liferafts, four circular lifebuoys, twelve lifejackets, a line-throwing apparatus and distress rockets and flares. It had all been inspected in January 1963 and was in order. Her navigation aids were adequate and in good order, and she was classed +100 A1 (Trawler) at Lloyd's. When she sailed on her final voyage, she was seaworthy in every respect.

Boston Pionair sailed from Lowestoft on a fishing trip on 6 February 1965 under the command of Skipper Brian Moyse and manned by a crew of nine hands all told. She commenced fishing the next day in the Horn Reef area in the company of another two trawlers, the *Boston Widgeon* and the *Roy Stevens*. The three vessels fished in that area until 12 February, by which time the *Pionair* had about 100 kits of fish on board. On the evening of 12 February, the wind was freshening and a weather forecast of north-westerly winds up to Force 10 was received and the three skippers decided to move to the westward to be nearer the land. About 1930 hours, *Boston Pionair* was seen to haul her gear and steam off on a course of about WSW. About an hour later, she was out of sight of the other two trawlers and was never seen again. The weather continued to deteriorate during the night of the 12th, and on the 13th, the skipper of *Boston Widgeon* estimated it was blowing a good Force 10, and on the morning of the 14th, the weather was very bad with very high seas and a north-west wind Force 9 or 10. About 0630 hours, the skippers of the *Widgeon* and the *Pionair* had a chat on the radio, and Skipper Moyse said he had been laying for an hour and a half, but by the look of the weather, he would have to start dodging again soon. After replying, and talking about fishing, the skipper of the *Widgeon* said 'Over' and expected a reply from Skipper Moyse, but got none. That conversation was the last that was ever heard from *Boston Pionair*.

The skipper of *Boston Widgeon* thought that maybe the *Pionair*'s aerial had come down, and later that day, both he and the *Roy Stevens* tried without success to contact the *Pionair*. On 15 February, Humber Radio sent out a message requesting all Boston trawlers to try to make contact with *Boston Pionair* but no contact was made. At first light on the 16th, a full-scale search was mounted. Two naval vessels, a Shackleton aircraft and seventy trawlers took part in the search, which was directed by Skipper Crisp of the *Boston Victor*. As a result of the search, articles belonging to *Boston Pionair* were picked up about 130 miles WSW of the position she was last seen.

A Court of Inquiry was held to investigate the cause of the loss. From the evidence, it was found impossible to state with certainty when and where the loss occurred. The probability is that the vessel was overcome by heavy seas about the western edge of Dogger Bank at some time on 14 February 1965.

1966

Only two casualties this year. Twelve men perished.

Hull	*St Finbarr* H308	1,139 tons	27 December 1966
Fleetwood	*Boston Wellvale* FD209	419 tons	21 December 1966

The *St Finbarr* was a modern, single-screw, refrigerated stern trawler. She was built in 1964 by Ferguson Brothers Ltd, Port Glasgow, and owned by Thomas Hamling Ltd, Hull. She was built to Lloyd's survey and classed +100 A1 Stern Trawler. Her gross tonnage was 1,139.34 tons, and she was 197 feet long, 36.05 feet beam, and 19.5 feet deep. Her main propelling machinery consisted of a Mirrlees National, type KLSSM8 eight-cylinder direct-injection diesel engine fitted with turbo charger, and developing 1,592 bhp at 300 revs per minute. A four-bladed controllable-pitch propeller was fitted and controlled from the bridge through a hydraulic system. A Laurence Scott generator was coupled into the main shafting system and was capable of developing 320 kW output at 220 volts direct current at 240 to 300 revs per minute. Air-conditioning equipment comprised one 0.1-hp galley supply plant with a control switch at the upper deck entrance and 4.5-hp air-conditioning unit. Radio communications and navigation equipment were all the most modern types and were all fully operational at the time she sailed. Life-saving equipment and fire-fighting appliances conformed with all mandatory requirements.

St Finbarr sailed from Hull on 16 November 1966 bound for the western North Atlantic fishing grounds with a crew of twenty-five men under the command of Skipper Tom Sawyers. When she sailed, she was seaworthy in every respect, with all equipment working efficiently.

On the night of 24/25 December *St Finbarr* was in position 55 degrees 15 minutes north, 55 degrees 45 minutes west, about 100 miles off the coast of Labrador. The weather prevented her fishing – a north-easterly gale, confused sea and heavy swell, and it was freezing hard. At about 0100 hours on 25 December, the men had finished repairing the damaged trawl and, apart from those on watch on the bridge and in the engine room, were sent below to rest. Later, as it was Christmas day and fishing was impossible, the skipper ordered Christmas drinks to be issued to the crew. The Court of Inquiry into her loss was satisfied that the amounts supplied were reasonable.

At about 0720 GMT, the assistant cook, Whitaker, went to the greasers' cabin to call greaser Smith for breakfast and watch-keeping duties, and repeated the call at 0730. On the second call, Smith jumped out of the upper bunk and followed Whitaker out, leaving the door open. On both occasions, Whitaker saw no signs of smoke and Smith wasn't smoking. At this time, spare hand Tognola was sleeping in his bunk in a cabin at the after end of the alleyway in which the greasers' cabin was situated. He was awakened by having difficulty breathing and leaped out of his bunk

St Finbarr. (P. Whiting)

into the alleyway, first calling spare hand Evans, who shared the cabin with him. The alleyway was filling with smoke, and they noticed flames coming out of the greasers' cabin from the top of the door parallel with the deckhead. They opened the door in the engine room casing and escaped up the engine room ladder, leaving the door open. About 0735, Third Engineer Grinlaw, who had been on watch since 0730, saw smoke coming into the engine room through the port-side casing door through which Tognola and Evans had escaped. He was unable to investigate the source of the fire because, by now, fierce flames were shooting from the alleyway through the door. He then attempted to inform the bridge by telephone. About this time, Whitaker reported to the skipper that there was smoke in the upper deck accommodation. The skipper attempted to go down to the upper deck accommodation but was driven back by smoke. He then ordered Evans, who had arrived on the bridge, to sound the fire alarm, which was done immediately. All accessible fuel tank valves were closed, the main engines stopped, and attempts were made to control the blaze using the deck water service, but by now the fire was out of control.

At 0740, the skipper sent out a Mayday call on the VHF radio, which was answered by the MFV *Orsino*, who was about five miles away. At about 0742, as another distress call was being sent, a sudden blast of hot air from the accommodation blew out the doors and windows of the wheelhouse. The forced ventilation was in operation at this time and was a contributory factor in the fire spreading so rapidly. The fire quickly spread to the bridge, and the skipper gave orders to prepare the lifeboat and liferafts to abandon ship. It was found impossible to handle the lifeboat. Electric sparks were seen on the davit and men received shocks. The two liferafts on the starboard side were launched, the rafts on the port side having already been damaged by fire, but one of them became detached and was lost. By this time, *Orsino* had moved close in, and her skipper shouted to the crew of *St Finbarr* to get in the liferaft and he would pick them up. About 0930, twelve men boarded the liferaft, which was then cast off and drifted over to *Orsino*. The weather was severe, and two of the men were lost boarding *Orsino*. A further ten men were trapped in the lower deck accommodation and perished, making a total of twelve men lost from the crew of twenty-five.

The skipper, mate and chief engineer stayed on board *St Finbarr* and sheltered in the net store in an exhausted condition. About 1030, the MFV *Sir Fred Parkes* fired a line across with a raft attached containing warm clothing, but the men were too fatigued to pull this raft alongside. Later, the mate of *Orsino* and her boat's crew boarded *St Finbarr* and revived and clothed the three men on board her. At about 1300, the generator stopped and the chief engineer, who was in a worse condition than the other two men, was sent across to *Orsino*. It was now possible to launch *St Finbarr*'s boat, and at 1400, the skipper decided to abandon her. She was still burning fiercely, and her fuel oil service tanks were on fire. He and the mate were transferred to *Orsino* using the *Finbarr*'s boat. Shortly after 1600, a boarding party established a tow-line, and at about 1930, *Orsino* began to tow the *Finbarr* stern first towards St Johns, Newfoundland. At about 0800 on 26 December, the tow-line parted, and towing was resumed at 1800. About 1925 on 27 December, *St Finbarr* finally sank in position 51 degrees 48 minutes north, 55 degrees 10 minutes west after having been towed about 203 miles.

After considering a load of technical evidence, the Court of Inquiry into the loss concluded that the fire had been caused by shorts in the electrical wiring. The heat generated had caused the plastic covering on the cable in the deckhead to melt, and an explosive mixture of gas formed in the space above the deckhead in the greasers' cabin. This gas was exploded by a spark and the resultant flash fire was spread rapidly by the operation of the ventilating system. It was revealed that although fire drills were logged as having been carried out, in fact, no drills had actually been carried out.

Boston Wellvale aground. (Boston's files ex P. Brady)

*B*oston *Wellvale* was a single-screw motor trawler built for Boston DSF Company at Beverley in December 1961. She was registered at Fleetwood as FD209 and worked the middle water grounds from that port under the command of Skipper Jack Chard. Later, she was transferred to Grimsby from where she worked in Icelandic waters. She was 139 feet 8 inches in length and 28 feet 4 inches in beam, and classed 100 A1 at Lloyd's.

On 21 December 1966, while under the command of Skipper Dave Venney, with her radar inoperative, she ran aground on Cape Arnarnes in a gale and snowstorm. At the time, she was proceeding to Isafjord to land a sick man and get the radar repaired. Water flooding into the engine room put the generators out of action, plunging the vessel into darkness. Oil lamps were rigged and attempts were made to inflate the liferafts, but heavy seas breaking over the vessel washed the rafts away. A shore party, alerted by the vessel's distress signals, had to use snow ploughs to reach a position from where they could fire a rocket line to the stranded vessel. A breeches buoy was rigged, and all seventeen crew members were got safely ashore. The insurance company decided that the ship was a constructive total loss. An Icelandic businessman, Eudmundur Marselliusson, bought the wreck for £150. In the summer of 1967, with the assistance of the Icelandic gunboat *Albert* she was refloated and towed to Hafnarfjord. Repaired, she was renamed RAN GK42 under Icelandic ownership, and resumed fishing.

1967

Only one ship lost this year.

| Aberdeen | *Juniper* A540 | 235 tons | 19 February 1967 |

The *Juniper* was a steel, single-screw motor side trawler built at Gateshead on Tyne by T. Mitchison Ltd in 1961 and owned by the Ashley Fishing Company, Aberdeen. She was 115 feet long, 25 feet in beam and 235 gross tons. She had one standard reflector-type compass and one overhead compass fitted in a binnacle sited aft side the standard compass. A spare compass to fit the overhead unit was carried. These compasses were in satisfactory working order and were adjusted on 8 November 1966. Her navigational aids included Decca Navigator, Decca Plotter, radar, Loran, two echo-sounders, direction finder, a Walker patent log and three hand lead lines. All were in working order when she first sailed, but the radar and the Decca Navigator both went out of order while the vessel was on the fishing grounds.

Juniper left Aberdeen on Sunday 12 February 1967 for a voyage to Shetland waters with a crew of twelve hands all told under the command of Skipper Terence Taylor. She was seaworthy in all respects and carried adequate charts for the voyage, and her life-saving appliances were in good order. She made her last haul early morning Sunday 19 February in a position about 11 miles NNE from Esha Ness and started off for home at 0230 hours. The wind was SE Force 4, a choppy sea and poor visibility with drizzling rain. Arriving a mile off Esha Ness at 0330 hours, Skipper Taylor was faced with a dilemma. The wind was freshening, he had a lot of fish on deck, and he had a market to catch. He could lay while the men cleared the fish off the deck, but this would almost certainly mean that he would arrive at Aberdeen too late for Monday's market. He could pass the Ve Skerries to the westward, but this would have placed the vessel in more open waters and made clearing the decks more difficult, if not impossible, and would have added a few more miles to the voyage. Or he could pass through the channel with Ve Skerries to starboard and Papa Stour on the port hand. This route involved passing through a narrow, unlit channel about 2 ½ miles wide, but would keep the vessel in more sheltered water and allow the deck to be nearly cleared before coming into open waters. The skipper chose the latter option and proceeded at full speed. The wind had increased to Force 7 by this time and visibility was very poor with heavy rain, with visibility from the wheelhouse further reduced by the fact that the deck lights had to be left on while the men were working on the deck. In the event, the vessel took the ground while doing full speed on Fogla Skerry at the north-west end of Papa Stour. The vessel began to make a lot of water and a Mayday call was sent out. The Aith Lifeboat arrived and, with considerable difficulty, managed to get alongside the wreck and take off all the crew. In doing so, she sustained considerable damage.

Juniper. (G. Coull)

At the Court of Inquiry, it was found that the stranding was caused entirely by the fault of the skipper. It was considered he may have allowed commercial considerations to override safety precautions. He had failed to stop and clear the decks when off Esha Ness before proceeding further and, knowing of deteriorating conditions, had attempted to proceed through an unlit narrow channel at full speed in poor visibility with radar and Decca Navigator out of action. He should not have been alone in the wheelhouse, steering the vessel and trying to keep a lookout with the windows closed and the deck lights obscuring vision forward. The proper course of action would have been to clear the decks off Esha Ness, set a proper navigational watch, switch off the deck working lights and proceed to the west of Ve Skerries, thus giving the dangerous rocks inshore a wide berth. The court suspended Skipper Taylor for two years.

Author's Note: This case is an example of the operational problems skipper's have in keeping to the watch-keeping rules with insufficient crew to comply and how commercial pressures are at loggerheads with safety. What was not mentioned at the inquiry was how long the skipper had been on the bridge. He last hauled the gear about 0200 hours. If he took the last tow (about three hours duration), we can say he had been on the bridge for at least seven hours up to stranding, and it is likely that, if fishing was heavy, he took the three or maybe four previous tows. It is quite possible he had been in the wheelhouse more than twenty-four hours. Where the ship grounded was under cliffs over 300 feet high, and if he had fallen asleep, he wouldn't have seen them. I can't think of any other explanation and think one of the assessors should have asked questions about this. But this would have brought manning levels into question, a topic owners are reluctant to discuss.

1968

Although only five ships were lost during 1968, the cost in lives was heavy, fifty-nine men being lost in a period of twenty-five days.

Grimsby	Notts County GY643	441 tons	4 February 1968
	Ross Puma GY646	355 tons	1 April 1968
Hull	St Romanus H223	600 tons	11 January 1968
	Kingston Peridot H591	658 tons	26 January 1968
	Ross Cleveland H61	659 tons	4 February 1968

The *Kingston Peridot* was a single-screw steam trawler built by Cook, Welton & Gemmell in 1948 for Kingston Steam Trawling Company, Hull. Her gross tonnage was 657.89 tons and her registered dimensions were 181.7 feet x 30.65 feet x 15.15 feet. She was classed with Lloyd's 100 A.1. trawler, and owned by Hellyer Bros, Hull. Her main engine was steam reciprocating direct acting with three cylinders. Steam was provided from a multitubular oil-fired return tube boiler with three fires and a working pressure of 225 lb per square inch. The propelling machinery developed 850 bhp, giving the vessel a speed of 13 knots. The electrical supply came from two 10 kW steam generators and one 10 kW diesel generator, all operating at 110 volts direct current. Life-saving equipment complied with the regulations and included two wood lifeboats each for thirty-three persons, three inflatable liferafts each for twelve persons, twenty-five lifejackets, four cork lifebuoys, twelve parachute distress flares, one line-throwing apparatus, one Aldis daylight signalling lamp. Navigation equipment consisted of two magnetic compasses and one spare, one Marconi Mark IV radar, one Fishgraph echo-sounder, one Kelvin Hughes MS 24J echo-sounder, one Loran LJ11 receiver. Communications equipment consisted of a Redifon 100-watt main transmitter operating on MF and HF and R/T on intermediate frequencies, two Marconi portable battery-operated transmitters, a Redifon R50M receiver covering all frequencies, a Redifon R55 receiver covering all R/T frequencies, a Marconi Gannet receiver with DF loop, a Mullard Discovery direction finder.

The *Kingston Peridot* sailed from Hull on the early afternoon of 10 January 1968 for a fishing trip to the Icelandic fishing grounds, with a crew of twenty men all told, under the command of Skipper Wilson. At the time of sailing, she was fit for a trip to Iceland under normal conditions likely to be encountered but had insufficient stability to cope with the exceptional conditions of storm or hurricane-force winds with heavy ice formation on her superstructure. On her outward voyage, she made no report until the evening of 14 January, when she reported that her ETA at Reykjavik was about midnight that night, and that the cook was ill. No report was received from her on the 15th, but on the evening of the 16th, she sent the appropriate report, and continued to send in at least one report daily until 25 January. On that day, she was

Kingston Peridot. (Grimsby Evening Telegraph)

fishing in the North Cape area and reported 'Fishing slack North Cape area. Steaming easterly 66.42 North 22.15 West.' At 10.45 on the morning of the 26th, the skipper of *Kingston Peridot* had a conversation with the skipper of *Kingston Sardius*, who was fishing on Kiolsen Bank, and said he had been fishing on the north-east corner of Skagagrunn, had fouled his gear, and intended to get it aboard, as the weather was getting worse. He was going to lay for a couple of hours to let the lads chop some of the ice off her and then steam to Kiolsen. It was arranged to resume contact in the evening after the schedule report had been sent in. However, the weather on Kiolsen Bank deteriorated, the wind reaching Force 8, and the skipper of *Kingston Sardius* decided to stop fishing, and about 1945, he instructed the wireless operator to contact the *Kingston Peridot* and convey to him this information. The wireless operator called the *Peridot*, but although he kept trying to make contact until about one o'clock the next morning, he was unable to do so. The conversation referred to above is the last time *Kingston Peridot* was heard on the radio.

Mr Rattray, an officer at the Meteorological Office at Bracknell, and Mr Sigtryggsson, the Director of the Icelandic Meteorological Office, gave the Court of Inquiry evidence as to the weather in the area west of Grimsey Island, where *Peridot* would have been, on 26 January. On the morning of the 26th, the wind was ENE Force 6 but by noon had backed to NE and increased to Force 8 to 9. At Grimsey Island, after 1500 hours, the wind backed quickly to NNE and increased strength rapidly to Force 11 or 12 by 1600 to 1700. At 1900, it was Force 12, decreasing slightly to Force 10 by midnight. On the morning of the 27th, the wind decreased to Force 5 or 6 with maximum gusts of Force 8. Throughout the 26th and 27th, there was continuous heavy snow falls and the temperature ranged between -10 and -14 degrees centigrade. When efforts by the owners and other vessels to contact the *Kingston Peridot* failed, a search by sea, air, and on the Icelandic coast was put in operation on 30 January. A partly deflated liferaft and four lifebuoys belonging to *Peridot* were found on the shore in position 66.10 North, 16.36 West, and hatch boards and oil slicks were seen just offshore.

Although it is impossible to be certain exactly what happened to *Kingston Peridot*, all the evidence suggests that, sometime during the afternoon of 26 January, a combination of heavy seas and a build up of ice on her superstructure overcame the vessel's stability and she capsized and sank. There were no survivors.

The *Ross Cleveland* was a single-screw steam trawler, built in 1949 by John Lewis & Sons at Aberdeen, for Hudson Bros Trawlers, Hull. Originally named *Cape Cleveland*, she was renamed when Hudson Trawlers was taken over by the Ross Group. Her gross tonnage was 659.27 tons and she was 174.4 feet long, 30.1 feet beam, and 15.15 feet deep. The vessel was classed 100 A1 (Trawler) with Lloyd's, had met all survey requirements, and was in good order and seaworthy in every respect when she left Hull on her last voyage.

Her propulsion machinery consisted of a steam reciprocating direct-acting three-cylinder engine, which developed 900 bhp and gave her a speed of 12.25 knots. The electrical supply was obtained from a 20 kW steam generator, and another of 8 kW, both producing 110 volts direct current. Her life-saving appliances complied with all the regulations in force at the time, and met all the IMCO recommendations. She was equipped with two 23-foot wood lifeboats each for thirty-one persons, two Elliot 10-man inflatable liferafts and another Elliot for twelve men, six circular lifebuoys, twenty-two lifejackets; one Schermuly Supreme line-throwing apparatus; twelve parachute distress rockets and an Aldis daylight signalling lamp. Communications and navigation equipment was adequate and comprehensive, comprising a Marconi Ocean Span transmitter, a Marconi Kestrel III emergency transmitter, a Redifon GR 286 Mk II VHF transmitter/receiver, two lifeboat portable radio telephones, and Atlanta receivers covering all frequencies. Navigational equipment included two magnetic compasses and one spare, one type 14/12 Kelvin-Hughes marine radar, one Redifon

Ross Cleveland as *Cape Cleveland*. (*Grimsby Evening Telegraph*)

type ' ... one Marconi Lodestone direction finder, and Simrad EH2A, and

⸍ 20 January 1968, bound for the
twenty all told, commanded by
s on 25 January, but the weather
⸍ Kogurgrunn off the north-west
was too bad to fish and the cook
and the cook and press the water
⸍ arrival, the weather was patchy
by breaks when she had to dodge
⸍ sent her the following message
Come for Monday's market. What
⸍d coming for Monday's market.'
⸍at the landing day suggested was
⸍bruary, a severe weather forecast
shelter in Isafjord. A considerable
⸍ost of them also decided to run for
Patrixfjord, and Dyrafjord. The first
⸍ing to lack of room, were forced to
⸍inued to get worse, and all the ships
⸍ away as possible. These conditions
⸍pers reported hurricane-force winds
⸍ss Cleveland was unable to use her
⸍ngston Andalusite, who was close by
⸍dar. Ten minutes later, the Cleveland's
⸍rry Eddom, having climbed up to the
⸍en decided to come head to wind and
⸍id being driven ashore on the western
⸍nes half ahead, she failed to respond.
⸍ut Ross Cleveland heeled over to port
⸍ a position 3 miles off Arnarnes Light.
the bridge, managed to get out of the
⸍b aft along the casing where two men
struck by a sea and washed overboard.
⸍ on to it by the two men already on it.
⸍vho was wearing protective clothing was
⸍re and found shelter under the lee of an
⸍im next morning and guided him to the
⸍nd put to bed. The other two occupants
⸍s the only survivor.
⸍evidence as to the state of the weather
⸍lusite stated he was only two cables from
⸍ded wind speed was over 120 miles per
⸍l. He rang the engines full speed, and put
⸍d and give assistance, but Andalusite took
⸍er back head to wind for the safety of his
⸍n Garnet stated that his vessel was heavily
⸍orthy, despite the crew's efforts to clear the
⸍ at such a large angle that he thought she
⸍Kingston Emerald stated that he thought the
⸍e gusts, and after laying for a time, he had
to wind, the ship heeling 30 to 35 degrees.

Notts County. (Hull Daily Mail)

Notts County. Insurance surveyor assessing the iced up wreck. (W. Taylor)

That same night, the Grimsby trawler *Notts County* was driven ashore in the same area, and an Icelandic trawler was lost with all hands. The Icelandic Coastguard spokesman expressed the opinion that the weather conditions that night were so severe that it was very fortunate that there were not more casualties.

The *Notts County* was a single-screw side motor trawler built in 1960 by Goole Shipbuilding Company for Consolidated Fisheries, Grimsby, and registered as GY643. She was 441 tons gross, 137.2 feet long, 28 feet beam and 14.2 feet deep.

On 4 February 1968, *Notts County*, with a crew of nineteen hands all told, under the command of Skipper George Bures, was sheltering from hurricane-force winds with a number of other trawlers in Isafjord. Shortly after the *Cape Cleveland* capsized, she sent out a distress call. With her radar inoperative due to ice on the scanner, she had driven ashore. A liferaft was launched and one man boarded it, but it overturned. Then a sea washed the raft back on board with the man still in it. This man died of exposure shortly afterwards, despite the efforts of his shipmates to revive him. The Icelandic gunboat *Odinn* was quickly on the scene and positioned himself upwind of the wreck. Then, with complete disregard for his own safety, the mate of the *Odinn* boarded one of the gunboat's rafts and floated down to the stranded vessel. After assisting the fishermen to board the raft, it was pulled to the safety of the gunboat. Eighteen men were rescued. The mate had a broken leg caused by a block of ice falling on it and Skipper Bures had severely frostbitten hands, later having to have fingers amputated. But for the bravery and skill of the Icelanders, it would have been a greater tragedy.

Notts County was declared a total loss and the wreck was bought by an Icelandic businessman for £35. She was refloated but never went to sea again, and the rotting hulk is now part of the breakwater in Isafjord harbour. The crew of the *Odinn* were later honoured at a reception in Grimsby Town Hall when they were presented with a silver salver in recognition of their courage and skill.

St Romanus. (Grimsby Evening Telegraph)

The *St Romanus* was a single-screw steam trawler of riveted-steel construction. She was built by Cook, Welton & Gemmell at Beverley in 1950 for Belgian owners. She was bought by Thomas Hamling & Co. of Hull, and after an extensive overhaul was put into service in March 1964. Her gross tonnage was 600.47 tons and her registered dimensions were 170.25 feet x 29.2 feet x 14.5 feet. She was classed 100 A1 (Trawler) with Lloyd's and, a short time before sailing on her last voyage, had been subjected to survey. When she sailed, she was seaworthy in every respect, and her stability was satisfactory. *St Romanus* was propelled by a steam reciprocating three-cylinder engine served by a tubular oil-fired boiler with three furnaces and a working pressure of 220 lb per square inch. The engine developed 850 ihp, which gave her a full speed of 12 knots. Electrical power came from a 15 kW steam-driven generator and a 10 kW diesel generator, both working at 110 volts direct current. Her life-saving equipment met all mandatory requirements and comprised one 18-foot Class C boat for fifteen persons, four inflatable liferafts with a total capacity of forty-four persons, four circular cork lifebuoys, twenty-three lifejackets, one Schermuly line-throwing apparatus, twelve distress rockets and an Aldis daylight signalling lamp. Radio equipment comprised a Marconi Oceanspan VII main transmitter, a Marconi Atlanta main receiver covering all frequencies, a two tone R/T alarm, a Marconi 2273A receiver, a Redifon GR 286 radio telephone, a Hudson AF 102 receiver covering maritime VHF frequencies, Rescuephones survival craft radio telephones, and a Marconi Kestrel direction finder.

The *St Romanus* sailed from Hull on the early morning of 10 January 1968, bound for the Norwegian coast fishing grounds with a crew of twenty men all told, under the command of Skipper Wheeldon. She had no radio officer but the skipper had a Radio Telephone Certificate. At 1930 GMT that same day, the skipper reported that the vessel was 120 miles NNE of Spurn, and immediately afterwards, he had a link call to his wife, promising to phone again the next day. He didn't make that call, and from that time on, nothing was ever heard from *St Romanus*. She just vanished. On the evening of 10 and morning of 11 January winds of Force 8, occasionally 9, gusting to 10, were encountered in the area *St Romanus* would have been in, but during the afternoon of the 11th, the weather improved, the wind becoming about NNE, Force 5 to 6 by 1800 hours. From then, the moderation continued, and conditions improved considerably on the 12th.

At 0400 hours on 13 January, a Danish fishing vessel picked up an inflated liferaft belonging to *St Romanus* in position 57 degrees 57 minutes N, 0.1 degree 35 minutes E, but this was not reported until 20 January, when the vessel docked at Esbjerg. On 21 February, a lifebuoy belonging to *St Romanus* was found on the north coast of Denmark near Hirtshals. No other trace of *St Romanus* was ever found.

The Court of Inquiry into the loss was unable to discover the cause, but decided that she probably foundered near the position that the liferaft was found some time on 11 January. A disturbing feature concerning the loss of *St Romanus* is that, although she was presumed lost on 11 January, no search for her was instigated until 26 January, a delay of over two weeks. The owners operated a system whereby the ships were to report their position daily, but management made little effort to enforce the reporting procedure. In fact, another of the company's vessels, the *St Andronicus*, sailed from Hull on 9 January for the Icelandic grounds and made no report for five days. On 12 January, a telegram was sent to *St Romanus* through Wick Radio ordering her to report her position. Wick was unable to make contact, but repeatedly called her for about four days without success. On 13 January, Cromer Coastguard received a message from the Danish Sea Rescue Co-ordinating Service advising them that the liferaft, and its number, had been found, and on 26 January, Wick Coastguard received the same message. The number of the liferaft was sent to Hull Trawler Mutual Insurance Society, and it was quickly established that the raft came from *St Romanus*.

On 20 January, the owners sent another telegram to the missing vessel, and again it was not delivered. They waited until the 24th before informing the insurance company of the lack of information on the vessel. The insurance company then advised the Inspector of Fisheries of the situation, who ordered Flamborough Coastguard to pass the message to all stations, requesting information about *St Romanus*. On 26 and 27 January, an air search was carried out but nothing was found. Had the company enforced the reporting system, when no report from *St Romanus* was received on the 12th, it would have caused concern, and the search could have been instigated two weeks earlier than was the case. The fact that no distress message was sent suggests that whatever happened to the *St Romanus* was very sudden, and even if a search had started earlier, it is likely nothing could have been done to save the lives of the crew.

*R*oss Puma was built in 1960 at Selby by Cochrane's for Ross Trawlers, Grimsby, and registered as GY646. She was a steel, single-screw motor side trawler of 352 gross tons. She was 127.5 feet long, 26.5 feet in beam and 13 feet in depth.

She sailed from Grimsby in mid-March 1968 for a fishing trip to the Westerly fishing grounds with a crew of fifteen men all told under the command of Skipper Dennis Speck. On 1 April, when bound home, she ran aground in a snowstorm on the west side of the Orkney Isles, close to the Old Man of Hoy. Badly holed, and with water four feet deep in the engine room, a distress call was sent out by radio. With the trawlers *Ross Renown* and *William Wilberforce* standing by 600 yards offshore, the Longhope Lifeboat was quickly on the scene. The lifeboat moved in close to the wreck, striking the rocks and sustaining damage in the process. Unable to get alongside the stranded vessel, she floated a raft down to the wreck. The fishermen boarded this raft, which was then pulled through the few yards of surf to the lifeboat. All the crew were rescued, but *Ross Puma* was a total loss. Mr David Kirkpatrick, coxswain of the lifeboat, was later awarded a second bar to his Silver Medal for his part in the rescue. Sadly, the Longhope Lifeboat was lost with her crew of eight men the following year (20 March 1969).

Ross Puma. (Fishing Heritage Centre)

1969

Only one ship lost this year.

| Hull | *James Barrie* H15 | 666 tons | 27 March 1969 |

The *James Barrie* was built at Aberdeen by John Lewis & Sons Ltd in 1949 for J. Marr, Hull, as the *Benella* and registered as H15. In 1951, she was sold to Newington Trawlers Ltd, Hull, who renamed her *James Barrie*. She was a single-screw steam trawler with a gross tonnage of 665.87 tons. She was 180.5 feet long overall, 30 feet in beam and 15.1 feet in depth. She was classed at Lloyd's for hull and machinery as +100 A1 and +LMC respectively, and retained her class up to the time of her loss. She was propelled by a triple-expansion direct-acting steam engine producing 1,050 ihp, which gave her a speed of about 12 knots. *James Barrie* was fitted with a Donkin steam-driven hydraulic steering gear, and her pumping arrangements comprised two engine-driven pumps, two double-acting reciprocal pumps, and a steam ejector. Her circulating pumps could also be used for pumping out. Regardless of whether the engine room was flooded or not, the fish room could be pumped out at a rate of 14 tons per hour. Her aids to navigation comprised Loran, two echo-sounders, Marconi Raymark 12-inch radar, electric log, leads and lead lines. Her radar could be operated at ranges of 0.75, 1.5, 3, 6, 12, 24, and 48 miles. Radio communications equipment consisted of W/T, VHF and emergency apparatus, all of which was inspected by a Board of Trade surveyor in October 1968 and found to be satisfactory. On her final voyage, she carried a wireless operator. Her life-saving appliances were subject to Board of Trade survey in October 1967 and found to be satisfactory. This equipment comprised one lifeboat for thirty-one persons, twenty-two lifejackets, four lifebuoys, four inflatable liferafts with a total capacity of forty-four persons, one line-throwing apparatus, twelve distress rockets, and two Marconi portable radio transmitters.

James Barrie sailed from Hull, bound for the Icelandic fishing grounds on 26 March 1969 with a crew of twenty-one hands all told under the command of Skipper James Thomas Brocklesby. The mate and bosun held Certificates of Competency, but the third hand had no such certificate. At the time she left Hull, she was in a seaworthy condition with all her equipment in efficient working order.

Three watches were kept, the watchkeepers being the mate, bosun and skipper, the third hand being in the skipper's watch. At 1245 GMT on 27 March, Rattray Head was abeam about four miles to port, and Skipper Brocklesby altered course to make a position 2-3 miles off Duncansby Head. The weather at that time was fine with good visibility. There was light south-easterly breeze Force 4 to 5, and a slight sea running. At 1700 hours, the skipper called Third Hand Laing to the bridge, gave him a course to steer, told him to keep a good lookout for ships and to call him, the skipper, if there was any difficulty. The skipper then left the bridge to issue bonded stores. Between 1700 and 1800, the skipper made brief visits to the bridge and remained on the bridge from 1800

James Barrie. (P. Whiting)

to 1830. He should have been relieved by Mate Dunne, but the mate had been helping him issue bonded stores, and went for his tea. The skipper again left the bridge to issue bonded stores to the relief helmsman, who had missed the earlier issue, and again the third hand was left in sole charge of the bridge. At this time, the vessel was approaching the entrance to the Pentland Firth in gathering darkness. At 1845, Third Hand Laing saw what he thought was Duncansby Head ahead, and without calling or informing the skipper, altered course to starboard. At the time of this course alteration, *James Barrie's* position was calculated to be about 2.75 miles S by W of Louther Skerry. What was taken to be Duncansby must have been Muckle Skerry. Shortly before 1900, the third hand saw breakers ahead on both bows and called the skipper, who came promptly to the bridge. The engines were rung full speed astern but it was too late. The vessel grounded on Louther Skerry at 12 knots. Sounding round and inspection showed the vessel was not making water and was aground from the stem to amidships but had deep water aft and unsuccessful attempts were made to refloat her by running the engines astern. The trawler *Loch Doon* and Kirkwall and Wick lifeboats arrived on the scene and stood by the stranded vessel. At about 0300 hours on 28 March, efforts were made to move her kedge anchor aft in an attempt to refloat her on the high tide predicted for 0643, but at about 0600 hours, the vessel took a heavy list to such an extent that the starboard side of her deck was under water, and her main and auxiliary engines stopped. She remained heeled over and her crew boarded two inflatable liferafts. They were safely picked up by Wick lifeboat and taken to Wick. Throughout the 28th, the wind freshened and considerable movement of the vessel was observed. Men from Kirkwall lifeboat boarded her and found she had started to make water in the fore peak and net store. At the high tide on the morning of the 29th, *James Barrie* refloated and the lifeboat tried to tow her to Widewall Bay with the intention of beaching her. However, at 1245 on 29 March 1969, she sank off Hoxa Head at the entrance of Widewall Bay.

The Court of Inquiry into the casualty found the stranding was caused by the default of Skipper Brocklesby and Third Hand Laing. The skipper was suspended for two years and fined £100. The third hand was fined £25.

1970

Only one ship lost.

Granton   *Summerside* LH389   214 tons   6 May 1970

The *Summerside* was a steel motor side trawler of 214 tons, 116 feet long and 24 feet in beam, built by A. J. Mitchell & Co. at Peterhead in 1961, and at the time of her loss was owned by William Lister Ltd, Granton. She was fitted with radar, Decca Navigator, two echo-sounders, radiotelephone and VHF transmitter and receiver. She was supplied with adequate charts and publications for her voyage.

Summerside left Granton at 1130 hours on 28 April 1970 bound for the fishing grounds off Fair Isle with a crew of twelve hands all told under the command of Skipper Roland Frederick Wonnacott. Before leaving port, all her navigational aids were checked and found to be in working order. The vessel was seaworthy in every respect. She commenced fishing off Fair Isle on 29 April, but after thirty hours, steamed further north to fish off Muckle Flugga. On 4 May, the radar broke down and was of no further use for the rest of the voyage. She completed fishing at 0200 hours on 5 May 1970 and set a course for home. At this time, the weather was bad with a Force 7 wind freshening. At 0130 hours on 6 May, Girdle Ness Light was sighted about three or four points on the starboard bow and estimated by the skipper to be eight or nine miles distant. No attempt was made to fix the vessel's position by taking a running fix of the light. When Girdle Ness was abeam, the skipper set a course of SW by W. This course was an error, as it would take the ship into the land if continued.

The skipper went into the chartroom to get the 0200 weather forecast, and shortly after 0200 hours, the deckhand on watch reported to him that there was a reading on the echometer of 30 fathoms shoaling. At 0205, the skipper ordered the echo-sounder to be switched off, and it remained off until the stranding. He then returned to the chartroom. At 0230 hours on 6 May 1970, *Summerside* took the ground on rocks on the north side of Garron Point, about two miles north of Stonehaven. After running the engine full astern failed to refloat the vessel, a Mayday call was sent and answered by Stonehaven Radio. A Dutch ship, the *Prinses Margriet*, arrived on the scene and launched her lifeboat, but seas were breaking over the wreck, and it was too dangerous for the lifeboat to get alongside. Aberdeen Lifeboat also arrived but could do nothing. Attempts were made to launch the liferaft but it was carried away empty by the sea. Coastguards arrived on the shore, and a rocket line was fired to them from the ship. A breeches buoy was rigged and ten of the crew were pulled ashore. The skipper and chief engineer remained on board until low tide, when the ship was high and dry. Then they went ashore. *Summerside* was refloated on 14

Summerside. (W. Dodds)

September 1970 and towed to Stonehaven but was considered a constructive total loss and scrapped.

The Court of Inquiry found that the stranding and subsequent loss was due to negligence by the skipper and suspended his certificate for eighteen months, but recommended he be given a certificate of service as second hand to allow him to sail in that capacity.

1971

There were only two ships lost this year.

| Hull | *Caesar* H226 | 830 tons | 21 April 1971 |
| Aberdeen | *Janwood* A457 | 250 tons | 29 October 1971 |

The *Caesar* was a single-screw oil-fired side steam trawler built by Smith's Dock Company, Middlesbrough, in 1952 for Hellyer Bros Ltd, Hull. Her gross tonnage was 830.24, and she was 189.55 feet in length and 32.2 feet in beam. She was powered by a triple-expansion engine developing 1,250 ihp at 132 rpm. She had Donkin telemotor steering. Her compasses were last serviced and adjusted on 5 September 1970 and were fully compensated for all latitudes. She had the following navigational aids and communications equipment: one Decca RM 326 radar, one Decca Navigator, one Loran model LC 1, one Marconi Fishgraph, 2 echo-sounder, one Kelvin-Hughes MS 24 echo-sounder, one Marconi Lodestone D/F receiver, one Oceanspan III main transmitter, two Marconi CR 300 main receivers, one Marconi Kestrel reserve transceiver, one Marconi Alarm Generator, Marconi SRE System 1 Redifon GR 286 VHF R/T, one Redifon Hudson AF 102 VHF R/T installation. All this equipment was in good order when she sailed on her last voyage. She had ample life-saving appliances, which were last inspected by the Department of Trade and Industry surveyor on 4 September 1970, and she was classed for hull and machinery with Lloyd's and assigned +100 A1 Trawler and +LMC. She was supplied with a complete set of charts and the latest edition of the *Arctic Pilot*.

The *Caesar* sailed from Hull on 15 April 1971 for a fishing trip on the Icelandic grounds. She was manned by a crew of twenty hands all told under the command of Skipper Len Whur. In addition to the skipper, the mate also held a skipper's certificate, and the bosun held a second hand's certificate. This is in excess of statutory requirements. The passage to Iceland passed without incident, and 21 April found her fishing on Hali Bank off the north-west coast of Iceland. At about 1100 GMT on that date, part of the trawling gear caught on the stop valve on the winch, snapping it off. The chief engineer was unable to repair it at sea, so Skipper Whur decided to put into Isafjord. At 1130, a course of about 125 degrees true was set and the vessel proceeded at full speed. There was a north-easterly wind, about Force 7, on the beam. *Caesar*'s draught was calculated to be 12 feet 6 inches forward and 17 feet aft.

The following is taken with reference to the *Arctic Pilot*. In order to enter Isafjord harbour it is necessary to proceed down Isafjord-hardjup past Osholar Light and then to alter course to starboard to enter Skutulsfjordhur between Vellir Point on the western side and Arnarnes Light on the eastern side. This fjord is about 4 miles long in a south-westerly direction, and the inner harbour of Isafjord (Pollurinn) is separated from the large part of the fjord by a narrow channel which is entered about 2 ½

Caesar. (Fishing Heritage Centre)

miles from the mouth of the fjord. There are five pairs of leading lights as a guide to entering this inner channel, which are visible from the entrance into Skutulsfjordhur in clear weather, but they are not intended for use in entering Skutulsfjordhur. Many trawler skippers, including Skipper Whur, actually do use these marks to enter Skutulsfjordhur, but this is a dangerous practice, because if keeping on the line of the leading marks, the vessel will pass only about four cables off the eastern shore of the fjord in the vicinity of Arnarnes Light, and the *Arctic Pilot* specifically warns mariners not to approach either shore within about four cables. The correct approach is to enter the fjord, keeping in the deep water in the middle, and line up the leading marks about a mile from the entrance of the channel of Pollurinn. This is the vicinity the pilot would board. *Caesar* entered Isafjardhardup at about 1600 hours with the skipper doing the navigating. At 1640, she passed Osholar Light three miles off and course was altered to starboard to bring the vessel in towards Arnarnes Light. He had picked up the rear mark but only observed the front mark when the ship had come round on her new course. He then saw that the leading marks were open to the starboard bow and realised that the vessel was too far to the east. Immediately, he ordered the wheel to be put hard a-starboard, but before this order could take effect, the ship grounded. The time was 1720 and the position in which she stranded was 4.5 cables bearing 272 degrees true from Arnarnes Light – only two cables from the eastern shore of the fjord. Attempts were made to refloat the vessel using her engines but these attempts failed. Then, with the assistance of local fishing boats, a kedge anchor was run from her stern to try and pull her off. This also failed. During the night, another trawler, the *Ross Defiance*, arrived. She made two warps fast to the *Caesar*'s quarters, and at 0430, on the rising tide, the *Defiance* winched her warps tight and tried to tow *Caesar* astern while those on board *Caesar* hove on the kedge anchor. *Caesar* refused to budge, and the *Defiance*'s warps both parted. Next, it was decided to try to tow *Caesar* from ahead. Fresh warps were made fast to the port bow and the wire to the kedge was released to give a lead from the bow. At 0530, with the *Ross Defiance* towing and the kedge anchor being hove on, the *Caesar* swung about ten points to starboard and her engines were put ahead in the hope of breaking her free. But as she turned, a pinnacle of rock pierced her hull in the way of the stokehold, and she began to fill with water. The warps were cut, engines stopped, and operations ceased. The boiler fires were shut down, and fearing injury to personnel if the water reached the furnaces while they were still hot, the skipper gave orders to abandon ship. The skipper and mate returned later to *Caesar* after the boilers had cooled, but apart from battening down where they could, there was little they could do. The support vessel *Miranda* and the Icelandic gunboat *Odinn* took soundings and a diver's survey was made from the *Odinn*. These investigations revealed that *Caesar* was lying across two rock ridges, one under the bridge and the other under the fore end of the engine room. The captain of the *Odinn* carried out a pump test and found that four pumps with a total capacity of 80 tons an hour were unable to make any impression on the water level in the vessel. This confirmed that the hull was substantially holed. On 24 April, Mr Holcroft, a surveyor employed by UK Trawlers Mutual Insurance, arrived in Isafjord to inspect the ship and make recommendations on what should be done. By this time, the after accommodation had flooded, and a certain amount of oil pollution was being caused by oil escaping from the ship. He took immediate steps to prevent further escape of oil and recommended that further attempts at salvage should be considered. As a consequence, the insurance company entered into a salvage contract with Norsk Bjergningskompagni A/S, and the salvage vessels *Achilles* and *Parat* arrived at Isafjord. These two vessels were able to secure buoyancy pontoons to the *Caesar*, carry out substantial pumping and other work, and finally succeeded in floating her on 20 May. She was towed to the outer harbour at Isafjord where a diver's inspection showed a hole 9 feet long and 31 inches wide and a considerable amount of other damage to the hull. It was then considered that the vessel was a constructive total loss, and a decision was taken by the underwriters that she should be towed out to sea and sunk off Iceland. The Icelandic authorities were naturally concerned about the pollution that had already been caused and were anxious that no further pollution should occur in the future. They made it clear that the sinking must not be within 100 miles of the coast of Iceland. *Caesar* was prepared for towage and finally left Isafjord at 0250 hours on 31 May, being towed by the *Achilles*. All the survey equipment was removed from the vessel except a 5-inch diesel pump with two hoses. It was supplied with enough fuel to operate for 36 hours. *Caesar* was unmanned because it was considered too dangerous to leave anyone on board, as it would have been difficult to get them off in the event of bad weather. At 0615, it was observed that the pump was no longer pumping water over the side, and the skipper of *Achilles* decided it was not possible to board the *Caesar* and investigate the cause. His main consideration was that with the moderate swell, the difficulty of moving round a flooded darkened engine room, and the danger of the vessel capsizing made boarding too dangerous. *Achilles* continued the tow, trying to get as far from the coast as possible, and kept a watch on the after deck ready to cut the tow if *Caesar* sank suddenly. Throughout the day, *Caesar* sank deeper by the stern and took a starboard list. By 1910, the boat deck was in the water, and it was considered too hazardous to continue towing and the tow-line was slipped. At 0047 on 1 June, the *Caesar* sank in 110 fathoms in position 65.49 N, 25.57 W.

The Court of Inquiry into the casualty found that the initial cause was the wrongful act or default of Skipper Len Whur in the navigation of the vessel. In view of his unblemished record as skipper over many years, it was not considered necessary to suspend his certificate, but he was censured and ordered to pay £250 towards the costs of the inquiry.

Janwood. (G. Coull)

The *Janwood* was a motor trawler owned by the Leslie Fishing Company, Aberdeen. Built in 1960 by T. Michinson at Gateshead, her registered dimensions were length 115.4 feet, beam 24.4 feet and depth 11.6 feet, with a gross tonnage of 250 tons. She sailed from Aberdeen on 28 October 1971 with crew of 12 hands under the command of Skipper George Guthrie Ellington. Both her skipper and mate held skipper's certificates.

On 29 October, *Janwood* was fishing on Whiten Head Bank, north of Kyle of Tongue. She hauled the gear at 1900 hours and laid while a torn net was repaired. At 2000 hours, the skipper decided to steam to a new ground off Loch Eriboll. He rang for full speed and set a course of WSW. At this time, he was alone on the bridge. A few minutes later, the mate, Ronald Blanchard Garden, came to the bridge and took over the watch from the skipper, with apprentice deckhand Leahy, doing his first trip to sea, steering the boat. The vessel was 10-12 miles offshore, and the skipper estimated her position from his knowledge of the area without referring to the chart. It was a fine clear night with excellent visibility, with the lights on Cape Wrath and Strathy Point clearly visible. The skipper gave the mate the Decca readings of the destination and an indication of the time it would take to get there, and instructed him to set up the Decca Plotter for the next tow. He then left the wheelhouse and went to his cabin, taking no further part in the navigation until the stranding. After the skipper left the bridge, the mate made no attempt to fix the ship's position either by radar, cross bearings or Decca, nor did he notice the approach to Faraid Head, high ground that must have been visible. The *Janwood* took the ground at full speed just south-east of Faraid Head still on a course of WSW, causing considerable damage to her bottom. The crew took to the liferafts and were picked up by the trawlers *Mount Eden* and *Mount Everest*. *Janwood* was later salved, returned to service, and was finally scrapped in 1982.

The Court of Inquiry found that the stranding was caused by negligence in watch-keeping by the mate:

1. He failed to keep a proper lookout.
2. He failed to plot the ship's position on or after taking over the watch.
3. He failed to check the position by radar, Decca, or visual bearings.
4. He failed to notice the proximity of land.

His certificate was suspended for five years. The court also found the skipper in default and suspended him for two years. Evidence given to the inquiry indicated that there was a lack of firm and proper control of the issue of spirits aboard the *Janwood*.

1972

No ships or lives lost this year.

1973

Four ships and three lives were lost this year.

Grimsby	*Ross Tern* GY700	288 tons	10 February 1973
Aberdeen	*Navena* FD172	353 tons	6 December 1973
Hull	*St Chad* H20	575 tons	30 March 1973
	Ian Fleming H396	598 tons	25 December 1973

The *Ross Tern* was built by Cochrane & Sons at Selby for Ross Trawlers, Grimsby, being one of the 'Bird' Class of small motor trawlers. At the time of her loss, she was owned by British United Trawlers (Aberdeen). She was a single-screw motor trawler of 288 tons gross, 107.5 feet long, 24.5 feet in beam and 12.5 feet deep. Her navigational aids consisted of Decca Navigator Mark 12, Decca Plotter, Decca Radar 426, Kelvin-Hughes Sounder Type MS 44, Kelvin-Hughes Sounder Type MS 29. All this equipment was in efficient working order when she sailed on her last voyage, subject to possible inefficiency of the Decca Navigator after leaving port, and she was supplied with adequate charts and nautical publications for the proposed voyage.

She sailed from Aberdeen at 1100 hours on 9 February 1973 for a fishing voyage to the West Coast of Scotland fishing grounds, with a crew of eleven men all told, under the command of Skipper William Martin Mackenzie Gardner. The vessel was seaworthy in every respect. When the vessel left Aberdeen, three watches were composed, to be taken by the skipper, second hand and the second fisherman. The latter was uncertificated. The skipper was due to go on watch from 1800 to 2300 hours on 9 February, but he was not called and the watch was taken by two deckhands. He was awakened at 2045 by the stopping of the engines when Ross Tern was 4 miles off Noss Head. He went up to the bridge, set a course N by E for Duncansby, and then returned to his cabin and again fell asleep, leaving the two deckhands on the bridge. At 2245, the second hand, Frank Sinclair Sutherland, called him, and as the skipper seemed tired, he volunteered to take the ship through the Pentland Firth, an offer the skipper accepted. The second hand went to the bridge and took over the watch, and after rounding Duncansby Head at 2245, he set a course of NNW to pass about 1 mile north of Stroma. He intended to navigate visually, using the radar, and making no allowance for the effect of the tide. When the watch changed at 2315, he indicated Swilkie Point Lighthouse, confirmed the course at NNW, and instructed the second fisherman that when Dunnet Head opened, the course should be changed to west. He left the bridge at 2325 without making any check of the ship's position. A bearing and distance from Duncansby Head would have given him an accurate fix and would have shown the vessel was seriously off course, being far too much to the northward, and still in the dangerous channel of the Pentland Firth. He then left the bridge, going to his berth without reporting to the skipper. At 2345, the Second Fisherman noted that the radar was showing land about 5 miles on

Ross Tern. (Fishing Heritage Centre)

Ross Tern. (G. Coull)

the port beam. He could see nothing forward or to starboard due to a snow squall, and considering the ship was too far north and her position uncertain, he gave the skipper an urgent call. The skipper came to the bridge immediately, but before he could take any action, the vessel grounded on the east side of Tarf Tail, Isle of Swona, at about 2350, 9 February 1973. A distress call was sent out and the crew were all rescued by the Longhope Lifeboat. There were no casualties.

At the subsequent Court of Inquiry, it was found that the loss was caused by he wrongful acts of both the skipper and the second hand. Skipper Gardner was suspended for two years, and Second Hand Sutherland was suspended for four years.

The *Navena* was a steel, single-screw motor trawler built by Cochrane's at Selby in 1959 for J. Marr, Fleetwood, and registered as FD172. Her registered dimensions were 132.9 x 27.1 x 12.2 feet and 353 tons gross. In 1969, she was transferred to P. & J. Johnstone, Aberdeen. She was a well-found ship, seaworthy in every respect, and equipped with appropriate navigational aids, including radar and a Decca navigator. *Navena* sailed from Aberdeen at 0930 hours on 5 December 1973, bound for the fishing grounds off the Faroes, under the command of Skipper James Clark. Three watches were set, the watchkeepers being the skipper, the second hand and the second fisherman, each having two deckhands with him. On 5 December, the skipper had the watch from 1800 to 2300 hours, when he received the following weather report from Wick Radio: 'Westerly veering North Westerly 7 to severe gale 9 locally storm 10 in Faroes. Some Showers. Visibility good.' As a result, he decided to set a course to the east of the Orkney Islands. At 2300 hours, he handed over the watch to the second hand. The vessel was then several miles south-east of Copinsay and steering N by E. The skipper instructed the second hand to proceed until about one mile off the land, stop the engines, and allow the vessel to drive off to about 5 miles, then dodge back under the land again. He also asked to be informed if the wind changed and to be called to take the 0630 weather forecast. He then retired to his berth and did not come to the bridge again until after the

Navena. (G. Coull)

Navena aground. (J. Worthington ex *Aberdeen Journals*)

stranding. At that time. the wind was westerly Force 7, and increasing. The second hand was on watch from 2300 until 0400 hours on 6 December when he was relieved by the second fisherman, Thomas T. P. Hunter. The wind was still from the west. During his watch, the second hand had dodged in towards Deer Ness twice, checking his position by radar and the Decca Navigator. Visibility was good apart from occasional showers, and both Copinsay and Auskerry Lighthouses were clearly visible. In handing over the watch, he showed the second fisherman the ship's position on the Decca chart, gave him the instructions about dodging, and told him to call the skipper if the wind changed and for the 0630 weather report. He did not refer to tides. He then entered the skipper's berth and told him the watches were being changed and the vessel's position.

Shortly after taking over the watch, the second fisherman dodged into the land and stopped engines about a mile off Deer Ness to let her drive back to the eastward at 0530 hours. At this time, he noted that the wind had veered and was now blowing from about NW by W. Despite the orders he had received, he did not inform the skipper of the change of wind, nor did he take any notice of the tide, which had turned about 0500 hours and was now going southwards at about 4 knots. At about 0600 hours, the second fisherman allowed both deckhands to leave the wheelhouse, and he went into the radio room to write a personal message of no urgency, leaving the wheelhouse completely unmanned. Although land masses and breakers were visible, and although the radar was operating and *Navena* was drifting towards Copinsay Lighthouse flashing at a height of 260 feet, this southerly movement went unnoticed. The wheelhouse was still unmanned when *Navena* struck the rocks between Copinsay and Horse of Copinsay. Immediately after the stranding, the skipper came to the wheelhouse, checked the engines could not be used, and sent out a Mayday call. Weather conditions delayed Kirkwall Lifeboat, which, when it did arrive, could not approach close to *Navena*. In the event, the crew were all taken off by a rescue helicopter at about 1000 hours.

The Court of Inquiry found that the loss of *Navena* was caused by the grossly negligent conduct of the second fisherman in respect of totally inadequate watch-

St Chad. (P. Whiting)

Ian Fleming. (P. Whiting)

keeping procedures, culminating in complete abandonment of watch-keeping. Since he was not a certified officer, the court could only record his gross negligence. The court further found that the skipper's conduct involved serious negligence in that he allowed an uncertificated hand to be in charge of *Navena* during manoeuvres that involved her being close to land in the prevailing conditions of wind and sea and the prospect of changes of wind and tide, and for not giving clear warning of the care needed to allow for the change of tidal currents. Therefore, the court suspended his skipper's certificate for a period of eighteen months from 26 June 1974.

St Chad was built at Beverley in 1956 by Cook, Welton & Gemmell for Boston DSF Co. and registered as H20. She was a diesel-engined side trawler with gross tonnage of 575 tons, 165.3 feet long and 30.5 feet beam. She left Hull for a fishing trip to Iceland about 19 March 1973 with a crew of twenty hands all told under the command of Skipper W. M. Hastie. She ran aground near Ritur Huk, Iceland, in a snowstorm on 30 March 1973 while seeking shelter. The British support ship *Othello* and the tug *Statesman* heard her distress call and were quickly on the scene and standing by. Shoal water and heavy swell prevented the rescuers from getting in close, but an Icelandic small boat managed to get alongside the *St Chad* and ferried all her crew to the *Othello*. There was no loss of life, but *St Chad* was a total loss. *Othello* landed the survivors at Isafjord, from where, after a short stay at the Salvation Army Hospital, they were flown to Rekjavik for transport home.

The *Ian Fleming* was built at Beverley in 1958 for Icelandic owners and named *Fylkir*. She was acquired by Newington Trawlers in 1966 and registered at Hull as H396 and her name changed to *Ian Fleming*.

Ian Fleming was a single-screw motor trawler designed for side trawling. Her overall length was 193.7 feet, and she was 32.35 feet in beam, with a gross tonnage of 597.94 tons. Her internal combustion engine of 1,400 bhp gave her a speed of 12 knots and could be controlled directly from the bridge. Her hull and machinery were classed at Lloyd's, and she was in class at the time of her loss. Her navigation equipment included magnetic and gyro compasses, two radar sets, two echo-sounders, Decca Navigator, Direction Finder and Loran, all of which were in good working order. For communications, she had MF and VHF radio, which were surveyed and found satisfactory on 29 June 1973. She was fitted with a Donkin hydraulic telemotor steering gear and an Anschutz Automatic Pilot. Her safety equipment was subjected to survey by the Department of Trade and Industry on 17 August 1973 and passed as satisfactory for twenty-three persons. This equipment included four inflatable liferafts, which complied with the regulations.

The *Ian Fleming* sailed from Hull, bound for the Norwegian Coast fishing grounds on Friday 21 December 1973, with a crew of twenty hands all told, under the command of Skipper David Atkinson. At the time of sailing, the vessel was in a seaworthy condition and all her equipment was in a satisfactory working condition. Bonded stores had been loaded prior to sailing, which included ten cases of beer and four cases of lager, but no spirits. It cannot be established how much duty-paid liquor was brought on board by individual crew members. After passing Spurn Light Vessel, the vessel was put in automatic steering and remained so up to the time of her stranding. As she proceeded northwards along the Norwegian coast, no fire drills of lifeboat musters were carried out as they should have been, and on Christmas Eve, a certain amount of jollification took place after a day spent preparing the fishing gear ready to begin fishing early on the morning of 26 December.

At 0230 GMT on 25 December, the *Ian Fleming* was abeam of Andanes, off the north-west coast of Norway, and although a further seventeen hours passed before she stranded, no other position was logged, hence it is not possible to state definitely exactly what happened during this period. The persons whose evidence would have helped most were the skipper, the mate, the bosun and the radio officer, who were all concerned with events on the bridge during Christmas Day. Unfortunately, the last three of these witnesses had died before the date of the inquiry into the loss, and the evidence of the skipper was considered unreliable because he admitted persistently lying when he had said that hand steering had been used before the stranding. A number of the crew gave oral testimony, but the court felt that their evidence was not entirely credible. Some of them had sided with the skipper in his false story about the hand steering, and others gave the impression of being either prejudiced or irresponsible. On Christmas Day, there was a south-westerly wind reaching gale force at times. There was no sunrise or moonrise, but the visibility was otherwise very good. During most of the day, the skipper and mate shared the watch-keeping so that the men could have the day free of duty or work. Late in the afternoon, the skipper decided to proceed into Rolvsoy Sund to shelter behind Rolvsoy Island while the crew were having their Christmas tea. He made no navigation plan and passed between Skips and Revsholmen Islands doing 12 knots and probably navigating by radar.

At 1830 GMT, Mr Waudby, an uncertificated third hand, and Mr Caine, a deckhand, came on watch, the skipper remaining in charge of the watch. Neither of these men were briefed as to what was happening or what was expected of them. At this time, the vessel must have been about nine miles from Gavlodden, where she later stranded. The course being steered was 085 degrees, and an alteration of course to port must have been made. If the radar was on the 3-mile range, Havoy and Gavlodden would not have shown up on the radar, and for that reason, a wrong course may have been set. In the event, the *Ian Fleming* grounded at the foot of Gavlodden Light at approximately 1913 GMT. Although Rolvsoy Sund is in a compulsory pilotage area, there was no pilot on board, and this may, or may not, have been a partial cause of the stranding. Passage through the Sund is not particularly difficult, and the Court of Inquiry considered that Skipper Atkinson's conduct was carelessly negligent. He should have made a definite navigational plan, he should have instructed his lookouts as to what was going on and encouraged them to make reports, he should not have relied exclusively on radar, and he should have taken bearings of Gavlodden Light, which must have been clearly visible at over 10 miles.

How much alcohol was consumed that day aboard the *Ian Fleming* is uncertain. The court considered that the skipper was not drunk at the time of the stranding, but that during that day, and the previous evening, he may have drunk more bottles of lager than he remembered and probably drank tots of spirits offered him by his crew. There was a festive atmosphere aboard the ship and some drinking on the bridge. The court considered it likely that he may have dozed off, and his part in the festivities may have blunted his judgement and been a contributory cause of the stranding. After the stranding, three liferafts were launched, two from the starboard side and one from the port side. The port-side raft proved unusable owing to the prevailing weather conditions and its close proximity to rocks on the lee shore. Of the rafts on the starboard side, fifteen men boarded one of them, and five men boarded the other. The raft containing the five men capsized, and of the occupants, only the skipper and a deckhand were saved. The mate, wireless officer, and the second engineer died of exposure before they could be pulled from the water. The deckhand managed to climb back aboard the vessel and was rescued later. In all, seventeen member of the crew of twenty were rescued, and these men owe their survival to the skill and courage of the Norwegians, who put to sea in great haste on receiving the Mayday call the *Ian Fleming* had broadcast before she was abandoned. Because of the question of drunkenness and drinking on the bridge and because three lives were lost, the court considered whether the skipper should have his certificate cancelled. However, it was decided that they would be more lenient, and the court ordered that his certificate should be suspended for three years. In the event, the *Ian Fleming* was abandoned as a constructive total loss and subsequently sank on 5 January 1974.

1974

Five ships and thirty-nine men were lost this year.

Aberdeen	*Dalewood* A481	234 tons	3 March 1974
Fleetwood	*Wyre Majestic* FD433	338 tons	18 October 1974
Grimsby	*Victory* GY733	1,750 tons	2 May 1974
Hull	*Gaul* H243	1,106 tons	8 February 1974

The *Dalewood* was a steel, single-screw motor side trawler of 234 tons gross built in 1960 at Gateshead by T. Michenson for the Ashley Fishing Company, Aberdeen. She was fitted with magnetic compass, radar, two echosounders, Decca Navigator and Plotter and a radio direction finder.

She left Aberdeen at 1015 hours on 3 March 1974 bound for the Faroese fishing grounds under the command of Skipper Joseph Murray Parker. She was seaworthy in all respects and her navigational aids were all in satisfactory working order. At 1800 hours that evening, the skipper relieved the second hand on the bridge and took over the navigational watch. The skipper had two deckhands, Buchan and Gellie, on watch with him. One of the deckhands took the wheel and was given the course to steer by the second hand. The second hand then reported to the skipper, who was in his cabin, before leaving the bridge. Shortly after *Dalewood* rounded Duncansby Head, the skipper was called and came to the bridge. The weather was fine, a light wind with good visibility. He checked the vessel's position relative to the headland and lighthouse, both of which were visible. He instructed the deckhand to hold the present course until Stroma, then round Stroma, keeping a mile off until *Dalewood* came round to a WNW heading, then to hold that course until abeam of Dunnet Head, and then to steer NNW. After giving these orders, he then again retired to his cabin, where he remained until the time of the stranding.

At about 2120 hours, *Dalewood* ran ashore at full speed on rocks almost at the foot of Dunnet Head Lighthouse in a small cove on the west side. At the time of the stranding, deckhand Buchan was alone on the bridge, Gellie having gone down to make tea. It seems incomprehensible that the trawler managed to run ashore in clear weather with Dunnet Head Lighthouse, 346 feet above sea level, showing a four-flash light every 30 seconds, providing an unmistakable mark, while the headland must have been clearly visible on the radar. At the Court of Inquiry into the stranding, Buchan stated that 'he had drunk quite a few cans of beer', indicating that he was drunk and had probably fallen asleep at the wheel a considerable time before the stranding. This would seem to be the only logical explanation. After the stranding, Skipper Parker took charge, and after the vessel had been checked for damage, and it was found that she was filling with water, he put out a Mayday call. In this message, he mistakenly gave the position as Duncansby Head, which led the rescuers astray

Dalewood. (G. Coull)

and caused a delay in her being found. The distress call was received at 2129 hours and Scrabster Lifeboat immediately put to sea. Meantime, aboard the *Dalewood*, the order was given to abandon ship, and the crew left her in two liferafts. The men in one of the rafts were picked up by the naval tug *Cyclone* and those in the other by the trawler *Sealgair*. Those men picked up by the tug were transferred to the Scrabster Lifeboat, and all of them were landed at Scrabster. The only casualty was the chief engineer, John Gray, who sustained cracked ribs while climbing from the raft to the *Sealgair*, but *Dalewood* was a total loss.

It is obvious the Deckhand Buchan was criminally negligent, but he should never have been left alone on the bridge, nor should the bridge have been left in dangerous waters without a certificated officer in charge of her navigation. The court found that the casualty was caused by default and wrongful acts of Skipper Parker and suspended his certificate for three years.

The *Wyre Majestic* was built by Cochrane & Sons at Selby in 1956 and owned by Wyre Trawlers Ltd, Fleetwood. She was a single-screw motor side trawler with a gross tonnage of 338 tons, a length of 132 feet and 27.25 feet in beam. Her engine developed 736 bhp, giving her a speed of about 10 knots. She was fitted with all proper, modern navigational aids, including two radar sets. All her equipment was in good order and well maintained, and she was seaworthy in every respect. She had a crew of eight hands all told and was under the command of Skipper Derek George Reader. The skipper and mate held the appropriate Department of Trade certificates, and the bosun held an insurance permit to sail as bosun, but was uncertificated. She had been involved in experimental work in pair trawling for herring with a sister trawler, *Wyre Defence*, and this work involved short overnight fishing trips and short sea passages. In these circumstances, a 'watch on, watch off' system was reasonable. The mate took one watch and the bosun the other, but it was understood that the skipper was in charge of the bosun's watch.

Wyre Majestic. (P. Whiting)

Wyre Majestic. (P. Whiting)

At about 1100 hours on Friday 18 October 1974, the two ships put into Oban to land the previous night's catch. Both crews were employed landing the catch, a job that took about an hour. It was intended that the trawlers would remain in Oban over the weekend, while the men returned to Fleetwood by coach, but no berths were available, hence it was decided to sail the ships home to Fleetwood. About 1300 hours, some of the men, including the mate and bosun of *Wyre Majestic*, went to a pub in Oban, where they stayed until closing time at 1430. The mate drank in moderation, but the bosun admitted drinking three or four pints of Guinness and three or four whiskies. Both the trawlers sailed from Oban at about 1510 hours that day. On *Wyre Majestic*, it was the mate's watch. The skipper was on the bridge and navigated the vessel through Kerrera Sound, and thereafter remained on the bridge until 1800 hours. At 1630 hours, the two ships closed up and a box of provisions was transferred to *Wyre Majestic*. After the transfer was completed, *Wyre Defence* slowly moved ahead of her sister and was about two miles away at the time of the stranding. At 1800, the skipper went down for tea and returned to the bridge shortly before 1830. Between 1800 and 1830, the bosun was called to go on watch several times but did not turn out. Shortly after 1830, the skipper instructed the mate to go down and get the bosun out. Deckhand Falcon had come on watch and was steering the boat. The skipper drew Falcon's attention to the radar, the screen of which was visible from the steering position, and told him to call him when the echo of Rubh' A'Mhail touched the variable-range ring, which was set at 5 miles. At this time, Rubh' A'Mhail was 8 miles away, fine on the starboard bow. The skipper then left the bridge and did not return until after the stranding. On leaving the bridge, the skipper went to his cabin and laid down on his bunk. He intended to read but fell asleep. When the bosun came to the bridge, Falcon gave him the skipper's orders, and shortly afterwards, the bosun took the wheel. Despite the orders he had been given, the bosun ordered Falcon not to call the skipper. Shortly after 1900 hours, Falcon called the *Wyre Defence* on the VHF and spoke to Tom Watson, her skipper, and said, 'I'll bet we beat you back to Fleetwood.' Tom replied, asking, 'Is the skipper on the bridge?' The bosun took the phone and replied, 'It is all right, Tom, I am here,' which Skipper Watson acknowledged and advised, 'Make sure that Derek [the skipper] is out.' Unfortunately, this advice was ignored. The *Wyre Majestic* continued to proceed at full speed. The bosun ignored the fact that she had entered the red sector of Carraig Light, and the close proximity of lights from the distillery just west of Rubh' A'Mhail, and struck at full speed on the north side of Rubh' A'Mhail in Islay Sound at 1945 hours. Subsequent attempts to tow the vessel off the rocks by the Islay Lifeboat, *Francis Wotherspoon*, and *Wyre Defence*, and later by a tug, failed, and she was a total loss. The Court of Inquiry found that the skipper was at fault by failing to remain on watch when navigating in confined and dangerous waters with no one on the bridge qualified to navigate the vessel and in leaving the bridge with the vessel in sole charge of a deckhand. Fortunately, no lives were lost, and in mitigation, the court took into account the skipper's previous good service. It was ordered that Skipper Reader's certificate be suspended for twelve months. In disregarding the orders to call the skipper, the bosun, J. J. Pirie, showed a total lack of responsibility to his ship and his shipmates and was severely reprimanded for his conduct. Also, the insurance company forbade him from sailing as bosun for three years.

The *Wyre Majestic* had stranded on a previous occasion. She left Fleetwood on the morning of 30 December 1959, and at about 9.10 p.m. that evening, she ran aground close to the Mull of Galloway Light. The Court of Inquiry into this incident found that the stranding was due to fault by the skipper and the bosun. The bosun, Tom Sillis, had failed to ensure a proper watch was kept, or a proper course steered, due to him being in an unfit condition to take a watch on account of overindulgence of alcohol

Victory. (Welholme Gallery)

Victory abandoned on Kola Inlet. (W. Taylor)

the night before. He was ordered to pay £100 towards the cost of the inquiry. The skipper, William Clark, should have been on the bridge before the Mull came abeam and was suspended for twelve months.

*V*ictory was a large freezer stern trawler built by J. Lewis at Aberdeen in 1965 for Northern Trawlers Grimsby. She was 1,750 tons gross, 216 feet long, 41 feet in beam and 27.2 feet in depth. She was registered at Grimsby as GY733. On 1 May 1974, while fishing in the Barents Sea under the command of Skipper Wally Wilson, she caught fire. The freezer trawler *Kurd*, Skipper John Dobson, took her in tow and headed for Vardo, Norway. The crew were successful in putting the fire out, but on the afternoon of the 2nd, fire broke out again and got out of control. *Kurd* slipped the tow and took her crew off. *Victory*, now a blazing hulk, was taken in tow by a Russian warship and beached on the west side of Kola Inlet close to Murmansk. Several months later, she was examined by insurance surveyors. She was found to be lying on her starboard side and two-thirds submerged. She was then abandoned as a constructive total loss.

The *Gaul* was built in 1972 by Brooke Marine at Lowestoft as the *Ranger Castor* for the Ranger Fishing Company, South Shields. In 1973, she was acquired by British United Trawlers and transferred to Hull where she registered as H243 and her name was changed to *Gaul*.

She was a two-deck, factory freezer trawler designed to operate in the North Atlantic and Arctic and to fillet and freeze her catch at sea. Her gross tonnage was 1,106 tons, she was 216.75 feet long (186.5 feet BP), 40 feet in beam and 25.5 feet deep. She was classed at Lloyd's *100 A1 (Stern Trawler), Class *LMC for her machinery, and Ice Class 3 for her hull. She was fitted with all the latest navigational, communications and life-saving equipment, and when she sailed on her last voyage, she was seaworthy in every respect.

The *Gaul* sailed from Hull at 0600 hours on 22 January 1974 bound for the fishing grounds in the Barents Sea with a complement of thirty-six men under the command of Skipper Peter Nellist. On 26 January, she called at Lodigen to land the mate, Mr Petty, who was suffering from a rupture. She then proceeded to Tromso to pick up a replacement mate, Mr M. E. Spurgeon, who had been flown out from Hull. She left Tromso early in the morning of 28 January and started fishing the next day in position 71 degrees 50 minutes N, 29 degrees 10 minutes E. For the next nine days, *Gaul* continued fishing in the vicinity of North Cape Bank among a number of other trawlers. She was in frequent radio and visual contact with these ships and reported her position daily to the Hull office. At 10.45 on the morning of 8 February, the mate of the *Swanella*, Mr Bill Brayshaw, saw the *Gaul* about a mile away, and spoke to the mate of *Gaul* on the VHF. Later, at about 11.10, *Gaul* sent two private telegrams through Wick Radio. Those were the last times *Gaul* and her crew were ever seen or heard. On Monday 11 February, after *Gaul* had failed to report, a massive air and sea search was instigated, but no wreckage or oil slick was found. *Gaul* and her thirty-six-man crew had vanished without trace. On 8 May, three months after *Gaul* disappeared, a Norwegian ship, the *Rover*, picked up a lifebelt belonging to Gaul in position 71.25 N, 28.15 E.

At the time *Gaul* disappeared, the weather in the area was very bad. A formal investigation into the loss was held in Hull, which found that *Gaul* had capsized and foundered due to being overwhelmed by a succession of heavy seas.

Author's Note: For a detailed account of the loss of the *Gaul*, refer to my book *The Loss of the Motor Trawler* Gaul (Hutton Press, 1998).

1975

Two ships and two men lost this year.

| Hull | *D. B. Finn* H332 | 701 tons | 21 March 1975 |
| Aberdeen | *Ben Tarbert* A418 | 280 tons | 28 January 1975 |

The *D. B. Finn* was built at Goole in 1961 for Boston DSF Company, Hull, and registered as H332. She was a large single-screw side trawler of 701 tons gross, 188 feet in length and 32.7 in beam.

She left Hull, bound for the Icelandic fishing grounds with a crew of twenty-one hands all told under the command of Skipper Jim Brocklesby. But before she could commence fishing, on 21 March 1975, she was driven ashore in heavy seas and hurricane-force winds on a sandy beach at Hjorleifshofdi on the south coast of Iceland. All the crew managed to get ashore. The vessel had a damaged rudder and was making water. Attempts to salvage her were made by Icelandic gunboats, but it was not until six days after the stranding that she was refloated. A sandstorm was raging in the area for two days, and when the weather moderated, the first attempt failed when the *Ryr*'s towrope parted. In all, three attempts were made, and the *Aegir* finally succeeded in pulling her off and towed her 180 miles to Reykjavik. The cost of repairing the damage she had sustained was prohibitive, and she was declared a constructive total loss.

The *Ben Tarbert*, a motor side trawler of 280 tons gross, was built in Aberdeen in 1960 and owned by Richard Irvin & Sons Ltd, Aberdeen.

She left Aberdeen just before noon on 28 January 1975 for a fishing voyage with a crew of eleven men all told under the command of Skipper John Forbes. About an hour later, the trawler *Aberdeen Venturer* also left port. The *Venturer* was owned by the John Wood Group, Aberdeen. She had a crew of thirteen hands all told under the command of Skipper John Morrice. Shortly after leaving port, both vessels developed faults on their radar and both proceeded to Peterhead for repairs. Both vessels were told to lay offshore, and an engineer would be sent out to them. Arriving first, the *Ben Tarbert* dropped anchor in the entrance to the Bay of Refuge. A little later, the *Aberdeen Venturer* arrived and intended to moor to the *Ben Tarbert*. For whatever reason, the *Venturer* rammed the *Tarbert* just aft side of the bridge on the starboard side, causing a large hole in the ship's side in the way of the engine room. *Ben Tarbert* rapidly filled with water and sank inside five minutes. The incident occurred only 600 feet from Peterhead South Pier, and the pilot boat was quickly on the scene and managed to rescue most of the crew. However, two men, George Lemon, second engineer, and John Greig, a deckhand, were drowned. Peter Buchan, Peterhead Harbour traffic controller witnessed the incident and stated that the *Aberdeen Venturer* made no

D. B. Finn. (J. Worthington)

alteration in course or speed and was doing nine or ten knots at the time of impact. The skipper and second engineer, William Alexander Cormack, of the *Venturer* were later charged with culpable homicide, and the trial started on 30 August 1976 at Banff Sheriff Court. At the end of a three-day trial, both men were found guilty of culpable homicide. Skipper Morrice was fined £250 on the culpable homicide charge and a further £75 on a charge of failing to ensure the safety of his ship and crew. Cormack was fined £100 for failing to respond to orders on the engine room telegraph because he was drunk on duty and £175 on the culpable homicide charge. Before passing sentence, Sheriff T. M. Croan said that the fines should not be regarded as a measure of blame and were imposed on the ability to pay. He considered that Cormack was more culpable than Morrice, and that other people on board should take a share of the blame. Speaking for Cormack, his agent Mr W. M. Reid, Advocate, of Edinburgh, said, 'It is clear that at least three of his superiors knew of his condition before he was put on watch, and some culpability must lie elsewhere. The chief engineer, Thomas Brown, put Cormack on watch knowing full well his condition. He was almost a zombie sitting on a box in the engine room. He was not a free agent and was subject to the orders of his Chief Engineer. Is he to be found guilty of not carrying out duties of which he was clearly incapable?' After the verdict of the court, the Department of Transport was considering whether to hold a formal inquiry into the casualty.

EPILOGUE

In the preceding pages, we have described the circumstances of the loss of 125 trawlers and over 420 lives, almost all of them large trawlers from the main UK distant-water fishing ports – Aberdeen, Fleetwood, Grimsby and Hull. We have made no attempt to record the loss of smaller boats, ships under about 200 tons, nor have we attempted to catalogue the losses from the smaller ports. Had we done so, the tally of ships and men lost would have been considerably greater.

All around the coast of the United Kingdom from Falmouth in the South West to Lerwick in the far north, and all points between, there are numerous small harbours where fishing boats make a substantial contribution to the local economy. And in every one of these havens, there will be families who have had to mourn for their menfolk that the sea has taken. A glance at a few of the lost Lowestoft boats will stress this.

The motor trawler *Guava* LT73 was lost with her crew of eleven men in bad weather on 31 January 1953.

The trawler *Bucentaur* was lost with all hands on 21 May 1947 after a collision with the *Wilson Victory* in the North Sea.

That same month the trawler *SDJ* was lost with all hands. It was presumed she struck a mine.

The motor trawler *Gypsy Queen* LT166 was lost with her seven-man crew in January 1955.

Play Mates lost with all hands 90 miles from Lands End in March 1955.

The motor trawler *Susan M* lost with all hands in December 1957. It was presumed she hit a mine.

Suffolk Warrior LT671 sank after collision with *Hendrika Johanna* in the North Sea on 15 February 1969.

The UK distant-water fishing fleet has been decimated to the point where it no longer exists. In January 1996, there were 325 fishing vessels over 80 feet in length on the UK register, over two-thirds of them over twenty years old. A considerable number of these vessels are foreign-owned 'quota hoppers'. The boats capable of voyaging to the distant-water fishing grounds can be counted on your fingers. This UK total is smaller than the number of trawlers landing their catches at Grimsby twenty-five years ago.

In addition to these bigger boats, there are 2,053 inshore boats (vessels 32.8-79.9 feet) fishing. There are currently 15,375 regularly employed fishermen. In 1995, they brought home 658,287 tonnes of fish valued at £454,499,000.

The next time you have a plate of fish and chips, spare a thought for these men and their families. Some of them will have paid the ultimate price to get it to your table.

Memorial to lost trawlermen in Hull. (J. Williams)

Memorial to men of steam trawler *Crane* in Hull. (J. Williams)

Memorial to men of steam trawler *Crane* in Hull. (J. Williams)

ACKNOWLEDGEMENTS

A large number of people helped in providing information and assistance in the preparation of this book to whom we want to show our gratitude:

To the staff of the Reference Section at Grimsby Central Library for help in research.

To John Wilson and Mrs Moss at the Town Hall Archives, Grimsby, for help and access to the Grimsby Registers.

To the staff at Fleetwood, Aberdeen and Hull Libraries for help in researching contemporary newspaper reports and photocopying inquiry reports.

To Keith Warrs and staff at the Grimsby Fishing Heritage Centre for providing photographs and help with research.

To the Welholm Gallery, Grimsby, for providing photographs.

To Les Isles ex-*Red Gauntlet* and Roy Hanath ex-*Northern Spray*, now both living in Cape Town, for personal accounts of the loss of the *Red Gauntlet*.

To Northcliffe Newspapers (*Hull Daily Mail* and *Grimsby Evening Telegraph*), especially Stuart Russell of GET, for photographs from their archives.

To Sonya De Marco Page at the Marine Safety Agency Marine Information Centre for Board of Trade inquiry reports.

To my friend, the late William Taylor of Grimsby Trawlers Mutual Insurance, for the photographs and accounts of the wrecks he attended.

To all the following who supplied photographs: John Worthington, George Coull, Wilf Dodds, Paul Whiting, John Campell, Henry Taylor, Jim Williams, Jack Bayram, George Brown, Ken Waudby.

To the scores of ex-shipmates and their kin who wrote to us and provided dates of losses and personal accounts, which greatly eased the burden of research.

Without your help this history could never have been compiled and we are grateful to all of you.

John Nicklin, Cleethorpes
Pat O'Driscoll, London

BIBLIOGRAPHY

Aberdeen Press and Journal
Fishing News
Fleetwood Chronicle
Grimsby Evening Telegraph
Hull Daily Mail
West Lancs Evening Gazette
Yarmouth Mercury

Boswell, D., *Loss List of Grimsby Vessels 1880-1960*
Close's Fishing Grounds and Landmarks of Iceland, Faeroe, North Sea, West Coast of Scotland (3rd revised ed. [no date], compiled by Albert Close, London)
Cox, C., *The Steam Trawlers of Grimsby* (1988)
Crawford & Moir, *Argyll Shipwrecks*
DTI Inquiry Minutes
Gill, A., *Lost Trawlers of Hull* (Hutton Press)
Lloyd's Registers
Olsen's Fisherman's Almanac
Ritchie, G. F., *The Real Price of Fish* (Hutton Press, 1991)

APPENDIX

Ship	Tonnage	Port	Date of Loss
Aberdeen City	264 tons	Aberdeen	16 September 1963
Achroite	314 tons	Fleetwood	February 1963
Aucuba	211 tons	Grimsby	5 September 1951
Andradite	313 tons	Fleetwood	7 March 1957
Arctic Adventurer	565 tons	Hull	8 December 1964
Arctic Viking	533 tons	Hull	18 October 1961
Barry Castle	380 tons	Grimsby	1 November 1955
Belldock	236 tons	Grimsby	16 November 1953
Ben Tarbert	280 tons	Aberdeen	28 January 1975
Ben Barvas	235 tons	Aberdeen	3 January 1964
Benghazi	257 tons	Fleetwood	23 April 1947
Blue Crusader	274 tons	Aberdeen	13 January 1965
Boston Heron	314 tons	Milford Haven	3 December 1962
Boston Wellvale	419 tons	Grimsby	21 December 1966
Boston Pionair	166 tons	Lowestoft	12 February 1965
Braconlea	200 tons	Aberdeen	5 October 1952
Caesar	575 tons	Hull	1 June 1971
Carency	233 tons	Aberdeen	28 June 1957
Corena	352 tons	Aberdeen	September 1948
D. W. Fitzgerald	235 tons	Aberdeen	13 June 1961
D. B. Finn	701 tons	Hull	21 March 1975
Dalewood	?	Aberdeen	3 March 1974
Daniel Quare	440 tons	Grimsby	9 September 1955
Dhoon	323 tons	Fleetwood	12 December 1947
Doonie Braes	213 tons	Aberdeen	20 April 1955
Earl Essex	225 tons	Grimsby	24 April 1946
Ella Hewett	595 tons	Fleetwood	6 November 1962
Epine	358 tons	Grimsby	13 March 1948
Euclase GN51	295 tons	Granton	22 September 1955
Evelyn Rose	327 tons	Fleetwood	31 December 1954
Gaul	1,106 tons	Hull	8 February 1974
George H. Hastie	229 tons	Aberdeen	9 December 1958
George Robb	217 tons	Aberdeen	6 December 1959
Goth	394 tons	Fleetwood	13 December 1948
Grimsby Town	422 tons	Grimsby	23 April 1946
Hassett	349 tons	Grimsby	18 September 1953
Hildina	324 tons	Fleetwood	1 December 1953

Ian Fleming	598 tons	Hull	25 December 1973
Invertay	230 tons	Grimsby	10 March 1961
Irvana	296 tons	Fleetwood	23 April 1964
James Barrie	666 tons	Hull	29 March 1969
Janwood	?	Aberdeen	29 October 1971
Jean Stephen	212 tons	Aberdeen	18 January 1958
Juniper	235 tons	Aberdeen	19 February 1967
Kingston Turquoise	811 tons	Hull	26 January 1965
Kingston Peridot	658 tons	Hull	26 January 1968
Kingston Aquamarine	613 tons	Hull	11 January 1954
Koorah	227 tons	Aberdeen	11 February 1954
Kuvera	202 tons	Aberdeen	26 January 1950
Laforay	609 tons	Grimsby	8 February 1954
Leicester City	411 tons	Grimsby	22 March 1953
Loch Hope	274 tons	Hull	11 June 1947
Loch Lomond	310 tons	Aberdeen	23 October 1952
Lois	286 tons	Fleetwood	5 January 1947
Lord Stanhope	448 tons	Fleetwood	7 November 1963
Lord Cunningham	635 tons	Grimsby	20 December 1963
Lord Ross	265 tons	Hull	1 December 1948
Lorella	559 tons	Hull	26 January 1955
Luffness	271 tons	Granton	2 February 1958
Magnolia	260 tons	Grimsby	20 August 1952
Margaret Wicks	366 tons	Fleetwood	2 December 1963
Michael Griffith	282 tons	Fleetwood	31 January 1953
Mildenhall	434 tons	Grimsby	1 November 1948
Navena	?	Aberdeen	6 December 1973
Norman	628 tons	Hull	4 October 1952
Northern Crown	803 tons	Grimsby	11 October 1956
Northern Spray	655 tons	Grimsby	11 October 1964
Northman	199 tons	Aberdeen	11 December 1956
Notts County	441 tons	Grimsby	4 February 1968
Ogano	265 tons	Grimsby	24 April 1950
Osako	260 tons	Grimsby	21 April 1956
Pintail	198 tons	Fleetwood	2 April 1949
Pollard	350 tons	Grimsby	17 February 1950
Preston North End	419 tons	Grimsby	14 April 1950
Prince Charles	514 tons	Grimsby	23 December 1955
Rangor	200 tons	Aberdeen	17 January 1964
Red Gauntlet	410 tons	Fleetwood	10 August 1947
Red Falcon	449 tons	Fleetwood	14 December 1959
Reggio GY368	285 tons	Grimsby	6 November 1955
Remindo	358 tons	Grimsby	28 April 1955
Revello	230 tons	Grimsby	7 December 1959
River Leven	202 tons	Grimsby	13 December 1953
River Ayr	202 tons	Aberdeen	16 April 1959
River Lossie	201 tons	Aberdeen	27 March 1953
Riviere	226 tons	Grimsby	10 June 1953
Robert Limbrick	273 tons	Milford Haven	5 February 1957
Roderigo	810 tons	Hull	26 January 1955
Ross Kenilworth	442 tons	Grimsby	May 1962
Ross Tern	288 tons	Grimsby	10 February 1973

ALSO AVAILABLE FROM
AMBERLEY PUBLISHING

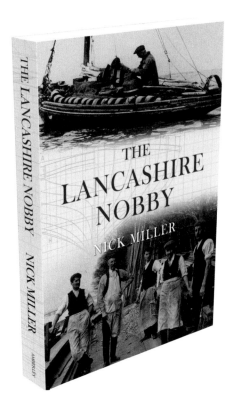

THE LANCASHIRE NOBBY

Nick Miller

Price: £16.99
ISBN: 978-1-84868-490-4
Binding: PB
Extent: 288 pages

ALSO AVAILABLE FROM
AMBERLEY PUBLISHING

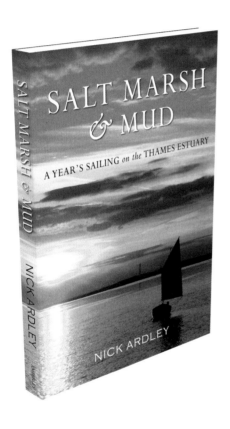

SALT, MARSH AND MUD
A YEAR'S SAILING ON THE
THAMES ESTUARY

Nick Ardley

Price: £16.99
ISBN: 978-1-84868-491-1
Binding: PB
Extent: 192 pages

ALSO AVAILABLE FROM
AMBERLEY PUBLISHING

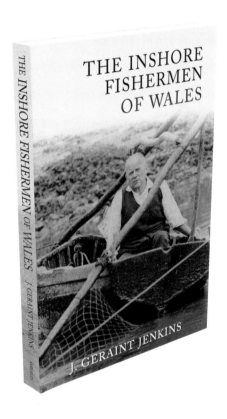

THE INSHORE
FISHERMEN OF WALES

J. Geraint Jenkins

Price: £17.99
ISBN: 978-1-84868-158-3
Binding: PB
Extent: 176 pages